Getting Through

YVONNE RODNEY

REVIEW AND HERALD® PUBLISHING ASSOCIATION

Since 1861 | www.reviewandherald.com

Published by Review and Herald® Publishing Association, Hagerstown, MD 21741-1119

Review and Herald® titles may be purchased in bulk for educational, business, fund-raising, or sales promotional use. For information, e-mail SpecialMarkets@reviewandherald.com

The Review and Herald® Publishing Association publishes biblically based materials for spiritual, physical, and mental growth and Christian discipleship.

The author assumes full responsibility for the accuracy of all facts and quotations as cited in this book.

Unless otherwise noted, texts are from the *Holy Bible, New International Version.* Copyright © 1973, 1978, 1984, International Bible Society. Used by permission of Zondervan Bible Publishers.

This book was
Edited by Penny Estes Wheeler
Designed by Ron J. Pride
Interior designed by Tina M. Ivany
Cover photo © 2008 Jupiterimages Corporation
Typeset: Bembo 11/14

PRINTED IN U.S.A.
12 11 10 09 08   5 4 3 2 1

Library of Congress Cataloging-in-Publication Data
Rodney, Yvonne, 1959-   .
  Getting through / Yvonne Rodney.
    p. cm.
  1. Church work with youth—Fiction. 2. Conduct of life—Fiction. I. Title.
PS3618.O3574G48 2008
  813'.6--dc22
                              2008028996
ISBN 978-0-8280-2386-3

To order additional copies of *Getting Through,* by Yvonne Rodney, call **1-800-765-6955.**

Visit us at **www.reviewandherald.com** for information on other Review and Herald® products.

For Mama and Joy,

two spunky women whose journeys through pain
challenged my faith in remarkable ways,
and whose legacies demand that I not give up.

Acknowledgments

- Toronto West (T-West) church family: you provide the right kind of soil to nurture the potential in your members.
- My T-West children: I expect great things from you, or there will be no more feasting at my table.
- Marilyn, Sharon, Diane, and Susan, who keep me accountable, provide cheek-hurting laughter moments, back-bracing talks, and memories to last a lifetime.
- Michele, who labored with me through the developmental stages of this book and has been a solid sounding board for most of my crazy ideas: I am blessed to know you.
- Greg and Nathifa, Marsha, Rhenee, Paul, and Nick, who took time to read the manuscript and provided useful tips and words of wisdom.
- Andy, your encouragement means a lot.
- Leroy, Norma, and all my relatives: I cannot imagine life without you. Thanks for listening, pushing, challenging, and always loving me.
- Dennis, my husband, who made me realize that there might never be a "perfect" set of circumstances in which to write but just to start somewhere, and who stayed out of my way so I could. I love you!
- Jeremy and Jessica, my children: supporters and critics, joyfully celebrating each milestone with me (and to think I was reluctant to have children!).
- Jeannette Johnson, Penny Wheeler, and the Review and Herald team, who helped me navigate this new landscape.

And thanks be to God,
who continues to provide inspiration and to open doors
far beyond those of my shortsighted visions.

Contents

Introduction

On a Friday evening in April, days before Easter, a good man suddenly dies. His death ushers in a series of events that beg for the promise of an Easter Sunday miracle. Set in twenty-first-century Toronto, Canada, *Getting Through* deals with the pain of loss—loss through death, and loss through betrayal. It asks some tough questions: Why doesn't God intervene in the suffering of His people? Why do bad things seem to happen to good people? And then it gets even more personal: When trouble comes to a Christian home, what happens? How do you cope? What if you can't forgive a loved one who has caused you pain?

Getting Through also explores premarital sex. If it's really wrong, why did God allow us to crave it before we get married? What harm is there, really, in having protected sex before one gets married? It also explores friendship—friends helping friends. Requiring accountability. Not letting them get away with wrong. Supporting each other during the bad times as well as the good.

Though the book deals with several tough issues, in many ways it's simply a good read. There is humor and fun, the triumph of life over death, and the very real hope of heaven. It touches on issues faced by real Christians, and while the characters are fictitious, their issues and questions, culled from lived or observed experiences, are not.

On a personal note, I find myself, in my twenty-first-century life, struggling to relate the gospel of Jesus Christ to my contemporary circumstances. As someone who has chosen to practice a Christian lifestyle because it makes sense to my soul, I've discovered that faith is a daily exercise. Even as I was writing this story, I spent many hours rebelling against God's unwillingness to accede to my demands to deliver my friend from death. He didn't. But He got me through. And so I accept. And I trust, even though I still do not understand.

I asked God to help this book find its way to those who would benefit from the story. Because you're now holding a copy in your hands, guess what? You are an answer to prayer! But the message here is not just for you—it speaks to me, too. I know nothing about your situation, but I continue to believe in a God who does. He will get you through any current, or future, situation; and He chose this moment to bring you this missive. If you receive a blessing from it, give Him thanks, and ask Him to direct you to whom you should pay it forward.

—Yvonne Rodney

He said to them,
"How foolish you are, and how slow of heart
to believe all that the prophets have spoken!
Did not the Christ have to suffer these things
and then enter his glory?"
—Luke 24:25, 26

Friday

Chapter One

Scott

"Brian, am I hearing you right?" asked Scott, the youth leader. "Are you saying that it's not realistic for God to expect today's young people to abstain from 'fooling around' before marriage? That *everyone* is doing it, and if a Christian girl older than 16 says that she's a virgin, she's a liar?"

"Yeah–you got it," replied Brian.

Scott turned to Brian's sidekick. "Is that what you believe as well, Damon?"

Damon shrugged halfheartedly. "I guess so," he said, looking to Brian for confirmation.

Scott Henry surveyed the faces of the nine young men ranging in age from 17 to 23, most of whom were finding the carpet very fascinating at the moment. Todd Williams, a studious second-year biology student at Hamilton University, indicated to Scott that he was going to the washroom. Those who had not seen Todd's gesture looked up with expectation at the sound of his footsteps, but as the door clicked shut the silence returned. Scott patiently waited for the silence to take over the room until it became uncomfortable.

It had taken him a long time to develop enough of a relationship with these young men from New Haven Ministries to get them to be open with him. Many wintry Thursday nights shooting hoops and summer evenings on the soccer field. Two months ago, after hearing them complain about how boring Friday nights were at home, he'd asked if they wanted to get together Friday nights to shoot the breeze. Talk about stuff that was on their minds—men to men. His appeal to their manly egos worked. Their one condition was that Scott would not become preachy. Since then, for almost five months, they'd met every week and were getting more and more comfortable speaking their minds around each other.

Brian the Brave, as he was dubbed by his friends, was one of the more outspoken members of the group. Sporting a well-toned footballer physique, he had a commanding presence and was handsome to boot. Some of the more reticent guys deferred to him. As for Brian, he enjoyed the limelight and being a rabble-rouser. How much of what he said he actually meant and how much he was saying simply to be provocative, Scott was still trying to figure out. He suspected a combination of both.

He continued to wait in silence. Obviously tonight's topic had touched a raw nerve. Still no one spoke. The carpet and then their fingernails seemed to require their full attention, and they all looked up expectantly when the creak of the door announced Todd's return.

"Say, Scott—well, not just you, Scott, but everybody—I was thinking as I was in the washroom—"

"Are you telling us that you need to go to the can to think?" Brian teased. "Ya sure you want to be making this confession here with us, or should we arrange for you to tell Oprah?"

"Or maybe Dr. Phil," piggybacked Damon.

"You think you're funny, don't you?" replied Todd. "And yes, some of my best thinking is done in the can. Maybe you should try it sometimes. It might improve your vocabulary and your B.O."

The guys howled with laughter. It was not often that someone got one up on Brian.

"You wound me, man. Just be warned—'one good turn . . .'" Brian joked.

"But seriously, guys, as I was saying before I was rudely interrupted, if what Brian says is true, why do we bother wasting our time coming to church? Aren't we being hypocritical? Since supposedly nobody's waiting till they're married to have sex and nobody thinks it's realistic of God to expect us to wait, what's the point of doing anything else the Bible says? Why not kill someone if they make you mad? After all, we see a lot of killing for sport on TV, we hear of it in the news, even right here in Toronto—every day people just killing each other. Young guys just like us."

"Who said anything about killing, man? How'd we get from sex to killing?" argued Brian. "Why do you always have to take something simple, Todd, and make it so convoluted? See, I know a big word or two," he added.

"Yeah, Todd, that's right," piped in Damon.

"Shut up, Damon!" chorused identical twins Larry and Les.

"I am *not* making things convoluted," Todd countered. "I am taking a statement that you made and following it through to its logical conclusion. Like I said, if what God expects from us as Christians is unrealistic, such as no sex before marriage, then why bother to do any of the other things He asks us to do?"

"Well, it's easier not to kill someone than to say no to sex," muttered Larry, the more practical of the twins.

"Listen, I'm not a lawyer or any great philosopher or a preacher . . ." Brian began.

"Philosopher?" whispered Damon to Brian.

Brian glared at him. "Whatever! I just call it the way I see it. All I'm saying is that I like the dames and if they're willing, I am always able—if you get my point. That's all I'm saying, man."

"Even if some guy feels that way about your sister?" Malcolm, a college senior, questioned.

"Is this a pick-on-Brian night? Where do you come off bringing my sister into this? She's just a kid!"

"Kid? She's at least 16 and definitely not ugly, if I might say so myself," returned Malcolm.

A few of the guys grinned.

Brian brought his pivoting chair crashing down on all four legs and glared at Malcolm. "If I so much as catch you holding my sister's hand, Malcolm Goodwin, I will see to it that you never hold anyone's hand again!"

"I don't get it, man. Why are you so upset about this? Your sister's a woman. Some guy's gonna see her in the same way you talk about other girls," Malcolm persisted. "Those girls you sleep with are all some other guy's sister or some other man's daughter."

Brian's eyes were angry slits. "Malcolm, you just shut your mouth. I've got 'nuff dirt on you, so don't come off being preachy to me. The same goes for a few more of you. You can clam up here if you want, but you know that you've done what I enjoy doing with the girls—pardon me—women. And if you haven't, you want to do it. Now go pick on someone else, PUH-LEEZ!"

Scott waded into the discussion, a thinking look on his face. He kept any tone of censure from his voice, for after all, this was a free-for-all kind of chat.

"Todd has raised some good questions. How do we decide which of God's commandments to keep and which to discard? Why do we come to church? Then, as Larry said, it *is* harder to resist sex than to resist killing somebody. So should God not expect us to do things that are difficult?

These are all very good questions to discuss at another time, but how about we hone in on this one? Brian said that some of you have done it already and that those who haven't want to. So here's my final question for the night. If we really want to have sex outside of marriage, is that the same as actually doing it?"

"Well, I kinda see Brian's point," Sammy, a high school senior, jumped in. "I've just turned 17, and no, I haven't done it yet, but I want to. Man, sometimes I see a babe—I mean girl, woman, whatever—and she's dressed in some 'come here' kinda outfit, and my mind just goes there. There should be a law cautioning women not to dress like that. It messes up men's heads—well, let me speak for myself. It messes up my head. So no, I haven't done it yet, but sometimes, man ..." His voice trailed off as he rolled his eyes back with a sigh.

"Then why don't you?" asked Todd in his quiet questioning way.

The question hung high and long in the room. Then Sammy answered.

"Because I know it's wrong and I'm kinda scared. Man, what if the girl gets pregnant? Me a dad at 17! I can barely wake up at nights to go to the bathroom. How could I get up to feed a wailing kid at 2:00 a.m.? Plus I gotta write my bestseller by the time I'm 25, which leaves me only about seven years! So, I take a shower and ..." His words disappeared in a mumble.

"What's that you mumbled?" asked Brian.

"I said I pray a lot," Sammy confessed sheepishly.

"Does that really help?" Les quizzed.

"I guess so, 'cause I usually fall asleep praying about it, and so far I've been able to resist. But that doesn't mean the urge goes away."

"Resist! When do you have time to resist anyone?" Larry laughed. "Every time I see you, you've got your head down scribbling something in that notebook. Do you even know what the female gender looks like? Man, I've seen a few girls giving you the eye, but your head is off in another universe."

"Really? Like who?" asked Sammy brightly.

"Start looking for writing material in the eyes of the women sitting next to you, Sammy. You might learn a thing or two," encouraged Larry.

Scott took a deep breath. "How about we call it a night, guys? It's going on 10:00, and we need to be out of here. Everybody cool with that?"

All agreed.

"Oh, and by the way," Scott continued, "let's note that there was some heated discussion tonight, but this is why we got together in the first place. Not to agree with each other all the time, but to talk and argue and challenge each other. So if you're feeling a bit hot under the collar now, think about why you're feeling that way."

Everyone stood up to leave, but not until they'd bowed their heads for Scott to pray. It was one of the few things he insisted on—that they asked God to be with them as they began and ended their discussions.

Schooled as his features were in calm, a great heaviness weighed on Scott's heart. How could he reach these young men with the transforming love of God? Yes, they had grown up in the church. Most of them considered themselves Christians, but was Brian right? Were most of them sexually active, and if so, with whom? The girls from their church? So tumultuous were his thoughts that Scott forgot he was the one who was supposed to be offering the closing prayer.

Into the stillness Sammy's voice began. "Holy Father, thank You for bringing us here safely. Thank You that we have this time to talk with each other." He paused and, after taking a deep breath, continued: "Help me to be an example for You in all parts of my life. I'm weak and tempted, Father, but help me to be strong and to do Your will. In Thy name I pray. Amen."

A quiet group filed out of the meeting room at the church.

"Anyone need a ride home?" Scott asked as he paused to turn out the lights. Everyone indicated they were OK except for Brian.

"My folks have the wheels tonight. They went to visit a neighbor who's in the hospital, so I told them I'd bum a lift off you."

"No problem, Brian," responded Scott.

"Cool, 'cause I have a question to ask you."

Scott clicked open the door to the car, and after fastening seat belts, both men checked for oncoming traffic as he eased out of the parking lot. April's chill could be felt in the air. Winter was still resisting the gentle but persistent shove of spring.

On the CD player the resonant voice of a popular musician sung about saints being just sinners who fall down and get up again. They listened to the song in silence until Scott's tenor joined in. When the final strains faded, Scott glanced at Brian.

"What did you want to ask me, O Brian the Brave? And how did you get the Brave part added to your name, by the way? Because you have a big mouth?" Scott teased.

"That's a crazy story for another day, man. Don't distract me. I want to ask you a serious question. It's kinda personal—I mean, you might not want to answer it. Listen, forget it—it's none of my business."

"Is the answer important to you, Brian?"

"Yes. No. Man, I don't know. I suppose so. I'm just kinda curious about somethin'."

"What's that?"

"What?"

"The thing you're curious about?"

"Oh. Yeah. Well, it's like this. You're old but not *that* old yet. Did you do it 'fore you got married to Charmaine?" he asked, quickly backpedaling. "Man, this is a personal question. You don't have to answer if you don't want to— I mean, I'll understand."

Scott drove in silence for several blocks. Then heaving a huge sigh, he said, "Yes, Brian. I did."

Brian looked up in shock. "You DID? But you're . . . like kinda a pastor . . . or something. You pray all the time. Man, you sound like God is like your best friend and all. You did it! Way cool! I mean—"

"Don't get bent out of shape about this, Brian. I did it. And I think it was one of the biggest mistakes of my life."

Scott signaled a right turn and pulled the car off the road into a mall parking lot. "When are your folks expecting you home?"

"They won't be expecting me for another hour or so. Why, you need something at the mall? Everything's probably closed."

"No. But I need to talk with you about what I just admitted."

Brian wanted to crow. He hadn't expected . . . Wow! He didn't know what he'd expected. "It's all right, Scott. I was just being nosy. You don't need to tell me about your private life."

"No, I don't need to tell you about my private life, but I will not be dishonest with you. You asked me a straight-up question, and I gave you an honest answer. So yes, I do need to talk to you in particular, and maybe the rest of the guys if it comes to that, about this."

"Why me in particular?"

"Because about 12 years ago Scott, the Self-acclaimed Stallion, was busy strutting his stuff just like Brian the Brave is doing now."

"Cool!" Brian checked his reply. "I mean . . . really?"

"Really."

Gaining confidence, Brian asked, "So what's the big heavy about that being the biggest mistake of your life, man? I mean, you had some fun before you settled down. We both—nudge, nudge—know there's not going to be any sex in heaven, and at the rate the world is going we better make sure we get—" Brian broke off, laughing. "A brother in crime! This is way too cool."

But Scott was not smiling. His face set in lines of regret, he stared into a past filled with memories he wanted erased. Slowly, as if moving caused him pain, he turned to Brian.

"Brian, if I only knew then what I know now, I would have waited. I would have kept myself for Charmaine only. If only I had known."

Sobering, Brian asked, "What's the big deal, man? You sound like you committed some kinda major crime."

"But that is the big deal, Brian. I did commit several grave sins. Against God. Against Charmaine. Against the women I slept with. And against my own body."

Brian threw up his hands. "I don't get you guys, man! What's the big deal about it? You all talk as if it's some great big no-no, but it's totally amazing!"

"Nothing is wrong with sex, Brian. God invented it, and as you have experienced, it is a pretty awesome experience. One that once we start, we can become addicted to. That is exactly what God intended. But here's the part you're not going to like, and I didn't want to hear either."

"And what's that?" Brian asked in a voice like rolled eyeballs.

"It should stay within the confines of a married relationship."

Brian yielded no quarter. "Then why did God give me these strong urges? I'm no way ready to be married yet. If we shouldn't have sex before we get married, then we shouldn't crave sex before we're married. Is God trying to make us crazy or what? I figure, why resist? If I can get it, I'm gonna have it, and that's how I see it."

Scott opened his mouth, but Brian was still talking.

"You're a good example, Scott. Even though you're not old like my dad, you've lost the urge, man. You don't remember what it's like to be like us.

Even more arguments for me getting what I can now. I can straighten things out with God later when I'm an old guy like you and have had my fun."

Scott rested his chin on the steering wheel. He felt very tired. As he looked out into the April night he asked, "Will you at least let me tell you—even though I'm 'old'—my reasons for saying that I think it was one of the biggest mistakes of my life? Mistakes for which I still feel the repercussions to this day?"

"All right, lay it on me. But don't be raining too hard on my parade, old man!"

Chapter Two

A Death in the Family

R obert and Len Baptiste sat at the kitchen table in silence, the poured tea ignored as each reflected on their hospital visit.

"I didn't expect him to look so . . . so . . . reduced," Robert quietly interrupted the silence. "It was a bit of a shock."

Tears filled Len's eyes. " 'Did not our hearts burn?'* That text comes to mind, and even though I know that the context is wrong, that's how I felt when I looked at him. Like my heart was on fire. Weak and yes, reduced as he was, his faith was still strong and his hope in God steadfast. That's how I want to be, Robert, when my end comes."

Giving Len's shoulder two gentle pats, Robert rose heavily. "I'm going to give myself a long soak. My head's been aching on and off all day. Coming?"

"I think I'll just sit here for a few more minutes."

"OK, I'll get things started," Robert said as he moved tiredly toward the back of the house.

Suddenly aware of the quietness, Len looked at the clock on the microwave and realized it was only 9:30. The kids should be home soon. Samantha had gone over to Candice's house to practice for the upcoming Easter play. She'd complained that she needed to work on her mournful appearance to get into the mood of Mary Magdalene. Len privately thought that the role called for someone with greater maturity than her young daughter, but had kept silent. Samantha had an excellent singing voice, and the role required a solo. Obviously her daughter's singing talent dictated the role.

Brian had said that he'd try to get a ride home with Scott. Len had no worries in that regard. Not only could Brian take care of himself, but also she trusted Scott to ensure that he got home safely. She applauded what Scott was trying to do with the young men of the church. It was nice that they had someone like Scott to talk with. Not a parent. Not a pal. A man young enough to be considered relevant, but old enough to have some wisdom to share.

O God, Len prayed, *they're growing up so fast. Have we set the right example for them, Lord? Place a hedge around my children, Lord. Forgive me. I pray selfishly. Place a hedge around all of our children. If they make mistakes, help them to know that You are a forgiving Father and that You love them dearly. I feel that Brian and Sam are growing away from me. I don't know how they feel about important things anymore, so that's why I wonder—have I done enough to model You to them? Have I? Help me to cast these cares upon You. And please watch over Mr. Singh in the hospital. Ease his pain, and keep his heart in the hollow of Your hand. Thank You for being our balm in Gilead. Amen.*

With a somewhat lightened heart, Len cleared the remnants of tea and stacked the cups in the dishwasher, the words of "Learning to Lean" softly creeping into song. With a start she remembered that Robert was waiting for her to join him in the bath. Quickly wiping the table and countertop, she threw the dishcloth into the sink and dashed to the bedroom to get fresh clothes.

Since their early married days more than 27 years before, they'd made a habit of showering together on Friday nights. Years ago when they lived in the two-bedroom apartment and the kids were still very young, they'd wait until the children had fallen asleep, then steal away to wash each other's backs. Now the luxury of the Jacuzzi allowed them to take long relaxed soaks accompanied by nonalcoholic wine and candlelight. Their kids considered this practice "Euuugh" for people of their advanced age. The practice continued, however, not needing their approval or consent. Len thanked God every day for the wonderful man she'd married. Few in words, but with a heart as big as his capable hands.

Locking the bathroom door behind her, Len noticed that one of the candles Robert had lit had started to sputter. So she took a fresh candle from the cupboard and lit it just before the dying one gave its last gasp. "Bet you thought I'd forgotten you," she said to Robert.

She looked over to catch his smile. His eyes were closed, and his head rested against the special bath pillow she'd made him as one of her "just because" presents.

"Yeah, I know. You're too tired to talk. I'll come rub your back. That'll make you feel better."

Len picked up a bottle of scented oil and tipped a liberal amount onto her palms. Sitting on the edge of the bath, she massaged her husband's tired arms and shoulders, leaning forward to reach his upper chest, too.

"Robert, you know what I've been thinking? We should take a holiday soon. Us, and the kids. They're growing up so fast. It'd be good for us all to get away together."

Robert's head tipped forward onto his chest.

"Robert?"

His head didn't move.

"Robert?" Len repeated, questioning.

"Robert!" Len felt a buzzing in her head.

"Oh, dear God!"

Frantically she felt his neck for a pulse.

None. None!

Dear God, dear God!

None at the wrist.

Nothing.

Jesus, help me!

With her heart sputtering like that of the extinguished candle, Len gently returned Robert's head to the bath pillow and rushed out of the room to call 911. She heard a familiar, detached voice provide the dispatcher with all the requested details and watched a steady hand return the telephone to its cradle, leaving fingerprints of moisture on the black instrument.

Then Lenore Baptiste returned to the bathroom to resume her ritual Friday night massage, humming "Taps" to usher in the Sabbath.

"Samantha Baptiste, will you stop fooling around and focus!" Candice was exasperated. "We've been here for an hour and a half, and have not yet managed a proper run through the song. Focus! Focus! The play is in only eight days!"

"All right. Keep your weave on. I'll give it a shot. But I just don't feel particularly mournful right now. Did I tell you that Sammy smiled at me today at school?"

"Yes, Samantha. You told me he smiled at you. You told me he SMILED at you, and you told me he smiled at YOU. Now you tell me HE SMILED AT YOU. Sammy is a nice guy. He smiles at everyone, but if you'll notice *I* am not smiling at you right now. So you figure it out. All I want you to do is pretend someone you love dearly has just been killed. You hoped you would have had more time with them, but now they're gone. That's what happened to Mary Magdalene, Sam. Jesus is dead. There is no Sunday morning. He's just dead. Sing about that pain, Sam. Forget Sammy for now. Focus on death."

Candice pressed the play button to start the CD track.

Shivering as if someone had walked over her grave, Samantha closed her eyes and let the music take over.

Candice watched in amazement, tears filling her eyes. *What a talent she has, Lord. A voice husky and strong—how does she do it!* She sang of pain and loss and despair as God let sin separate Him from His only Son, and let Him die. The final strains of the music faded into the silence.

"Wow!"

Samantha opened her eyes and smiled. "Happy now?"

Not waiting for a reply, she continued as if the musical interlude never happened. "Candice, you're a bit older than me. So tell me, how do I find out if a guy really likes me, like *likes* me?"

Shaking her head in despair, Candice answered, "Well, I suppose he looks at you a lot, and yes, he smiles at you. If he is brave, he will go out of his way to walk or talk with you, but each guy is different. I am only a couple years older than you and not an experienced woman of the world. Most times I don't even know what I'm having for lunch because my mind is busy organizing an event—such as this play, Miss Thing. So let's make a deal. I will tell you what little I know about guys if you will sing at the Easter program just as you did tonight. Deal?"

"Cool! Deal," agreed a happy Samantha.

"Now that you've worn me out, let's head upstairs for a snack."

"Good idea. I'm starved."

Just then they heard the telephone ring three times, and then Candice's mom called down. "Candice, could you tell Samantha that she's wanted on the phone? It's her mom, I think."

"What do you mean, 'I think,' Mom? You and Mrs. Baptiste are like best friends. You don't know her voice?" Candice loud-speakered up the stairs.

"Well, if it's her, she didn't say hello. She just asked for Samantha. Have you picked the phone up yet, Samantha?"

Samantha hurried to the extension next to the couch where she'd been sitting. "I have it, Mrs. Bolski, thanks," she said into the receiver. Then, "Hello? Mom? You sound kinda weird."

"Come home now, Samantha," croaked Lenore.

"I'm just about to leave. Candice and I are going to grab a snack, and then I'll be right there."

"Don't take time to eat, Sam. Come home right now. Please." Lenore's voice almost broke. "Put Gwen on the phone."

Samantha stared at the phone as if she'd never seen one before and passed it wordlessly to Mrs. Bolski, who'd arrived in the basement. She could hear her mom's voice still speaking as Mrs. B put the phone to her ear.

"Lenore, it's me. What's going on?" asked Gwen.

"Gwen, could you please bring Samantha home right now? Oh, Gwen, hurry. I have to go, but I'll see you in a few minutes. OK?"

Mrs. Bolski's finger pressed the off button, and her smooth round forehead wrinkled into a frown.

Walking over to Candice, Samantha picked at a strand of her friend's hair and watched it fall slowly back against the mass of curls. She repeated this motion several times, mesmerized. Her body shivered.

"Samantha honey, your mom wants you to come home now," Gwen Bolski gently prompted.

Samantha let fall another strand of Candice's hair, and turning, she walked woodenly over to the couch, collected her things, and without saying another word headed past Mrs. Bolski up the stairs and toward the front door. Gwen's eyes met those of her daughter, and both followed quickly on Samantha's heels.

At the front door Samantha stuck her foot halfway into one running shoe, then without warning made a U-turn toward the kitchen, thumping and sock-padding her way back into the house.

In seemingly one motion Gwen grabbed her keys, threw on a light jacket, and redirected the fleeing Samantha back toward the front door and her other shoe. She let go of Samantha and turned to her daughter. "Candice, I think you'd better come along with us," she said.

When Gwen opened the front door, Samantha whirled around and again headed back into the house.

"We need to practice some more, Mrs. B, and we didn't have our snack. The song maybe should be in a lower key. If I get Jim to lower the key, do you think the band will play it instead of me singing with a track? It would give the song a bit more feel. What if I forget where to come in? Mrs. B, something bad has happened, hasn't it? My mommy is upset. I need to go home."

"Yes, honey. I'll take you right now," said Gwen as she herded the girls out the door, a feeling of dread in the pit of her stomach.

---

* Luke 24:32, KJV.

Chapter Three

Brian the Brave

Charmaine laid aside her women's devotional reading and pondered the topic she'd just read. The author of the article had claimed God's promise recorded in Isaiah 43:2 ("When you pass through the rivers, they will not sweep over you. When you walk through the fire, you will not be burned") as her reminder through a particularly painful relationship breakup.

I'm so blessed, Lord, prayed Charmaine. *You have been so good to me. I don't know that I take the time often enough to thank You. I have a wonderful husband who loves me dearly. He truly does, Lord—of that I have no doubt. Watch over him where he is right now. I feel angry with him sometimes, especially nights like tonight, when it seems that others are more important to him than I am. I want him home on Friday nights, Lord, but I do understand the importance of what he is trying to do with the young men of the church. Please rid me of this selfishness and remind me again that I can, instead, use these precious hours as time for just You and me. Bring Scott safely home, and take away the remnant of any resentment I might still be feeling.*

She had just decided to return to her reading when the phone rang.

"Hello, Mrs. O'Henry!"

"Hello to you too, Scott Henry."

Charmaine's maiden name was O'Dell, and in the process of figuring out whether she wanted to hyphenate her last name when she married Scott, he had jokingly said, "Why don't you become Mrs. O'Henry? Then I can have a nibble at you whenever I get hungry."

"So am I on the same level as junk food?" was Charmaine's rejoinder. "Thanks a lot!"

Somehow the moniker stuck, and became one of those accidental endearments that develop between husbands and wives.

"Running late?" asked Charmaine.

Sounding a bit offbeat to her ears, Scott replied, "I stopped to have a chat with Brian; then I'm giving him a ride home. I should be with you in about 40 minutes, so don't you dare fall asleep before I get there to kiss you good night."

"Well, since you asked so nicely, I'll wait up. I'll go make myself that cup of hot cocoa that I'd convinced myself earlier I didn't need. See you soon, love."

"'Bye, hon."

He does love me, doesn't he, Lord? Charmaine resumed her prayer, not really questioning God, but affirming a truth. *Teach me to share. He's such a good man, but I told You that already. Others need him too. Use me. Use him. Use us both to become the people You mean for us to be. Thank You for this Sabbath, this weekly reminder that we are so special to You. Help me to worship You with my whole heart. Amen.*

Charmaine looked lovingly around the small living room. It was a charming two-bedroom apartment, albeit on the small side. However, it was close to the subway and afforded her and Scott the ease of getting to and from work without the car. Her love of Highland plaid could be seen in the forest green and warm burgundies that accented the room. Illuminated with the low setting of the tri-light lamp and made cozy by the smell of baking bread wafting from the bread machine, the apartment looked and smelled the epitome of warm comfort. Another thing to be thankful for. She put her books away and headed for the kitchen to prepare her treat.

As she passed through the living room, she paused to admire a photograph of Scott that sat on the shelf of their entertainment center. His short-cropped hair accented the strong lines of his cheekbones. White teeth flashed in response to her prompt to smile. She'd managed to capture him during a hiking trip with a hint of impishness in his eyes. She kissed her index finger and touched it to his face.

"Hello there, Mr. Handsome." The warm look in his dark-brown eyes gleamed back at her.

"Did I hear you call your wife Mrs. O'Henry?" inquired Brian as Scott closed the cell phone and maneuvered the car back into the flow of traffic.

"Yep."

And it's none of my business!"

"You said it."

"You love her a lot, don't you?"

"Yep."

"All right, I'm not that thick. Enough for tonight, but I might ask again. Just be warned."

"I'm warned."

"My dad and mom are old, but they still take baths together almost every Friday night after we're in bed. They light candles and bring out the massage oil, and we're not allowed to bug them unless there's an emergency."

"Cool. That's romantic," smiled Scott.

"You know my dad. He's so quiet. Mostly he lets Mom or us speak for the family, but he loves my mom a lot. He's told me that several times. He says he hopes that when the time is right I'll find someone to love just like that. It's kinda corny but, you know, kinda neat. I don't know what he'd do if anything bad happened to Mom."

"God always gives us the— Whoa!" Scott pulled off to the side of the road seconds after the night air was pierced by the wailing of an ambulance rushing to who knows where.

"Man, I hate it when they put on the alarm suddenly like that," retorted Brian angrily. "Sometimes I think these guys do it so they won't have to slow down or wait at traffic lights. It's enough to give you a heart attack."

"There are no traffic lights here, Brian, and hardly any traffic. That looks like a real emergency."

"Hadn't thought of that. But just last week after I'd driven Sam to her swimming lessons, I was waiting at the traffic lights at Yonge and Sheppard. Man, I almost jumped outta my skin when I heard this sound like a flock of geese with sore throats. It was a cruiser. Lights flashing and all, speeding through the intersection. As soon as he went through, the honking and lights went off. *That* is taking advantage!"

"Careful, Brian. Didn't I hear you say you were thinking about becoming a cop? Those are your future brothers you're bashing, man. Remind me again, which turn is your street?"

"Oh, next right, then the first right after that, then left onto Park Trail. Number 55."

"Got it! Wow, these houses are nice."

"They're OK. It'll be five years this Easter since we moved here. Wait a minute, lights are flashing down there on our street. Man, I hope Mr. Singh's OK. Come to think of it, it can't be Mr. Singh. He's in the hospital. He's our neighbor. Oh, it's our house. They're taking somebody out of our house. Stop the car, Scott! STOP!"

Brian dashed out before Scott could completely stop the car. Seconds later Scott leaped out too. *O God, help us. Help them*, he prayed as he ran smack-dab into a masked mummy in a white bathrobe. As it focused on Brian, the mask seemed to split down the middle into two distinct halves to reveal the face of Lenore Baptiste. She grabbed her son, pushed him away, then gently pulled him back and held his face in her palms.

"Brian, your daddy is gone!"

"Gone where? Mom, what's wrong with Dad? They're taking him to the hospital? What happened? I told him to get his cholesterol checked. He had those white rings around his pupils. Man! OK, Mom, I'll come with you to the hospital. Where's Sam? Come on, Mom, get some clothes on. Why are you just standing there? They're closing the doors of the ambulance."

"Dear God, dear God, dear God, dear God," Lenore whimpered dry-eyed as the ambulance quietly drove away without its pulsing lights to hold back the gloom.

"Mom, where's the car? We'll follow in the car. Did they say which hospital they're taking him to?"

Lenore came to attention in the driveway. She looked at her son. So like his dad to look at, but not quiet like his dad. Her eyes commanded Brian's full attention as she said, "Brian, love, your daddy died in the bath 40 minutes ago. He's dead."

Scott was just at the right place to catch Brian as he fainted dead away, a look of complete stupidity on his face.

"Dear God, dear God, dear God. Help me, help me," prayed Lenore aloud.

Scott became aware of arms helping him support Brian's weight. As they were making their way toward the front door, a car flew around the corner and skidded into the driveway.

"Mommy!" cried a voice. The small crowd parted as Samantha flung herself into the presence of her mother. Close on her heels were Gwen and Candice Bolski.

"Mommy, what happened? What's the matter? You said to come right away. What's wrong with Brian? Why are they carrying him?"

Lenore gathered her daughter into her arms and held on tightly. After a little while her lips could be seen speaking words into Samantha's ear. Words that caused the girl's body to grow still and shiver violently in the chilly April night. A scream rent the air, followed by a full minute of silence. Then, as if in a paused movie, the sound came back on as neighbors, gawkers, and new mourners entered the scene. And the world came to life at Number 55 Park Trail.

Chapter Four

Charmaine

C harmaine. It's me."

Of course I know it's you, Scott. Don't tell me you're going to be later than you said! I've had my hot cocoa, spent some time with God, and as soon as the man that I love comes home, all will be well with my world."

"I'm sorry, honey, but I can't be home anytime soon."

"Scott!"

"Charmaine, I'm at the Baptistes'. Robert is dead."

"What! I just saw him this afternoon. What do you mean he's dead?"

"They think it was a massive heart attack, Char. He died in the bath."

"Oh, no! I'll come right away."

"But honey, I have the car."

"That's OK. I'll call a cab. It's Park Trail, right?

"That's right. Number 55. Off Westmount."

"Oh, Scott! Poor Mrs. Baptiste! Poor kids! Scott?"

"Yes."

"I love you, honey. I really do. You're the best thing that ever happened to me. Have I told you that today?"

"I love you, too, hon."

"See you soon. One more thing. Are there lots of people there?"

"It's starting to fill up. Mrs. Bolski came with Samantha right after the ambulance left. Sam didn't get to see her dad, and she's taking it really hard. Brian passed out on the driveway. He's come around now, but I'm kind of worried about him. He's just been staring at the wall, and not even his mom is getting through to him. I know he's in shock still. Everyone is, including me. It feels unreal. I gotta go. I'll see you soon, honey. Be careful."

In two minutes flat Charmaine Henry had donned a pair of black pants and a sweater. The hard part was waiting the 15 minutes the cab company said it would take to send a car. One arrived in seven minutes, and Charmaine was on her way.

Dear God, she prayed, *help me to be helpful to this family tonight. It was a Friday night like this that Your Son died. You know the pain we are feeling right now. Comfort this family, Lord. And show me what to do and say when I get there. Please make me a blessing. Amen.*

A stranger opened the door to Charmaine's knock. "Hi. I'm Emily Price, a next-door neighbor," said the slim white-haired senior.

"I'm Charmaine, a friend of the family. Please tell me how I can help."

"I don't know, dear," Emily said, wringing her hands. "This is such a shock. Robert and I were talking just this evening in the driveway before they headed to the hospital to visit Mr. Singh. I saw their car drive in two hours ago, and now he's dead. It's a bad dream. A really bad dream."

"I know! It's awful. I saw him earlier today at the fruit market. It's so hard to take in. And the poor children and Lenore," mourned Charmaine. "I think I'll go find Samantha. I used to teach her in Sabbath school. God will see them through this. He's especially good with these types of tough situations."

"God!" spat Emily. "What good did He do to this poor family tonight? Taking an honest, good man like Robert Baptiste? He was hardworking, took care of his family, and loved his wife. How can you talk about God being good at a time like this? If He's such a good God, why didn't He take one of those thugs roaming the street molesting decent people trying to make a living? Tell me that, young lady!" On that note Emily Price stalked away, leaving Charmaine to come into the house and find the broken family herself.

Taken aback, Charmaine eased off the light jacket she'd grabbed on her way out the door and proceeded in the direction of voices coming from the rear of the house. Approximately a dozen people were already gathered in the family room, all speaking in hushed tones. Neither Scott nor any family members were to be seen. Unsure of the correct procedure for assisting a grieving family, especially with a wound so fresh, Charmaine was trying to decide what to do or where to go when the phone shrilled into the hushed quietness. After four rings she lifted the receiver. "Baptiste residence," she said.

"Yes, it is true. Mr. Baptiste died tonight. No, I don't know a lot of details, but I could call you back as soon as I know more. The family? I'm not sure where they are right now, but I will tell them that you called. 'Bye."

"Paper, paper, I need paper," muttered Charmaine. Ah, paper! She spied a small pad lying atop the telephone directory on the nearby shelf. She'd just finished writing the name of the caller when the phone rang again. The church's grapevine had been activated.

One call after another, the phone rang constantly for the next half hour. Writing furiously, Charmaine recorded message after message and gave directions to the house several times over.

Just when she thought she could not field another call without additional information, there was a lull. Seizing the opportunity, she dashed upstairs in hopes of at least finding her husband. At the end of the hallway she came upon a sight that broke her heart afresh.

No sound.

No tears.

Three people holding on to each other, each looking shell-shocked and extremely wounded.

A tired-sounding voice belonging to Lenore Baptiste greeted her.

"Hello, Charmaine. We're hiding. Robert is d—" Samantha's hand clamped over her mother's mouth.

"Don't say it, Mommy. Please." Not denying the reality, but not ignoring the raw need of her daughter, Lenore pulled her close and stroked her hair.

"Oh, honey," soothed Lenore.

Charmaine observed a stiffening of Brian's back. Wordlessly he released his mom and sister and left the room. Len's arms reached out to bring him back into her circle of care while still holding on to her daughter. A choice between two competing needs. Her face mirrored the struggle as her hands massaged comfort to the one still in its embrace.

Feeling like an interloper, Charmaine turned to leave, but Lenore's voice stopped her.

"Don't go, Charmaine. We need you to help us hold things together. What's the paper in your hand?"

"Well, I've been taking messages from callers, and I promised to get back to them with information and to let you know that they called." Charmaine read quickly through the list of names.

"The grapevine is activated," sighed Lenore. "What a large family we have. The Lord gives, and the Lord takes away.* I didn't light the candles with him tonight, Charmaine. We usually light the candles together. He died, and I didn't even know it. I was talking to him the whole time, and I didn't know.

I was massaging his back, and I didn't know till his head fell to his chest. I should have known. Should have felt something. He was my heart. Why did mine not stop beating when his did?" Lenore asked this question as if trying to figure out an intellectual curiosity.

Choking back a sob, Charmaine ran into the circle of embrace to provide comfort and find a task for Lenore's one empty arm. The prayer broke from her lips before she could think.

"O God, we need Your comfort now, Father, right now. Send Your angels to encourage Lenore and Samantha and Brian, Lord. You know their pain. I know You can exchange this blanket of grief and put joy in their hearts again, but tonight the pain is so sharp and new, and it hurts so badly. Comfort this family, Your children, Lord Jesus. Bless them tonight as they hurt, as we all hurt. Bear us up in Your hands."

"I want my daddy. Daaaddy! God, why did You take my daddy? I didn't get to say goodbye. I didn't get to say good night." Great, heaving sobs racked Samantha's body while Lenore's hands accelerated its comforting motions. And one solitary tear carved a new wrinkle down the right side of her face.

---

* See Job 1:21.

Saturday

Chapter Five

Today Is All We Have

G ood morning, honey." Scott reached over and drew his wife close to him. She looked as exhausted as he felt. "Have you been awake long?"

"For a while. I woke up at 7:00 and couldn't get back to sleep. I kept seeing Lenore and Robert in my dreams. He looked so alive, and then when I woke up and remembered, it took the sleep away for good. How about you?"

"Just let me hold you for a while." It felt good to lie against her warm body. Comforting.

Charmaine snuggled closer, burying her face within the crook of her husband's neck. He held her tightly, inhaling the scent of her and stroking her short, curly hair. She'd worn her hair longer when they'd first met, in a style that framed her face and half hid the dimples in her cheeks. He was captivated by the dimples. He would have loved her without them, but from then on he worked to invent ways to make her smile so he could see those lovely dimples. The long hair hiding them was always a source of frustration, but about a year ago she'd come home from the hairdresser with the short, sassy look she now sported. He missed the longer hair, but was compensated by the clear view of her cheeks and the artistic depression wrought by a smile. This morning, however, her cheeks were smooth and burrowed in his neck beneath his chin. Scott sighed. Neither one of them felt capable of smiling.

"I believe that when we die it *is* a sleep," said Scott, "but Robert's death has shocked me again into the realization of how frail we really are and how tenuous our hold on life is. We should know this, but at times we walk around so arrogantly it's as if we rule the universe. I know we can't spend all our time dwelling on dying, yet how we regularly misuse our time. How does God put up with us?"

Pulling her even closer, Scott continued, "Oh, honey, I am just glad that I can hold you right this very minute. I pray that I will never lose you. I know my hope is futile, but I am still amazed that you love me and are here with me right now. I'm glad it's not you who's dead. I know God will see me through when that happens, but just for today I am really, really grateful that I have you to hold. I love you, Charmaine O'Dell Henry."

Shifting her face in order to speak, Charmaine whispered against his chin. "And I love you so very much, Scott Henry." She kissed him tenderly on the chin, then exhaling loudly, she turned onto her back. "Are you going to church today?"

"I really don't feel up to it, but I'll go. The guys will probably want to talk about what to do for Brian and his family. Yikes! This is my week to teach the young adult class!"

On that note Scott released his wife, gave her a quick kiss on the cheek, and reluctantly dragged himself out of bed. He missed the look of disappointment on her face as he headed toward the shower.

Exhaling more forcefully this time, Charmaine reached for her women's devotional in search of other words of comfort.

Pastor Andrew Leonardo Simms—Pastor Al to the young people—stood before his congregation. It was going on five years since he'd come to New Haven Ministries. During that time it had grown from a small company into a thriving community of 500, with a healthy dispersion of young adults.

He finally could say that he knew almost all of his parishioners by name. He bolstered them. They bolstered him. But today his typical twinkling smile was missing. The pastorate weighed heavily on his back. These people, his flock, his fellow pilgrims, his friends, needed a word to ease the heaviness in their hearts. He too needed a word. One man's absence had left them stunned.

He prayed for strength.

"My fellow believers. My sisters and brothers. My friends."

He paused, the muscles in his jaw contracting.

"More than four years ago when I first entered this church, I was greeted by a quiet man who would eventually become my mentor, my supporter, my shoulder-gripper, and my friend. Robert Baptiste would meet me in the vestry every Sabbath morning, shake my hand, and then give my shoulder a grip. When this pastor needed a pillar—or wasn't even aware that he needed one—Robert was a quiet strength. Few in words, when he spoke he dropped nuggets of gold. I was made a richer man because of him.

"But this morning I had no handshake. This morning there was no grip

. . . no . . . grip on my shoulder." He could feel his throat closing up. He sucked in a deep, wet-sounding breath and soldiered on.

"Robert Baptiste died last night."

Pastor Al heard a few gasps of shock in the congregation. Apparently the usually effective grapevine had missed a few folks.

"While the cause is still being investigated, it is suspected that it was from a massive brain aneurysm."

He bowed his head and prayed for strength.

"So here we are this Saturday. A gaping hole in the middle of our hearts. And I for one am lost in the gap Robert has left behind. I can't imagine how Lenore, Brian, and Samantha must be feeling."

Somebody in the congregation was crying aloud. Pastor Al prayed for more strength. This death was too personal.

"If Robert were here right now, I'm sure he would quietly walk up to me and grip me on the shoulder. Then he would gently say to me—he always spoke gently—'Let not your heart be troubled . . .'"

His voice wobbled, but the congregation joined in with theirs to bolster him and each other, his tears joining those already flowing from fellow mourners. He tried again.

"'Let not your heart be troubled: ye believe in God, believe also in me. In my Father's house are many mansions; if it were not so, I would have told you. I go to prepare a place for you. And if I go'—what did He promise to do?"

The congregation answered back, using the familiar King James words, "'I will come again, and receive you unto myself.'"

"'That where I am . . .'"

They answered with one voice. "'There ye may be also.'"

"On days like this I long for heaven. Don't you?"

The congregation nodded in agreement.

"On days like this, when pain strikes with no apologies, I long for heaven. Death is the enemy, and a vicious one at that! Today it has left us reeling in its wake."

He forcefully calmed himself and continued.

"Yet even in the midst of this hard pain, let's comfort one another. Let's bolster our family. Let's allow death's sting to swell us up into a community of perseverers. Death will not make us give up, give in, or give over. We serve a death-surviving God."

A chorus of amens and hallelujahs filled up the room.

"Yes, let's weep because the pain is hard. But let's also remember: Joy comes in the morning."†

Sister Reese shot up out of her seat and got her praise on. Pastor Al waited for quiet.

"Last week, last Saturday morning, I received my last grip from Robert. I did not know then it would be the last. But it was. My fellow believers. My family. Grip each other today. Put away the stuff that's standing between you and someone else. Grip your child. Grip your wife. Grip your husband. Grip your friend. Though we like to pretend otherwise, tomorrow is not promised. Today is all we have. And while you are gripping those around you, tighten your grip on God. And be assured that even though our fingers may get tired and we lose our grip on Him, He will never let us go if we ask Him to hold on to us."

Pastor Al reached under the podium for the box of tissues and sat down. He felt the presence of his wife beside him, comforting. Quiet crying could be heard among the congregation. Then the organist started a hymn, and those capable of singing joined in.

When peace, like a river, attendeth my way,
When sorrows like sea billows roll—
Whatever my lot, Thou hast taught me to say,
It is well, it is well with my soul.‡

After the song an elder prayed, and church was dismissed.

Still they sat, drawing comfort from each other and making plans to bring comfort to the immediate members of the grieving family.

◆ ◆ ◆ ◆ ◆

"Hey, Scott, can I talk to you for a minute?" Todd stopped Scott as he was locking up the youth room.

"Sure, Todd. What's up?" Todd's normally serious face was even more studied today.

"Man, that's an awful thing to have happen to Brian's dad. He was so quiet and all, but I really liked him, and I know that Brian was really close to him. How's Brian taking it?"

"He was in shock, but trying to be stoic." Scott and Todd walked out to the parking lot. "It's too soon to tell how he'll come through this. When I

Today Is All We Have

left his house early this morning, he was just staring at the wall and not say-ing a thing. He kinda waved goodbye when I left, but I don't think he was aware of what he was doing. I don't know. I think women have it right. They cry or talk about how they feel. Men suck it all in."

"So what do we do, Scott? How do we help him?"

"Hang around and wait to catch him when he crashes. 'Cause he will."

"You headed over there later?"

"Yeah. Charmaine stayed home today, but we'll both go over later. You want to come with us?"

"I want to go, but I don't want to at the same time. You go ahead. Let me round up a few of the guys and see what they want to do. I know they're feeling as uncertain as I am, but we all want to do something."

"OK. Just think of what you would want someone to do for you if you were in Brian's place. And if you don't have any words to say, just hang around long enough to let him know you're there. Keep in touch, especially after the funeral. That's when the crash most likely will happen."

"Thanks, Scott."

"No problem, Todd. As Pastor Al said today, that's what God put us here for—to be a comfort to each other."

■ ■ ■ ■ ■

"Mom, what are we going to do about the Easter play?" Candice asked her mother Sabbath afternoon.

Church had been a place of mourning, and now many folks were visiting with the Baptiste family. A rehearsal was scheduled for the next evening, but Candice wondered if anyone's heart was in it anymore. It was difficult going on with business as usual in the middle of so much heartache and pain. Her own dad was long gone, and she was used to that, but poor Samantha. How was she going to cope? Plus, hers was a pivotal role in the play. Candice could not see how Samantha could continue in the production. It was too much to expect. She was too broken up, and the play was now only seven days away.

Gwen thought for a while before answering. "Now more than ever, peo-ple need to hear about death. Think of it. Jesus was in the tomb on a day like today. His family and friends were feeling the sharp pain of separation that we all feel right now. Imagine how His mother felt. Imagine how Lazarus,

Martha, Mary, and His disciples felt! The Easter story should be told. I think we all need to hear it anew."

"But Mom, this is going to be so hard. I was yelling at Samantha last night to sing as if she'd lost someone very dear to her. I said that to get her into the mood. And now her dad is dead." She gasped at the thought. "He probably was dying as I was yelling at Sam. Oh, Mom! I didn't mean it. Look what has happened."

"Don't do this to yourself, Candice! How could you have known? Life happens, honey, and sometimes death comes—often without so much as a knock on the door. For those who die in the Lord, it is not the end.

"As hard as it is for the family and friends to go on, we have the hope that we'll see our loved ones again. That is what Easter does for us, Candice. It reminds us in the middle of Saturday that there is coming a Sunday morning. The One who has power over death and the grave is the One who tells us that one day He will come again to receive us unto Himself."

She gave her daughter a slight smile. "Can you focus on that during your preparation for the play, dear? Maybe it will help you to convey the message in a whole new way. Saturday's sorrow does not last forever."

"I'll try, Mom. But it's so hard. I want to go over and stay with Sam, but I don't even know what to say to her. How will I ask her if she is able to sing for the production?"

"Have a plan B, love. But don't underestimate Samantha. Focusing on this production may give her a way of working through her own pain. After all, Mary Magdalene's life, the role Sam's playing, was not an easy one. God does not delight in our hurting, Candice, but He can use hurting moments to draw us closer to Him—if we let Him." She paused, unconsciously shaking her head. "When your dad left, I thought I would not survive the pain. But God has used that pain to make me a stronger person. Go on over to Sam's. I'll be by later on. I need to make a few casseroles for the funeral dinner."

It was a good 40-minute walk to the Baptistes', and Candice could have taken the bus, but she needed the time to think. She had no idea how to help her friend other than just being there and holding her hand. It felt so awkward. All of the things she thought of saying didn't seem to be the right things. Life should stop when someone died. Yet the sun was still making its way across the sky, and life went on as usual for most, while for others, such as the Baptistes, it had come to a full stop. All too soon she was turning in the driveway of Number 55 Park Trail.

The house was even more full than last night. People seemed to be in every nook and cranny, while Sam was nowhere to be seen. Mrs. Baptiste stood in the family room with a group of women from church, looking and talking as if she were the one doing the comforting. Candice was amazed. Mrs. Baptiste looked up, saw her, and excused herself from the group.

"Candice, how are you, love? How was church today? We couldn't come because none of us had a lot of sleep last night. Sam just woke up from a nap and should have showered by now. Why don't you run up and see her? I'm sure she'd like to see a friend. Just earlier she was reminding me that she has a rehearsal tomorrow."

"She still wants to be in it?"

"I think so, but why don't you talk to her yourself?"

Seeing Candice's hesitation, Lenore hugged her. "This is a tough time for all of us, Candy, but God will see us through. If I didn't believe that, I could not go on. Help us remember that, especially this Easter. Now go on up and stop looking so tragic. Death came to our house yesterday, and it is at some- one else's house today, and will be somewhere else tomorrow. Help us keep the hope alive so that we will not fall apart."

The host mask on Lenore's face slipped a little, and Candice caught a glimpse of sequestered pain. Jerking her neck as if to snap her head back to reality, Lenore smiled and pointed a still-amazed Candice up the stairs to her daughter.

Brian lay on his bed and stared into an empty place. It asked nothing of him. That was perfectly fine. He had nothing to give. Around the periphery of the place were images of people connected to him, but not a part of him, mouthing words that had no meaning, made no sense. Some of them touched his body—hugged him, even—but they were far, far away, irrelevant sentries around the empty place. He watched himself, and he watched them. And he felt the nothingness gain weight.

---

* John 14:1–3, KJV.
† See Ps. 30:5.
‡ *The Seventh-day Adventist Hymnal,* no. 530.

Chapter Six

The Alabaster Box

Charmaine's Sabbath had not been restful. Why today of all days could she not find peace and comfort? She should have gone to church with Scott. That's what she should have done. Church would have provided a distraction from whatever was ailing her.

Today, with time on her hands and death on her mind, she looked at herself, and did not like what she saw. Today, with pain in her heart over the Baptistes' loss, she could not understand why her husband, the man whom she loved more than she was afraid of death, did not choose to stay with her and hold her. Instead, he'd chosen to put those deserving young men and their needs above hers.

Seeing Sam's door slightly ajar, Candice knocked softly. The plush beige carpet that covered the upstairs rooms and hallway caressed her bare toes. "Hey, Sam, it's me, Candice."

A husky voice answered. "Come in, Candice. I'm up."

Candice tiptoed into the room and sat down on the bed of her friend. She felt awkward in this place of death and mourning.

"The kindergarteners sent you a few cards. Jonathan especially asked for you and offered to send you his beloved 'blankie' to help you feel better."

Samantha was touched by Jonathan's offer as well as the gifts of love from the class she assisted in teaching. "Oh, Candice, I'd take him up on his offer if I thought it would make things better. Having you here and knowing that others have our family in their thoughts make me feel less lonely. This death thing is awful, Candy. I woke up this morning thinking about nothing in particular, and then all the memories came crashing into my head. My daddy is dead, and the sun still came up this morning. How can that be? I want the world to stop, the sun to stand still or something. My dad's death should have caused something big in the universe to break."

"What exactly happened, Sam? Last night I heard that it was a heart attack, and today at church I heard it was something else. It was all so sudden. Your dad wasn't sick—was he?"

"Not that I know of. Mom says that they'll do an autopsy, but if it wasn't a heart attack, then it might have been an anuri—something."

"Aneurysm. Yikes! I don't know what to say, Sam. I feel so helpless," blurted Candice.

"If Daddy were here, he'd say something like 'Words are not the only ways of comforting.' He had this thing about too much talking and saying nothing." Sam chuckled softly. "He would also say that what I just said was a prime example. Dear God, I don't think I can survive without my dad. He was always there for me, Candy. He always came to my room to watch over me. Sometimes I'd pretend to be asleep, and he would just stand there and look at me. Sometimes he prayed over me, and if I was asleep or pretending to be, he would kiss his two middle fingers and lay them gently on my cheek and whisper, 'Good night, my precious.'

"Why did he have to die, Candy? Who will call me precious? Who will pray for me and teach me about life? I don't want him to be dead! I want him to be downstairs sitting on his chair and quietly holding up our home. I want Mom to be back to buzzing around as usual, making space to entertain the usual Sabbath crowd. But he's someplace alone lying in a cold box, and Mom is . . ." Sobs took over her body.

"Easy, Sam. I'm sorry; I'm so sorry." Candice tightly hugged her sobbing friend for whose grief she had no balm. And because she had no words, she relaxed her hug and gently rocked her back and forth, humming the tune to the Easter song "Alabaster Box." She felt Sam react.

"That's it! Why didn't I figure this out before?" With tears still spilling from her fountain of grief, Sam abruptly broke the embrace, a look of wonder in her eyes.

"What's it?" asked a bewildered Candice.

"The alabaster box. You were just humming that song!"

Used as she was to Sam's conversational and emotional gymnastics, Candice was having difficulty connecting the dots this time. Seeing the confusion on Candice's face, Samantha explained with the wonder of new discovery still on her face.

"The alabaster box had oil. Mary poured the oil on Jesus to prepare Him for burial. On a Saturday like today, Candy, Jesus was lying in a cold place just like my dad. The disciples and Mary and every one of His friends were mourning just like us. All of Saturday was about death and pain. Mary's song must have been the saddest song of all. All day Saturday they had no idea what would happen on Sunday morning! I need to get ready for the Easter program, Candy. I know now what you were asking me to sing about. Saturday is a wretched and awful day of death. No hope, no promise of a Sunday. Just think, Candy, they had no clue! That particular Saturday had to be just like today. Full of pain and death! I understand now." Tears flooded her eyes anew. "I am living Easter Saturday."

"Are you sure you're up to this, Sam? This is a rough time for you and—"

"I—" Sam interrupted with a sob. "I won't have to try to borrow the emotion. I just need to focus my sorrow and grief and pour it into the music. I can do this for my dad. I can do this. Call Mom for me, Candice. I have to tell her. I can do this."

Candice hurried to do her bidding and soon returned with a frantic Lenore on her heels.

"Sam, what's the matter?"

Her teary-eyed daughter turned to her full of knowing wonder. "Mom, Easter Saturday was just like today!"

Sensing no immediate crisis, Lenore's overtired heart downshifted to its regular hyperrhythm. "Say that again?"

Samantha explained her new discovery to her mom, finishing with "Don't you see, Mom? They had no clue. They didn't know that Sunday morning would change everything. That's what we need to tell the people during the Easter program, Mom. We need to show them how awful Saturday was so that they can really appreciate the miracle of Sunday morning. We are living through a Saturday like that one."

Lenore stayed quiet for a long time, her head bowed.

Samantha misunderstood. "I'm sorry, Mom. I didn't mean to hurt you. I thought that this would . . ."

Lenore drew her daughter to her and placed her two middle fingers over her lips. "Don't apologize, Sam. I was just taking time to thank God in the middle of this saddest of days for your reminder that Saturday's pain does not last forever. We can hang on to that, Sam. Thank you, girls, for the reminder. *Please, God, give us the patience to endure, no matter how long it takes, for the Sunday morning miracle and the subsequent descent of the Comforter."*

Lenore opened her eyes just in time to see the haunted face of her son retreat from the doorway to return to his own grief.

How can they pray and be grateful to God in all this? Brian slammed the door and flung the pillow against the wall. God! Well, he had a thing or two to say to this God. What did his dad ever do to deserve a death such as this? His dad was the best of God's followers. And God did this to him. Starting now, he had no place for this God. *Sorry, Dad! I know you'd be disappointed to hear this, but God cannot love and allow pain like this. After all this family has done for Him!*

Scott felt at loose ends. Too much sorrow. Too many things he could not fix. He really should get home to Charmaine, but Brian's haunted face from the night before was still with him. Without even knowing that he'd made a decision, he found his car headed for the Baptistes' home. Memories, like a recent but fleeting nightmare, brought a shiver to his spine. Life was so short. Was it only last night that he'd driven up this street planning a future that had turned on its head? Was it only yesterday that Robert was making his own plans for tomorrow? His heart beat dully in his ears, marking time to the ultimate solo dance. *Death is not natural*, he thought.

He eased his body from the car and mustered what little joy he had. The dregs created a slight smile, which he gave to Lenore, who greeted him at the door. Her exhausted voice sounded as if it were at war with the serenity in her eyes. He folded her in his arms as words deserted him. She hugged him back with the kind of intensity that spoke of repressed tears and banked pain. He felt her body shudder and asked the inane question that came from inadequate words.

"Are you going to be OK?"

He felt the escape of a sigh against his neck, almost reminiscent of Charmaine's early-morning sigh.

"I will be fine, Scott. I really will. God has already sent me many messages of encouragement today. Your hug is one of them. Thank you so much. Now come on in and help me mingle with my comforters. By the way, where is Charmaine?"

"She stayed home today. I'm on my way back from church, but wanted to drop in and see if there was anything you need. And I wanted to touch base with Brian. He's been on my mind a lot today."

"I'm glad you came by." She sighed. "I hope you can get him to open up. He will not allow himself to be comforted, and if I know my boy well, this is going to be a rough time for him. He's shut down, Scott, and when he does that, we just have to wait it out."

"Do you mind if I go up and see him anyway?"

"Why would I mind? Go right on up," Lenore directed.

Scott climbed the stairs and knocked softly on Brian's door. "Hey, Brian, it's me, Scott."

A full minute later the door opened. Entering the room, Scott saw that the blinds were still drawn and the bed made but rumpled. Perching himself on the edge of his bed, Brian looked the picture of dejection. He'd slept in his clothes, his face looked haggard, and he moved as though his whole body hurt. Scott wanted to put his arms around the young man, but Brian's aura welcomed no intruders within his personal space. Scott chose to respect that.

"Did you manage to get some sleep?"

"A little, I think." Brian cleared his unused voice.

"The guys at church told me to say hello, and I think some of them are going to drop by to see you."

"Yeah, thanks," said Brian dully.

Resisting the awkwardness of death in the room, Scott plowed on.

"Your dad was a very special man, Brian. I know you already know that, but I just wanted to say the words aloud. When I moved to this area and started to come to our church, he introduced himself and invited me to one of the men's retreats they were having that summer. I'd never been to one of those things before, so he took me under his wing. I remember we were in the middle of a discussion group about the role of men in the home, and I must have been spouting some opinion about how Charmaine and I were so in love that I couldn't imagine doing anything to hurt her or putting the needs of others above hers."

Glimpsing what looked like a flicker of interest in Brian's eyes, Scott continued.

"I remember him looking me in the eye and saying something to the effect that sometimes we hurt the people we love without even meaning to, and that the important thing is what we do about the hurt when it happens. He talked about the importance of making and taking time to talk—and mostly listen—to the person you're married to, and doing nice things for them to remind them that they are loved. Those words of your dad's have helped me a lot."

A reluctant smile visited Brian's mouth. "That's Dad, all right. He should have been a scholar."

"But he was, Brian. He just didn't get a Ph.D. from a university. God, in His wisdom, knows why He allowed him to go now, but I know we can trust Him to see us through the pain."

Brian jumped up, his dark eyes blazing in the dimly lit room. "Don't talk to me about God, Scott. Let's have that clear. I don't want to hear about Him or talk about Him. As far as I'm concerned, God died with my dad last night."

"You really don't mean that, Brian. After all, your dad lived his life for God and for others. He was truly a good man!"

"So why did God snuff him out just like that? Why? No warning. No time to prepare yourself. Just like that," Brian snapped his fingers, "and Dad's gone—leaving a big fat hole in our family that will never be filled. Answer me that! If that's God's love, then I don't want to have anything to do with it or with Him!"

"But death is a reality of living, Brian—"

"Save it, Scott. I respect you and all, but save the preaching for someone looking for a crutch."

Recognizing that any more talk of God would further antagonize his young friend, Scott walked over to the window. He wanted to let in some of the light, but instead turned his back to the window and again faced his young friend.

"How's Samantha doing? I didn't see her downstairs when I came in."

"Sam will be fine. I'll make sure they're fine. That's what Dad would want. I'll do what I can for them. Just none of the God stuff."

Scott walked over to Brian, who'd again sunk down on the edge of his bed.

"Do that, my friend. Your mom and sister need you, and you need them." He ventured a quick, light touch on his shoulder. "I promise I will not talk to you of God unless you bring the subject up. But I'll be praying every day for you to find your way back to your faith. Now, I'd better get home before Charmaine starts to worry. We'll be back tomorrow to help with the preparations for the funeral."

A gentle shoulder grip and back slap, and Scott let himself out of the room. Even as he walked away his mouth moved silently in unsolicited prayer for his young friend.

Charmaine busied herself setting the table in preparation for lunch. The barley vegetable soup would be a nice beginning to the Sabbath meal. She dawdled over the preparations, anticipating that Scott would be a bit late coming home. Death had a way of causing people who typically don't talk to you to want to connect. She silently talked to God again about her feelings of deprivation, chastising herself for resenting the very attributes that had attracted her to Scott in the first place. But she couldn't help it. She felt so alone.

Why does everyone always have to come before me? Why can't I be the— What? The only one who matters to Scott? Is that what I want? And why? He loves me. I know he does. So what more do I want of him?

Exclusivity, a voice answered.

But I can't want that, Charmaine argued back. *That's selfish and un-Christlike.*

Be honest with yourself for once! You want him exclusively. You wanted him to stay with you today because you were scared. You did not tell him that. You did not say what you needed, but you felt it, and then got angry when he left you for the guys.

O God, I am selfish. I don't want to share my husband, but I don't want to be selfish. What am I to do?

The ringing of the telephone interrupted Charmaine's private debate. "Hello."

"Hi, hon. I'm coming home right this minute. See you soon."

"OK, lunch is almost ready. Anyone coming with you?"

"No. I just want to be with you today. We can come back to be with Lenore and the family later, but right now I just want it to be us."

"Me too. See you soon, love."

Catching a glimpse of her face in the mirror as she hung up the phone, Charmaine noticed it was smiling.

He loves me.

On her way to the kitchen to check on the status of lunch, the phone rang again. Guessing it was Scott calling back to say that he was bringing someone home with him after all, she answered with a lilt in her voice, "Yes, Mr. Henry?"

"Is this the home of Scott Henry?"

"Who's calling, please?"

There was a pause. "I'm sorry, but are you . . . are you his wife?"

Feeling a touch of alarm, Charmaine responded, "Yes. Is something wrong with Scott? Was there an accident?"

"Oh, dear me," answered the voice. "This is not going to be easy. Can I leave a number for you, dear? Have your husband call me as soon as he gets in. Here's the number. It's long distance, I'm afraid."

Charmaine wrote down the number with a feeling of undefined dread. "Are you sure that I cannot help you in any way, Ms. . . . ?"

"It's Turner. My name is Lana Turner. Just like the actress. I am Emelia's mother. He will know who it is." And with that, the phone went dead.

Charmaine pondered the strange call, but could fathom nothing except the continuing feeling of disquiet.

Gwen Bolski put the last mound of grated cheese on the macaroni pie and inserted it in the oven. "There. That's done." She set the timer for 45 minutes and the temperature for 375 degrees and started to clean up the kitchen. Her mind turned to Lenore. What could she say to her to help her friend? Probably nothing. Being there for the long journey back from the edge of insanity was what was needed.

Lenore's faith was strong. Gwen knew that. She'd been there in the past to bolster Gwen. The words she had spoken, the phone calls at the right moments, the hugs that communicated love and care given at the right time. Always.

Stephan had taken her heart and almost her sanity. Or so she thought at the time he'd left her with a young child to rear on her own. Not quickly, but quietly, bit by bit for a year, he'd distanced himself from them. Missing dinners, then days. All the time promising a moon he could no longer deliver.

Two years later he wrote to ask for deliverance in the form of divorce papers. That was the day Gwen lost her footing. She'd been so sure that he'd eventually come back. So sure.

It was Lenore, and God, and angels, and little Candy who made sure that she walked again. Now Lenore was the one who would need a step trainer. Maybe not today. But soon.

Scott bounded into the apartment. "Where's my favorite girl?"

Charmaine ran to greet him. He swung her up in his arms and kissed her breathless.

"I should have stayed with you today, hon. I missed you by my side." Sitting them both down on the couch, he cupped her face in his hands and looked deeply in her eyes. "Charmaine Elizabeth O'Dell Henry, will you still take this man to be your lawful wedded husband? To love you and cherish you as long as life lasts?"

Charmaine was overcome. Without warning, her eyes filled up with tears, and with a full and grateful heart she answered, "Yes, my love, I will, and I do."

Their loving became a dance of healing. Later they made their way to the kitchen to salvage what remained of lunch. They fed each other soup and continued to murmur words of endearment as they ate—hardly any space separating one from the next.

"I could die now a happy man," murmured Scott.

"Please don't talk about death. Let's think about life and about you and me and us and happiness. Just for a little bit longer."

"But it is my happiness that's talking, love. It's my happiness to be with you and to be so thoroughly loved by you. Especially when you kiss me like this."

At 73, Emily Price, neighbor to the Baptistes, would be the first to admit that she lacked patience. Others might have said of her that she did not suffer fools gladly. At this moment, however, she was seated in Lenore's living room right next to her friend's pastor. The man had been going on and on for what seemed like forever about God's so-called goodness, mercy, and love. Throughout his monologue the eight or so adults around the room nodded respectfully in his direction. Obviously, they too believed this drivel.

Emily wanted to fling something breakable against the wall. Hard! Had her Thomas been here, he would have seen the danger signs and reached over to press her hands. But he wasn't. Instead, Emily suddenly stood up. The pastor turned at her abrupt move, smiled, and, mistaking her rise for an imminent departure, pronounced a blessing on her. She felt her face flush.

As Emily struggled to reel in her desire for some kind of violent protestation, she thought of her dearly departed Thomas. That was not sufficient. She then thought of her mother, long departed, resting in peace there in the family plot in Glasgow, Scotland. She would not embarrass them. She certainly would not. Plus, dear Robert would . . .

She must not think of that. She would make tea. Pots and pots of tea. That's what she'd do. Mumbling something she hoped was polite, she ejected herself from the room.

Wow, that was close! Sure, the pastor seemed like a nice man, and he had kind eyes, but she could not have abided another second of his constant references to God. She wondered where he went to school to learn to God-talk like that. Dear Robert would have patted her hand and told her that he'd come by tomorrow to cut her grass. She liked quiet people, even if they had to believe in God. But even though the pastor had kind eyes, he really did talk too much.

Sunday

Chapter Seven

A Voice From the Past

Happy Sunday morning to you, my gorgeous! Today I am going to make you breakfast. Belgian waffles à la Scott! Your only decisions will be how many you want to eat and your choice of topping."

Flipping onto her back, Charmaine stifled a yawn. Then stretching lazily like a cat, she turned her back to her husband. Soon, however, her voice took on a tone of extreme concentration.

"Choice of toppings? H'mm, tough decision. Frozen yogurt might be nice, or blueberries. No. Make that strawberries. But then again, raspberries have such a nice tang. But since it's my choice, and the sky is the limit . . ."

"I did not say that," protested Scott.

Undeterred, Charmaine continued, ". . . yes, since the sky is the limit and my husband will do anything for me, and since he spent a good part of yesterday and much of last night telling me how much he loves me, I really should consider sliced bananas with chocolate syrup . . . or maybe hot buttered apple slices with a sprinkle of cinnamon and brown sugar. Ooooo, yes. But then, why just settle for waffles? How about French toast and a cheese-and-tomato omelet?"

Smacking her lips loudly in anticipated pleasure, Charmaine focused on her culinary wonderland.

Scott groaned. "Help! I've created a monster. How did that happen? Beside me a minute ago was a woman who told me she loved me with all her heart, and just like that"—he snapped his fingers—"she has turned into this beast who just wants more and more. How do I shut her up?"

Scott assumed a listening pose. "You think that will do the trick?" he asked. He seemed to listen again, then nodded. "Then who am I to question?"

Scott turned onto his left side, reached across the three- to four-inch gap, and gently pulled his wife close. She snuggled up against him. He whispered a question somewhere in the vicinity of Charmaine's ear.

"Am I on the right track?"

Charmaine could picture him listening for a response. Loving the game, she still kept enunciating her various menu possibilities.

Her husband's voice continued. "Oh? I should do a bit more of this? I'll get right on it."

Thus prompted, Scott splayed light kisses against Charmaine's neck. The kisses moved closer to her earlobe. She paused in her musings. Reversing the trail of kisses, Charmaine sighed and snuggled even closer, her talking finally stilled, her eyelids closing.

With a quick move Scott extricated himself from his snuggling spouse and jumped off the bed. His beloved's eyes flew open in shocked confusion.

"Belgian waffles with a choice of strawberries and blueberries coming right up, my lady."

He fled from the room, managing to close the bedroom door just in time to avoid a well-aimed pillow.

Then poking his head back in, he chided. "Tsk! Tsk! Such violence does not become you, dear."

He pulled the door closed again in the nick of time as another speeding missile connected with the wood.

Whew! That was close.

A frustrated Charmaine allowed her imagination to work out best and worst case scenarios for revenge. The one she decided on put a smile on her face and gave her the energy needed to rise, change the bed, and head for the shower.

Ah, life was good!

* * *

"Wow! This table looks good enough to eat," complimented Charmaine as she entered the dining area.

Sure enough, Scott had really outdone himself. A white rose stood jauntily in a bud vase at the center of the table. Tumblers filled with what looked like freshly squeezed orange juice sat to the right of their best china plates. A bowl of the promised strawberries (sliced), a blueberry compote, and even a pot of her favorite hot chocolate completed the picture. He'd gotten out the cloth napkins, too!

Waltzing in with a plate of freshly made waffles and humming a merry tune, an innocent-looking Scott placed the plate on the table with a flourish. Bowing deeply from the waist, he announced, "Madame, breakfast is served."

As Charmaine started to pull out her chair, her husband intervened.

"Allow me, please."

He saw to it that she was comfortably seated and then ensured her napkin lay perfectly on her lap. Finishing his ministrations, he seated himself opposite her. Reaching for her hand across the table, he smiled beatifically at her and bowed his head.

"Let's thank God for the food. Dear Father, today we come to You celebrating our love and the gift of life. Thank You for my beautiful wife—crafted and created in Your image. May our love continue to shine like the light in her eyes, and may I never take her for granted. We eat this meal now to nourish our bodies and pleasure our palates, and we do it with thanksgiving. In Jesus' name we pray. Amen."

Scott was rewarded with the sight of his wife's two dimples in full display. Eyes shining with joy, Charmaine whispered, "I love you, honey. That was a really nice prayer."

"Thank you, dear," Scott said with a wink. "Now if you will pass your plate to me, I will serve you. One or two waffles?"

"I'll start with one, but I'm sure I'll be able to do justice to another. And by the way, my love, while all of this is making me feel so special, you are hereby forewarned that I haven't forgiven you for that little trick this morning. Maybe not today or tomorrow, but one day soon I will repay."

"Promises. Promises! Eat your waffle, dear, before it gets cold."

"Yes, my lord and master," Charmaine giggled as she brought a forkful of waffle saturated with blueberry sauce to her mouth. Closing her eyes in ecstasy, she purred, "H'mm! This is delicious. What did you put in this sauce? And the waffles just melt in your mouth."

Using his best stage whisper, Scott responded, "The angels shared their recipe with me. You see, I was still working under divine inspiration while I was making breakfast. You, my beloved, are eating angel-food waffle and foretaste-of-heaven blueberry compote. Consider yourself blessed among women."

"Oh, you are in fine form today. I don't think I'll ask about the hot chocolate. I'm just gonna shut up and do justice to this heaven-sent meal."

"In that case, *bon appétit!*"

Reclining in the comfort of the couch, with Scott's head resting on her lap, Charmaine remarked. "What a lazy day this has been. It's 4:00 p.m., and we have not done a single thing since breakfast."

"Not quite true. You cleared the breakfast table, and then we walked over here to the couch and sat. Seriously, though, sometimes we need down days like this. Life can get crazy with all the running around we do unless we take time to chill." He let his gaze drop from Charmaine's face. "Robert's death is a painful reminder that life is short, and we need to take time to cherish the people in our lives."

"Poor Lenore and Samantha. I wonder how Brian is doing," Charmaine sighed.

"He was pretty angry when I left him yesterday. But everyone deals with their anger differently. Losing a parent must be very hard, but losing a dad such as Robert must be devastating for Brian. I just wish he would allow someone to get close to him. He's gone into his Brian-the-Brave mode. Totally macho."

"How did he come to be nicknamed Brian the Brave?"

"I asked him that on Friday night, but he said it was a long story. To tell the truth, because we were busy discussing other things, we never did get back to the reason."

"What things?"

"Such as who in their group is having sex and who isn't, and whether God is being reasonable in asking singles to abstain. Stuff like that."

"That's deep stuff. What did you tell him?"

"That God makes rules for a reason, and—" Scott's thought was interrupted by the ringing of the telephone. After two rings the answering machine clicked on.

"Hey there, Scott. Hi, Charmaine. It's Sammy. Scott, me and a couple of the guys were thinking of going over to visit Brian tonight. Since you're kinda our big brother leader, we wondered if you wanted to come too. Call me on my cell when you get this message. Thanks."

"That's so sweet. Honey, we can finish our talk later. Go call him back," Charmaine urged. Then suddenly she sat upright. "Oh, where is my brain! I completely forgot to tell you that a woman called yesterday asking for you.

She wanted you to call her back as soon as possible." She leaned across Scott, saying, "I wrote down her name right beside the telephone. Hold on, let me get it. It had something to do with the movies."

Scott sat up reluctantly. "Someone wants me to be in the movies?"

Charmaine left to get the message pad.

"No, silly," she laughed, flipping through the pages of the pad. "The woman's name has something to do with the movies or acting. Here it is. It's Turner. Lana Turner. She asked me if I was your wife, and said she was Emelia's mom, and that you would know who she was."

He frowned. "Emelia? The only Emelia I know is Emily Fernandez, and I haven't seen or heard from her in years. It couldn't be her mom."

"Well, I don't know an Emily or an Emelia, so you'll just have to call and find out."

"I'll call as soon as I talk to Sammy." Looking a bit perplexed, Scott left to return Sammy's call. Charmaine heard him thinking out loud as he dialed Sammy's number. "Emily Fernandez. I wonder what became of her."

"Sammy. Scott here. Yeah, we're doing OK." A pause. "Listen, I'll be dropping by the Baptistes' later today. But who knows, a visit from you guys might be good for Brian. Yesterday when I spoke with him, he was pretty sore." Another pause. "Just do what you'd like done for you if the circumstances were reversed. If you don't have anything to say, just be there for him, OK? Catch you later!"

Staring at the message pad in his hand, Scott proceeded to make his second phone call. In the process of dialing, he called out in surprise, "This is a long-distance number, Charmaine." The phone was ringing, so he did not catch her response. After four rings a voicemail system prompted him to leave a message after the tone.

"This is Scott Henry. I understand from my wife that you called yesterday, so I'm returning your call. Sorry I missed you. I should be home for another couple hours, but if you don't reach me today, leave a message, and I will try to call you back soon. Have a blessed day!"

"So who is Emily Fernandez?" questioned a curious Charmaine, hugging her husband from behind.

"She was a Latino woman I dated years back," replied Scott as he tidied up the pieces of paper atop the phone table.

"Was she pretty?"

"Yeah, I'd say so. She was a really nice girl."

"Why did you stop seeing her?"

Scott turned around to face Charmaine. He looked off into the distance, trying to remember. "I don't recall all the details, but I think she was ready to get serious and I wasn't, so we called it quits."

"Poor girl. A fellow victim to the Henry charm. But I don't recall you ever talking about her."

Scott pulled his wife closer to him. "Why would I do that, honey? I used to date her, and stopped dating her years before I met you. You wouldn't be feeling insecure about my love for you, would you?"

"Well, sometimes a wife may start to wonder—"

He didn't allow her to finish. "Listen to me. No one else can hold a candle to you or even come close to rivaling the place you have in my heart. No one! Not only do I love you like crazy, but when I married you I made a covenant before God and with you to continue to love you till the day I die. So tell me, Mrs. O'Henry, why would I even talk about a girl from my distant past, h'mm?"

Smiling into his eyes, Charmaine conceded. "You're right! I forgot. I am blessed among women."

Scott playfully kissed her on the tip of her nose. "And I'm blessed even more."

Chapter Eight

Rehearsal of Hope

"OK, people! Let's get started." Candice clapped everyone to attention. "This is our first dress rehearsal, and I want to be able to see the whole play in action tonight. We'll run the three acts from top to bottom, mistakes and all. Before we start, however, I have a few announcements, so listen up! We rehearse again on Thursday night at 7:00. Not 7:30 or 8:00. Seven p.m. sharp! Next, tonight before you leave, make sure you see my mom about your costume. That's Sister Bolski for those of you who do not know who my mom is. Make sure your costume fits properly. We want no embarrassing accidents during performance. Do not take the costumes home. Just make sure that they fit. Those of you acting in the historical scenes, please lose your modern-day accessories. Back in Galilee there were no watches or brand-name running shoes. Are there any questions?"

Seeing no raised hands, Candice continued. "Thank you. I am glad to see that you are all paying attention and that I have been crystal clear. Musicians, please take your places."

Candice saw Jim, the piano player and band leader, waving at her from the band pit.

"Sorry, Candice, but the drummer isn't here yet," he said.

"Then we'll have to proceed without him," Candice replied.

"Give him five minutes. He should be here shortly."

"I'm sorry, Jim, but we have a lot to cover tonight," said Candice. Seeing Jim's look of resignation, she relented. "On second thought, all of you can take a five-minute washroom break. Once we start, I don't want to hear that excuse. Everyone should be back here by 7:20 on the nose. Let's move!"

Everyone made a mad dash for the door—even the more senior members of the cast shuffled out with a bit of pep in their steps. The annual Easter trial was about to begin. Candice prayed for patience and fortitude.

Lenore wished the people visiting would stay forever. If they could only stay and keep talking, giving her busywork so that she did not have to go upstairs and face the bedroom, the empty side of the bed that would never be filled again by the man who'd anchored her for more than 27 years. Was it only two days ago that they were sitting together and planning for a future that was not guaranteed? two days ago that life was normal and dreams were possible? And now . . . Now she must walk on without him, and she was not ready to take even the first step.

I must stay strong for my children and model what I told Candice yesterday.

"Is there anything I can do for you, Lenore? Tell me there's something I can do. I feel so completely helpless around death." Lenore brought her mind back to reality to find Emily Price, her next-door neighbor, by her side.

"Hi there, Emily. How about giving me a hug? I came in here to get something, and lost track of what I was supposed to be doing. You're sure you don't want to visit some more with the folks from church? I can see to things here."

"Here with you is just fine. Just fine," replied Emily as she grabbed a loaf of banana-nut bread from the counter and proceeded to knife her way through each slice. Lenore recognized the signals. Someone had obviously upset Emily.

"Emily, did someone say something to disturb you?"

"I am fine in your kitchen, Lenore. I can use my hands and make myself useful. Anything but face all those people from your church. They make me crazy with all their singing and talking as if they're going to see your husband and my dear friend sometime soon. And that pastor of yours—I mean no disrespect, but he's been talking nonstop since he got here! Counseling and encouraging, mind you, but it's way too much talk. That's what I loved about your husband, Lenore. He kept his views to himself, but showed them in actions. Death is depressing, and I want no part of it."

"You and I can certainly agree on that, dear," said Lenore. "I too want no part of it, but it didn't give me a choice. Since you're finished with the banana bread, why don't you help me cut up some of this cake? Then you can start a big pot of tea to feed those people who are making you crazy.

This will definitely give you a few minutes of peace from the crazy talking."

Glancing at Lenore to see if she was putting her on, Emily Price reached for the kettle. Just then the doorbell rang, letting in another batch of comforters and well-wishers.

"Dear God, let them stay forever," Lenore whispered.

⚑ ⚑ ⚑ ⚑ ⚑

"Claire, what did I tell you in rehearsal not ever to do while on stage?" bellowed Candice.

"Turn my back to the audience?" admitted an already-repentant Claire.

"Give the girl a medal, somebody! Now, Claire, please do not let me see your back again for the rest of the time you're on stage. People, people! You guys act as if you've never heard of this play before or seen this stage. Work with me here. No. Let's do better. Let's take a few moments to talk to God. My patience is wearing thin, and you don't need me yelling at you. Brother Simmie, could you please pray for us?" A few of the onlookers sitting in the pews continued chattering.

"Quiet on the set, everyone!" Candice bellowed again.

Brother Simmie intervened quickly. "Certainly, Ms. Director." He waited for silence. "Let's all bow our heads. Dear Lord, our hearts are heavy with grief, but we want to perform this play as a tribute to You. You have shown us such love, and this play allows us to keep on remembering afresh the sacrifice You made to redeem us. Be with us now as we speak our parts and act our roles. Let Your message find a way to emerge from our frail frames to do nothing but bring glory to You and draw those who will come into a closer relationship with You.

"Bless young Candice and the rest of the crew as they direct this project. Give them the patience they need, and thank You, Lord, for the awesome talent you have given them. Please be with the Baptiste family in a special way right now, as they and we deal with the loss of our dear brother Robert. Console us as only You can, we pray in Jesus' name. Amen."

"Thank you for that prayer, Brother Simmie," said a subdued Candice. "Before we get back to the Gethsemane scene, I apologize for my earlier testiness. Claire, I know you can do this role. You aced it many times in rehearsal. Let the meaning of the message take over. This is true for everyone.

Think about your role and how that character is feeling. If you are a Roman guard, then think about how you would conduct yourself. Be the best guard you can be. If you are a follower of Jesus, then put the passion of bewilderment, wonder, confusion, fear, anger, or whatever emotion your character is feeling into the role. Do it so that the audience will feel as if they have been transported to that time and place. Now, let's start again."

Gwen Bolski arrived just in time to hear the tail end of her daughter's speech. Sometimes she had to remind herself that Candice was only just shy of 18. As usual, she had everyone organized and motivated to take on the rather daunting task of what had become an annual project—the Easter musical. Mom, of course, got the role of costume designer and fitter. Too bad her dad was not around to see her. But that was water under the bridge. Tonight was not a night to visit the land of might-have-beens.

Seeing that Candice had her hands full, Gwen turned to walk back upstairs, deciding that her costume question could wait until later. She stopped as she heard voices in the seniors' room, and listened.

"It's cancer, I tell you. He died from cancer. It had to be," insisted a voice Gwen did not immediately recognize. Then it clicked. That must be Sister Agnes.

"No, they said it was his heart. An aneurysm of his heart," replied the patient voice of Sister Percival.

"What's that, you say? A hernia?" yelled Brother Marcus.

"Aneurysm. Not hernia," Sister Percival corrected.

"He had cancer in his hernia? I didn't know you could have that," Brother Marcus continued to shout.

Sister Percival sighed. "He was the best of men. Quiet. I am sorry to hear that it was his heart that failed him, because he had one of the best hearts I knew. That is the kind of man I would have married if he'd asked me. I don't know how his poor wife is going to get along. They were such a nice family, but death comes for us all sooner or later."

"I sure hope God takes me before I get any of that hernia cancer business. I don't want to die from any strange diseases. I want to die from something that people know," said Brother Marcus.

"Be quiet, Marcus. You're talking foolishness as usual," responded Agnes.

"What's that, you say?"

"Turn up your hearing aid!" yelled Sister Agnes.

"Let's calm down, everyone," said Sister Percival. "Remember we're here to pray for the Baptiste family and those who are participating in the Easter program. We want the community to learn more about us and God through this production." She then went over to Brother Marcus and asked him to turn up his hearing aid. This he did, smiling sweetly.

"Are you still sure you don't want to marry me, Florence? After all, we're not getting any younger, you know."

"I am quite sure, Brother Marcus, but just to be on the safe side, why don't we both pray on it?" she said gently.

Resigned, Brother Marcus remarked, "You always say that."

Deciding to leave well enough alone, Gwen continued on her way upstairs.

Upstairs in the master bedroom, Samantha tried to avoid looking at the two photographs of her dad that sat on her mother's dresser. This was hard to do, seeing that her mom kept staring at them as if she wanted to talk to him. She'd been doing that when Samantha entered the room, and she was still doing it.

As for herself, Sam felt empty. She'd felt that way since Friday. She thought she'd cried enough tears to fill a river, but still the tears came. Everything made her cry. But her mom remained tearless. Samantha wished she could get her to cry. Anything but that, that . . . that efficient emptiness Mom carried around with her now.

Samantha had to break the silence. "Mom, I feel really bad about missing tonight's rehearsal. I'm supposed to be singing."

Lenore, reluctantly taking her eyes off the photographs, focused on her daughter. Her mother's heart ached for her. With her swollen, red-rimmed eyes, her daughter looked nothing like the girl of days past. Recalling the comment Samantha had just made, she walked to her and pulled her close.

"I am sure that under the circumstances, no one expects you to be there tonight, Sam. They will understand. And I need you here to help with all the things that need to get done. We need to start talking about the funeral service. Pastor Simms brought a program outline for us to look at and make whatever changes we want. He said that the church would take care of the rest. And I have to select some clothes to take to the funeral home tomorrow, and tomorrow night we have the viewing, followed by the funeral on Tuesday. So much to do. Call your brother, dear, and let's get started."

"I don't want to do it."

"Pardon me?"

"I don't want to do it, Mom!"

Lenore's head hurt, but she asked patiently, "What don't you want to do, Sam? Call your brother or help plan the funeral service?"

"Neither. I mean both! Brian is acting as if I did him some wrong and . . . and I'm not ready to say goodbye. If we start planning his funeral, well, it . . . it means that Daddy is really gone, and I can't do it, Mom. I just want him back downstairs sitting in his office or coming up to say good night to me." Samantha's plaintive voice filled up her mom's room and spilled out to Brian's room at the other end of the hallway.

"What's going on, Mom?" Brian asked, rushing into the room.

"We need to make funeral arrangements. Sam is upset."

Action! Something to do instead of staring at his bedroom wall. Brian jumped into the plans as if granted a lifeline. He turned to his sister, impatient with her tears.

"We're all upset. Come on, Sam. Suck it up, and let's just get it done. You don't have to like it, but it's gotta be done, so let's get it over with before someone comes up here to find out why we're not downstairs. What do we have to do first, Mom?"

Lenore picked up the program draft and sat down on Robert's side of the bed. Brian plopped down beside her.

The first words on the page that greeted her eyes were sunrise and sunset. The hand holding the paper started to shake. She switched the paper to the other.

Brian reached over and patted her hand just as his father would have done—the silent giving of comfort. Lenore bit down hard on her teeth and pressed on.

"OK. First of all, how do you see the service? A lot of music, speeches, what?"

"Whatever we do, let's keep it short," responded Brian.

"That will be hard to do, dear. In his quiet way your dad had an impact on the lives of a lot of people. Many will want to say something. Pastor Al has already prewarned me."

"Yeah. I guess they will," Brian said with a nod. "In that case, let's make it a celebration of his life."

"We could include texts and songs that he loved, and ask his favorite singers to sing and musicians to perform," whispered a subdued Samantha, coming to sit on the other side of her mom.

Lenore hugged her. "You know, of course, that you're his favorite singer. Do you want to sing a song for him? You don't have to, but it might help."

"I don't know, Mom. I know I told Candice that I understood what Saturday means, but I can't sing 'It Is Well With My Soul' when I feel so upset."

"But honey, God understands our sadness and pain. He understands even when we become angry at Him because of that pain. He Himself cried when Lazarus died. He then asked the Father to glorify Him by bringing Lazarus to life. Maybe Jesus wept because He was not sure it would be His Father's will to bring Lazarus back, but of course God did. If you feel too upset to sing about peace, sing instead about hope."

"Let me think about it. I know Daddy really loved the song 'We Shall Behold Him.' Maybe by Tuesday I'll be able to sing that."

"Then we'll leave space in the program for you to sing it if you feel like it. How's that?" Turning to Brian, she asked, "How about you? Do you want to say anything at the funeral?"

"I'll carry the coffin. I'd prefer not to say anything."

"Are you sure, love?" prompted Lenore.

"Very sure, Mom. Can we get on with the rest of the program?"

After giving his hand a squeeze, Lenore continued. "We can use the Scripture reading suggested here. Your dad would like that. Then we can ask Scott to say a few words, the senior choir to sing, and then I think I want to say something."

"Mom, are you crazy? Nobody expects you to say anything when it's your husband's funeral. And with Dad dying so suddenly, you won't be able to do it. You'll start bawling, which I'm sure will set off everyone else."

"I won't cry, Brian."

"How do you know that?"

"I just know. I haven't been able to cry since Friday. I will just talk about

Robert as if it's our anniversary and I am sharing with others what he means to me. I have no difficulty doing that."

"But what if you break down, Mom? What about that?" Brian kept on.

"Well, then, I will just be behaving like a grieving wife. Don't worry about me. God will help me through. I need to do this."

"OK, it's your funeral," intoned Brian.

"No, dear. It's our funeral."

Rising from the bed, Lenore walked toward the closet. "We need to select some clothes to take to the funeral home tomorrow."

"Can I beg off doing this part?" squeaked Samantha.

Brian's response was short and testy. "Come on, Sam. We all need to do this together. Mom needs our help, so let's just get it over with. Like I said, nobody likes doing this, so let's just get it done fast."

"Why are you being so mean?" wailed Samantha.

"I am not being mean," yelled Brian. "I'm being practical!"

"You're not being practical! You're being insensitive and cranky and, and—mean."

For a minute Lenore felt the room spin. She closed her eyes and breathed deeply until the feeling passed. When she opened her eyes, only Brian was in the room.

"Mom, you OK?"

"Where's Sam?"

"Probably in her room. Let's get the rest of the stuff done; then I'm going for a run. I need some air."

Chapter Nine

At a Loss for Words

Sammy switched off the ignition to the VW Bug and turned to the other guys in the car, "Did anybody bring a card?"

"Nobody said anything about a card. I thought we were coming to visit Brian. And his family," defended Larry.

"It never crossed my mind. Man, I'm not sure I want to go in there. This death thing makes me uncomfortable. I'm sure I'm gonna say something stupid," Damon complained.

"Then don't say anything at all," remarked Larry.

"Am I supposed to hug him, or what?"

"Damon, get a grip! We can't duck out now. Besides, Scott's coming by as well. He'll know what to say. He's good at stuff like this. Why don't we take cues from him? Remember, this is Brian we're talking about here," Sammy told him. "Our friend."

"How come Todd's not here? He usually thinks deep thoughts and can be counted on to say something intellectual," whined Damon.

"I told you before," Sammy snapped. "Todd had to work. He said he'll visit later in the week. Now, come on, let's go in."

"I think we should wait till Scott gets here," said Les, anchoring his body more firmly in the seat.

"What's that going to accomplish?" questioned Larry. "Get your lazy butt outta here and stop being Chicken Little. People die every day, and one day it'll be your turn."

Mumbling under his breath, Les reluctantly unbuckled his seat belt and opened the door. "At least if I'm dead I won't have to find words to comfort myself."

Dragging their feet, the boys slowly made their way to the Baptistes' front door. As Sammy reached for the doorbell, the door was yanked open and Brian came crashing through, head down, butting Sammy hard on the nose.

"Oomph! Hey, man," Sammy yelped, "what'd you do that for? I think I broke something!"

"Stung again by Brian the Brave! Way to go, man!" Damon raised his hand to give Brian a high five, but dropped it at Brian's glare.

"What are you doing here?" he demanded.

"We came to see you. What kinda question is that?" Damon said, affronted.

"Yeah, we're sorry to hear about your dad, and just wanted to let you know that we're here if you need us. Your dad was the best," said Sammy.

"Well, the best is dead. I gotta get outta this house for a while. All those people in there are driving me crazy. My dumb sister starts crying every time you look at her, and my mom is acting as if this is some big party she's throwing."

Turning to Sammy, Brian said, "Sorry 'bout your nose. I didn't see you. You OK?"

"I'll live, but if you gotta get out, how about we take you for a spin? We could go cruising down King Street for a while."

"Sorry, guys, but I'm not good company right now. I need to take a run or hit something. Go on in the house. Mom'll be glad to feed you or something. I'll try to be back in a little while. I'm outta here!"

With that, Brian took off as if chased by killer bees.

"That's gratitude for you," Damon puffed. "We come all this way to comfort him, and he runs off."

Watching the quickly diminishing figure of Brian, Larry commented, "Running might be the best thing for him. He was close to his dad. Talked about him a lot. The guy must be going through hell."

"That's still no excuse to run out on your friends," Damon muttered.

"I told you we should've waited for Scott," griped Les.

Trying to be the voice of reason, Sammy said, "Listen, guys, Brian said he'd be back soon. Let's just go inside and at least say hello to Mrs. B and Sam. We can wait inside till Scott comes. Anyone have a problem with that?"

"Maybe you just want to comfort Samantha, eh, Romeo!"

"Damon!" yelled an exasperated Sammy. "Never mind. Arguing with you is a waste of time. I'm going in. You guys can stay here if you want."

Sammy disappeared into the house. Larry looked at his twin. "I'm going in too. I would suggest you do the same. After all, we can't very well go anywhere without Sammy. He's got the car and the keys."

"Good point," agreed Damon as he pushed past Larry to get in. Les reluctantly followed.

Brian's lungs were on fire, but still he ran, pushing against the pain, letting the thud-thud-thud of his footfall lull him into a coma of nonthought. Pushing, pushing until his lungs started to scream. Only then did he cut the pace to half. Still he ran. Getting away was all that mattered.

Go back, my son.

His dad's voice was in his head. Brian increased his pace.

Go back and help your mom and your sister. I am counting on you, son. I am counting on you. Remember, God will be with you. No trial will come that He will not be there to bear with you.

Brian slapped at his head and stopped suddenly. He needed to nip this in the bud. "Stop right there, Dad. I'll go back for you. I'll help Mom and Sam for you. Just don't give me any of that God foolishness now. I don't want to hear it."

He could hear his dad's voice as if he were right there beside him.

Run to comfort, my boy. God is the Comforter. Run to Him.

Without another word of protest, Brian shut the voice down. Turned off the audio clean. But the face of his dad remained on the screen of his mind, patient and quiet as usual.

With a force of his will, Brian then shut off that screen and resumed his run.

Backwards.

Toward home.

"Hey, Charmaine, let's get going. I'm sure the guys are there by now."

"I'm coming, I'm coming. Let me get a towel to wrap this coffee cake in. It's still hot."

"I'm sure they have lots of food there, honey."

"Maybe," Charmaine murmured as she wrapped up the cake. Handing it to Scott, she reached in the front closet for a light jacket and slipped her feet in comfortable shoes, still talking. "But I need to bring something. At times like this words are not enough—you feel the need to do something. And I'm sure that it will get eaten in no time. There must have been a lot of people there yesterday, and there'll be more today. Food is a source of comfort, you know."

"Yes, dear," agreed Scott, opening the door. On the elevator down to the underground parking he worried. "I hope the guys aren't waiting outside for me. They want to go, but don't know what to say or do."

"And they need their big brother to help out," noted Charmaine.

"Is that what I've become? A big brother?" Scott opened the car door for Charmaine and ensured she was comfortably seated. Then giving her the coffee cake to hold, he made his way to the driver's side, started the engine, and backed the Honda out of the parking space.

Continuing with the discussion as they drove, Charmaine said, "Those young men look up to you, honey. They respect you. When they start calling on you to accompany them on difficult assignments like this one, that's how you know that they hold you in a position of high regard."

"I surely pray that I'll represent God to them in all my actions. Some of these guys . . . their dads aren't around, you know. We need more men to be there for them, to help them navigate the passage into manhood." He braked as a squirrel dashed across the road, then continued his thought—"talking to them about what that all means."

"Isn't that the truth!" Charmaine concurred.

As they drew near the Baptistes' home she saw that the driveway was full and the nearby street parking spots were already taken.

"I think we're going to have to find a parking space further down the street," she told Scott. "Looks like a lot of people are here. I surely hope Candice has all her crew at church for tonight's rehearsal."

"Except for Sam," replied Scott. "I don't think she'll be there tonight, but she's definitely one gutsy kid. Yesterday, even in the middle of her tears, she was determined to still participate in the production. Tuesday's funeral will be a trial for them. A trial for all of us."

Seeing a parking space about a block down on Park Trail, Scott parked the car. Walking back toward the Baptistes' house, he paused, taking Charmaine's hand.

"Let's pray before we go in, love. Brian is sore at God, and the family is reeling, and the guys don't know how to help. I'm not sure even I know what to do to help, especially with Brian, but God can give us the guidance we need.

"Heavenly Father, a husband and father has died. You know that. We, the members of the immediate and extended family, are at a loss for words. We need You to help us to be providers of comfort tonight, Lord. Let no words come out of our mouths tonight that are not reflective of You. We ask, and believe, and thank You. Amen."

Tucking Charmaine's hand in the crook of his arm, he walked on with purpose. "Now, let's go in and let God do His thing."

Charmaine rang the doorbell and was greeted again by Emily Price.

"Good evening, Mrs. Price. Good to see you again."

"How do you know my name, young lady?"

"Remember? I met you Friday night. I was the one you told that you didn't want to hear any God-talk from."

Still blocking the entry to the house, Emily groused, "How am I to keep all these people straight in my head? Almost everyone who's been in this house talks like you! However, I do recall that you made yourself useful in taking messages. Come in and stop letting the cold draft into the house. It's not good for my arthritis. What this family needs is not so much talking but more people doing things to help. The family is not doing well at all. Young Brian went charging out of the house just a few minutes ago, leaving those four young men who came to see him all by themselves."

Turning to Scott, she commanded, "You should go over and do something with them." And to Charmaine, "You come with me. We can slice that coffee cake you have there. Don't look at me like that. While my eyes are not what they used to be, nothing is wrong with my nose. I can tell that is the recipe from the *Best Housekeeping* magazine. Autumn edition!"

Picking up her dropped jaw off the floor, Charmaine managed a wink at Scott and followed Emily into the kitchen.

Scott spied the guys sitting awkwardly in a corner of the living room and moved in their direction. Les was the first to see him, and even a blind person could not mistake the look of relief on their faces.

"Hey, guys. You made it, and you're here for your friend. That's great!" Scott greeted them.

"Yeah, right," said a sarcastic Damon, still smarting from Brian's rude behavior toward him earlier. "That friend almost broke Sammy's nose and ran off down the road, making us feel like we're the enemy."

"What's this about Sammy's nose?" asked Scott. "I heard that Brian went out, but I heard nothing about a confrontation with Sammy."

"Don't listen to him, Scott," Sammy said, glaring at Damon. "It was an accident. Brian was charging out the door at the same time I was about to ring the bell. We had a little collision. My nose is sore, but it will be fine. And Brian said he'd be back soon. Said he needed some air."

"Have you spoken to Samantha or her mom?" Scott asked, looking around.

"No, we haven't seen them. Les decided that we should wait for you before we do or say anything stupid. An old lady keeps coming out of the kitchen to offer us tea," added Larry.

"Maybe we should have asked for cake instead. She probably has cake in the kitchen."

"Damon, how can you think of eating at a time like this?" hissed Les.

"Well, I'm kinda hungry. I hadn't had dinner when you came to pick me up, and Sammy, our driver here, refused to stop for me to get somethin' to eat."

"OK, guys. Charmaine is in the kitchen, so I'll go see what I can rustle up. Is Damon the only one who's hungry?"

Looking a bit shamefaced, Les said, "I could do with a bite. Nothing major. A little somethin' will do. But no tea."

Helping them to save face, Scott said, "I'll bring 'something,' and whoever feels like eating can do so. How's that?"

Without waiting for an answer, he headed for the kitchen. Minutes later the boys had food.

■ ■ ■ ■ ■

Pastor Al; his wife, Judith; and baby Jess dropped in around 8:00 p.m. to help keep the vigil. Lenore was again making her rounds among the guests. Walking over to the guys, she hugged them each.

"Thanks for coming to sit with us. It helps, you know. It helps to make the pain bearable. To know that you are surrounded by friends. Brian should be out of the shower by now and will be down to see you in a few minutes."

"He's back? I didn't see him come in," said Damon.

"He probably used the side door. This is very hard for Brian. It's hard for all of us, but he and his dad were like this." She held up intertwined fingers. "Just be there for him. And talk to him about everything as normal."

Sammy asked, "How is Sam . . . I mean . . . how is Samantha doing, Mrs. B?"

"Sam is upstairs . . . no, here she comes now. I'll leave you young people to visit. Thanks again for dropping by, and please remember to keep us in your prayers."

Lenore moved on to another group of guests.

A limp-looking Samantha came over to greet the guys. Sammy's heart did a flip and flutter. She looked so lost. He wished he could give her a hug, but if there was a moment to do so, it passed quickly.

Damon, however, had no such compunction. He walked boldly over to her and said, "I'm so sorry about your dad, Sam." And then he hugged her. A bit too long in Sammy's estimation. Walking back to his seat, Damon winked at Sammy.

The creep!

Sam hesitated as if she did not quite know what to do with herself. Finally she sat down on a chair beside Sammy. He shifted his chair a bit to make sure she had enough room. She misunderstood and started to rise. Desperately Sammy blurted, "No, don't go. I was just making space for you to be comfortable."

"I never thought of myself as fat. I don't need that much room."

Seeing a situation with the potential of spinning out of control, Sammy worked to rectify it. "You're not fat. You're perfectly fine just as you are."

"And by that you mean what?" questioned a somewhat confused Samantha.

The other guys were trying hard not to snicker at Sammy's predicament, but he dug his way out by changing the subject.

"It means that I am glad to see you and wanted to let you know if you need a friend or someone to talk to, well, I am available."

Tears started to pool in Samantha's eyes. "That's so very sweet of you, Sammy. Thanks." She leaned over and gave him a quick hug. "Everyone has been so nice to us. Sorry, guys, I don't mean to cry on you, but I can't seem to stop the tears. Excuse me." She hurried off back upstairs.

They all watched her go, feeling helpless and inadequate. The food in Les's mouth turned to chalk, and his appetite vanished. "See what I mean?" he stated. "When you come to comfort people in mourning, it's like you're walking a minefield. You never know what's going to set them off."

"Set what off?" asked Scott as he rejoined the group.

Larry summed it up. "Sam came to sit with us. Damon hugged her, and then she sat beside Sammy. Sammy told her she was fat but that it was OK by him, and offered to be her friend. She gave him a hug and started to blubber and ran back upstairs."

"That's when I said you never know what's going to set people off," Les added.

Scott looked at Sammy. "You told her she was fat? What's wrong with your eyes! I thought you liked Sam."

Sammy glared at Larry. "I do like her! All of this was a big misunderstanding. And I did not tell her she was fat. She assumed I thought she was fat because I moved over to give her more space when she sat beside me. I was just being considerate. Now she thinks I think she's fat. But she's not. She's just fine, and I do mean it about wanting to be a friend to her. She's a really nice girl."

"Who's a nice girl? Don't tell me that you guys are having a conversation about girls without me?" said Brian, walking toward the guys. He'd changed clothes and looked a bit less haunted than earlier.

"Hey there, Brave. You should shower more often. It looks good on you," joked Scott.

"Funny guy. Sorry for my foul mood earlier, guys. How's the nose, Sammy?"

"Still in one piece. Gonna be fine," responded Sammy. "Just remind me not to butt heads with you. You have a very hard head, man." The guys laughed, feeling a bit more relaxed as they recovered some of their usual banter.

"So who's the nice girl?"

"Your sister," smirked Damon. "Sammy thinks she is."

"And you think different?" asked Brian with an edge to his voice.

"No, man. I think she's nice. Very nice. I really like her nice," gushed Damon.

Les, Larry, Sammy, and Scott had a good laugh at Damon's expense. Brian did not laugh.

Looking hard at Damon, he said, "Good. As long as we understand each other. Just make sure you 'like her nice' from a distance."

"Sure, man. Sure thing. If that's OK with you," responded Damon.

Sammy secretly smiled as he recalled Samantha's hug. He felt a poem coming on.

Chapter Ten

The Rock of Sisyphus

A tired Candice and her mother locked up the church close to 10:00 p.m. The parking lot was almost empty as they got into their compact station wagon. Deftly executing a U-turn in the parking lot, Gwen headed the car out of the drive and into traffic. Remembering her earlier question for her daughter regarding the costumes, she waited for Candy to debrief before she broached the subject.

"I came close to losing it tonight at practice. Everyone was acting so sluggish and difficult, and everything took more time to do. Finally, when I caught myself yelling at Claire, I had to ask Brother Simmie to pray. After that, things went a bit smoother, but now I feel completely worn out."

Taking one hand from the steering wheel, Gwen reached across to pat her daughter on the knee.

"You're doing a great job, honey. I came downstairs earlier to ask you about the costumes for the second act, and overheard you apologizing to the cast. I like it that you take responsibility for your actions and are not afraid to say you're sorry. This mom was very proud of her daughter tonight."

"Thanks, Mom. Sometimes I feel like Sisyphus, rolling a rock to the top of the hill all by myself, only to have it roll back down."

"Well, you are not alone. I pray for you constantly. The seniors were in their room praying for you and the cast. Many people have told me how much they admire what you're doing with the Easter production. Best of all, remember that God is always there for you when you feel discouraged."

"And sometimes He speaks through your mom to say the nicest words of comfort to help you put things back into perspective," replied Candice.

"Thank you, dear," said Gwen. "That's what moms are for. Something else to keep in mind, Candy. Robert's death has hit the church family really hard. Not only was his death sudden, but in his very quiet way he was one of the pillars of our church. When a pillar collapses, the whole church is affected. You and the cast members are all being affected by it, which I'm sure contributed to some of the difficulty you experienced in rehearsal tonight. Keep that in mind at your next rehearsal. Take a few minutes to let people talk about how they're feeling, and then help the cast channel their grief into a fitting tribute to the Baptiste family and to God. I think if you do that, the audience cannot help being blessed."

"Now, why didn't I think of that? It never occurred to me that my own crankiness was because of my sadness. I do miss him. I can't even imagine how Sam must be feeling."

"We all miss him, honey. He was quite a man. After your father left, I thought—never mind. Now, about those costumes."

"What did you think? What were you going to say? You always start talking about Dad and then stop in midsentence. I really would like to know how you felt and what you went through."

Gwen did not respond. Signaling to turn onto their street, she maneuvered the car into the garage.

Thinking she had offended her mom in some way, Candice apologized.

"Sorry, Mom. Am I being insensitive? You don't have to talk about it if it's very painful."

Gwen turned in her seat to face Candice. "I never talk to you about your dad?"

"You do talk to me about Daddy. But never about how you feel or felt about him. Those are the conversations that get the hiccups."

"The hiccups, eh? I hate when people do that to me too. It is very annoying," Gwen teased.

"In that case I should get a medal, 'cause you do that a lot," replied Candice. Then she added, "But only when you talk about your feelings for Dad. You must have really loved him."

Gwen nodded, a burning in her throat. Clearing her throat, she said softly, "Yes. I really did. Ah, honey, if it's important to you, then I guess I can tell you about how I feel and felt where your dad is concerned."

"But not if it's going to hurt you, Mom."

"Some hurts are for good causes. I think this is one of them. Let's both grab a quick shower and talk over a cup of chamomile tea. Just remember that we can't be up too late, because tomorrow is a work and school day."

"In that case, I'll be showered and dressed in five minutes."

"This I have to see to believe," laughed Gwen as Candice opened the front door and dashed down the corridor to her room.

Gwen locked the door and leaned her head against it.

Dear God, what do I say? Help me tell this right, and keep me strong in the telling. Gwen continued to pray as she filled and plugged in the kettle. She then went to her bedroom and entered the ensuite bathroom to start her own shower. Leaving the tap to run for a bit, she stopped to stare at her reflection in the mirror, talking to the image that shared her brain.

Why is it that after all these years you still haunt me, Stephan? Why do I still miss you? Her brain amended that statement. *Of course, not with the out-of-one's-mind craziness that I had when you first left, but yes, I still miss you. You completed me, and have left me half full and half a woman.*

Despite some occasional bids for her affection, no one had been able to make her feel the way he did, so she had elected to remain single and yes, sometimes lonely. Now her daughter wanted to hear how she felt. How she feels still.

Just talk about what you're comfortable with sharing, a voice seemed to whisper in her ear.

"OK, I can do that," said Gwen.

Maybe you'll find some healing in the telling, the voice continued.

"Maybe," responded Gwen.

"Mom, I'm out of the shower. I'm going to make the tea," called Candice from the hallway.

"Be right out!" she called out to her daughter.

Well, thought Gwen, *I guess the die is cast.* Serious brown eyes looked back at her through the misted mirror.

■ ■ ■ ■ ■

When Gwen arrived in the kitchen a few minutes later, she found tea steeping in the pot and cookies neatly arranged on a plate. Her daughter, wrapped in her "comfy" bathrobe, was already seated at the table and stirring sugar into her own cup of tea.

"Aren't we the eager beaver," teased Gwen.

Grinning, Candice owned up, "That's me! You know I can't resist a good story. Plus, I've been waiting years for this. Years!"

"Is that so? And what exactly have you been waiting 'years' to know?" asked Gwen as she sat across from her daughter.

"The love story between you and Dad. It has to be a good love story because you're not bitter, but you haven't given any other man the time of day. Last year I was starting to have hopes for Mr. Richardson, but he got the gentle rebuff too."

"I did no such thing. Well, I guess I did." Looking a bit flustered, Gwen finally said, "I'm not sure I know where to start."

"Why don't you start with Mr. Baptiste?"

"Robert Baptiste? What does he have to do with this?" questioned a puzzled Gwen.

"Remember in the car, on the way home from rehearsal, you said, 'After Dad left, Mr. Baptiste,' and then you did one of your hiccups."

Gwen's chocolate-brown face lost its puzzled look. "Ah, I remember now. What I was going to say was I heard from Lenore that Robert prayed for me every night during that first year after your father left. She said he mentioned me specifically by name each night."

"He did? Wow!" replied Candice.

"He used to come by every morning in the winter to shovel the driveway. Every weekend at church he or Lenore would take you along with Samantha to the children's program so that I would have some time to study and pray with the adults. I remember one time in particular that many people, including us, had their basements flooded. Robert rallied a few of the men from the church and cleaned up the mess. They replaced the drywall, carpeting, and anything covered with mold. It took them a week of evenings, but they made sure we had a nice snug home in no time. Robert would not even hear of me paying them for the work."

"Wow!"

"Yeah. Wow is the right word. He was quite the man."

"And Dad?"

Reconciled now to this conversation, Gwen did not dither. "He was quite the man, too. I felt that I had no choice but to fall in love with him."

"What did he do? What was he like?" asked an eager Candice, a cookie paused halfway to her mouth.

Gwen stirred her poured tea, thinking. "That's hard to describe. It was more how he made me feel. The first time he kissed me, I literally thought that I was transported to another universe."

Seeing her daughter's look of skepticism, Gwen added, "I know it sounds overly dramatic, but it's true. When I was with your dad, I was the only star in his universe. He had a way of focusing on me so exclusively that I could not help feeling special, totally loved, desired and desirable. We dated for about six months, and when he asked me to marry him, I had to."

Eyes widening from shock, Candice squeaked, "What do you mean you had to? Were you pregnant?"

"Absolutely not! Despite modern-day trends, I believe that sex should wait until one gets married. I had to marry him because he completed me. Sometimes I would feel so close to him that I had the strongest urge to crawl under his skin and merge with the beat of his heart."

Seeing her daughter's raised eyebrows, Gwen responded, "I'm not sure how else to explain it, but that's how I felt."

"So how did Grandma and Grandpa feel about him? Didn't they think you were rushing things?"

"No. I was 28 years old at the time and living on my own. They really liked Stephan."

"They had no objections to his being White and not being a Christian?"

"What do you mean he was not a Christian? I would never marry someone who did not share my faith. And no, even though he's Caucasian, my parents saw that he really loved me, and they were content with that."

"But if he was a Christian, how come he left you, Mom? How come he left us?"

Oh, dear God, here comes the hard part.

"I don't think he wanted to leave us, Candice. No, I'm not explaining this right. He wanted us, but he wanted other things as well. I recall when you were born, how he cried. I had never seen him so moved. He could not believe that this miracle we had created together, formed by God, was his child. He just kept holding you and staring at you with tears streaming down his face."

"Wow!"

"You're saying that a lot tonight," teased her mom.

Candice shivered. "He really loved me that much?"

"He loved you that much, honey. Sometimes I'd find him late at night in the rocking chair with you cradled in his arms, supposedly rocking you to sleep. He would tell me that he heard you fussing, but I think he just loved holding you."

"So how did it all fall apart, Mom?"

Gwen did not respond. She seemed to be far away in her mind.

"Mom?"

"Yes, dear. Sorry about the wool gathering. What did you say?"

"What happened, Mom? What happened to all the love that was in our home? Why did Daddy leave?"

Gwen's eyes filled up with tears. "Because . . . because in the end we were just not enough. He needed more."

"More what?" questioned Candice, an edge to her voice.

"More highs. More novelties. More challenges. I suppose if I had dated your father longer than those few months, I would have discovered that he was a seeker. Someone who would have made a great frontiersman. Once he sets his mind to a task, he concentrates on it till he feels he's explored all there is to know. Then he needs to move on.

"Just when he was starting to get antsy in our marriage, I became pregnant with you. And so you see, that was another *new*. New emotions, new responsibilities. But after a while, life is all about repetition, isn't it? The same bottles have to be made every night, the same diapers have to be changed, the same routine of waking up and going to work have to be followed, and the same wife needs to be loved."

Candice wished she'd not started this conversation. She could feel herself getting angry. "But you said he was a Christian! Shouldn't a Christian husband have more staying power than that? Shouldn't he know that his commitment to his wife and child is for a lifetime, and stay because that's what he should do?"

"Those are very good questions, and ones I have wrestled with God over. In the end, despite the fact that it meant letting some sun go out of my life, I had to let him go. If you and I were never going to be enough for him, I did not want to be 'settled' for. I wanted more too. I wanted him to want to be with us to the exclusion of all else."

"Oh, Mommy!" Candice was on the verge of tears.

"That's the gist of the story. Please remember, however, that your dad loves you. He calls you faithfully from wherever he is, visits when he can, never forgets your birthday, and continues to provide for you financially. He would do the same for me, but I wouldn't let him. And one more thing before we go off to bed, honey."

Candice blinked back the tears. "What's that, Mom?"

"Remember the parable about the sower and the seed? Some fell on dry ground, some fell on the wayside, and some fell on good soil. Well, some people really want to do God's will, but if they don't take time to nurture their relationship with Him, they're not able to develop strong roots. These people are easily choked by life and constantly make bad decisions despite wanting to do well. Make sure that when you find a guy you take time to discover if he has strong roots."

Candice wiped her eyes. "Thanks, Mom. You've given me a lot to think about. If I have more questions about Dad later, do you mind if I talk to you about them?"

"Anytime, dear." Musingly she added, "You might not believe it, but there are days I miss him something awful. But God is good. He sustains me. And after all these years, my resolution has not changed. I am not willing to settle. I still want my love for him and his love for me to be enough."

"You want more, too."

Rising from her chair, Gwen brushed the hair away from her daughter's forehead and gave her a light kiss. "Yes, I too want more. Good night, love. Get to bed. Tomorrow is another day."

Trying to hide a yawn, Candice rose from the table and gave her mom a hug. "I'll wash up these things first. Thanks for talking with me, Mom. Good night."

As she washed the dishes, Candice thought about her dad. She saw him maybe twice each year. Always on the move, he faithfully kept her supplied with postcards from his different destinations. It had been she and Mom for so long that she could barely recall what having him home was like. And while she longed for him to be there for her, she had learned to go on without him.

After hearing Mom talk about him tonight, she felt a stirring of memories. Daddy taking her to see the children's theater production of *The Wizard of Oz*. Daddy making snow angels with her, and Daddy driving her and Mommy into the country and telling her star stories.

"See those three stars there, Candy Plum?" he'd asked, pointing to a pattern of stars. "Those are the 'I can do all things' collection. When you feel as if you can't do something, look for those stars and remember that you can. And see that one over there by itself? That one is the Lonely Heart star. When you feel lonely, look at that star and remember that even though it is alone, it is still shining."

And then he'd start reciting passages from Dr. Seuss's book *Oh, the Places You'll Go!* and she would sing-song it right along with him.

Oh, Daddy, why couldn't we be enough? Candice's heart cried. "I'm lonely for you. I am still trying to shine."

Drying her hands, she turned off the kitchen lights, ignored her conscience's reminder to brush her teeth, and crawled into bed.

That night she dreamed of stars falling, falling out of the sky. In the dream she saw a miniature replica of herself racing madly around with a too-small hat in hand, trying to catch the falling stars and missing most. Giving up in despair, she sat down to cry. A moon drifted over and said gently, *Don't cry for the ones you missed, little one. It's not your job to catch them all. Just catch as many as you can.*

The moon drifted back the way it had come, but before fading completely, it winked at her. The face in the moon was her daddy's.

Monday

Chapter Eleven

The Phone Call

G wen woke up from a pleasant dream. She'd been at a concert with someone whom she could not quite recognize, but with whom she felt comfortable. No. She'd felt loved. In love. The performance was outstanding, and she had risen with the crowd to shout "Bravo!" and beg for an encore. Now the dream was fading, and she wondered about the invisible person who was her companion.

"Ah, well, back to reality."

She reached for her Bible study guide, read the section for the day, and then began her morning conversation with God. As she prayed, she thought of Lenore. She asked God to comfort and sustain her friend and her family. She thanked God for His constancy and asked Him to make her a blessing to someone that day. As was her custom, she paused for a few more minutes to listen for God's instructions, and when she was finished, she reached for the telephone and dialed Len's number. It was early, but if she knew her friend, she would be up by now—if she'd even slept at all.

A tired voice answered.

"Hey there, my friend. How are you holding up?"

"Up is a bit too much for me right now, but I'm holding on, Gwen. I'm holding on. I'm just a bit tired, that's all."

"Have you been able to sleep?"

"A bit here and there."

"I wish I could help you bear some of the pain, Lenore. But you know I'm here for you whenever you need me, and even when you don't. I'm praying constantly for you that God will sustain you. My devotional reading today reminded me that He is able to do abundantly above all that we can think."

"Thank you for the reminder. I do feel Him sustaining me every hour of the day. I couldn't get through without Him and without my friends and family."*

"So what is on the agenda for today?"

"Well, at 10:00 I have to bring clothes to the funeral home for them to dress Robert. Then the children's schools have to be notified, and . . ."

"I'll drive you to the funeral home."

"But Gwen, you have to work."

"I'll go in later. This is not something you're doing alone."

"But—"

"Don't argue with me, Len. Get dressed, and I'll see you at 9:30. And we need to get something for you to wear to the funeral. When we're through at the funeral home, I'm taking you shopping. Is that OK with you?"

"Gwen . . ."

"I take that to be a yes. See you soon." Gwen hung up the phone and prepared to support her stubborn friend in her time of need. She called her work to inform them that she'd be in at noon, and went to rouse a still-sleeping Candice.

Scott kissed his wife, sprang out of bed, and headed for the bathroom singing a song about a beautiful morning. Charmaine groaned, flopped over onto her tummy, and pulled two pillows tight over her head. She'd married a morning person. Some mornings she wished she could press a mute button and silence him. How could anyone be so chipper in the morning! There should be a law somewhere that prevented morning people from marrying those of dissimilar ilk.

The ringing of the telephone further rattled her already-jarred nerve endings.

"Fie on you!" her nerves screamed at the caller.

Scott flung open the bathroom door and rushed to the rescue. Glancing at his distraught wife, he picked up the cordless receiver, answered a chirpy hello, and respectfully closed the bedroom door so she could have her much-needed morning space.

Summoning her resolve like the Little Engine That Could, Charmaine gingerly removed pillow number one from her head, followed by pillow number two. Cracking one eye open, then the other, she turned slowly onto her left side.

Good girl.

She visualized her hand removing the layers of bedding wrapped around her, preparing her body for its eventual exodus.

Deed followed thought.

Atta girl!

Next she imagined her body slowly rising into a sitting position onto the side of the bed.

That too happened after deep concentration.

Now all that was left was for her to stand up and stiffen her spine.

She did. Then swayed. She was *so* not a morning person.

Grabbing on to the wall for support, Charmaine willed her muscles to work. Then moving slowly and with deep concentration, she shuffled her way around the bed, opened the bedroom door, and, with hair flattened down one side of her head and face as sour as wine grapes, she navigated her body to the bathroom. Somewhere in the back of her mind she registered the muted voice of her husband coming from the direction of the living room.

Water. Let there be warm water left.

There was.

Ah! Life is beautiful.

Letting first her back and then her face take the full blast of the warm spray, Charmaine came to life. Bit by slow bit, the day took on a more appealing aura. Yes, life was beautiful.

Thank You, God, for waking me up this morning.

■ ■ ■ ■ ■

When Charmaine emerged from the bedroom some 30 minutes later, she was a different woman. Gone was the pariah from hell, the soured face, and the hairdo with issues. In her place was the beautiful woman whom Scott loved next to God.

Watching her transformation every morning reminded him of the power of grace and its ability to take the worst in people and make them brand-new. Not that he would share that bit of observation with his beloved. Some things were better kept to oneself.

As Scott sat at the table, half perched on a partially pulled-out chair, he watched his wife walk toward him looking even more beautiful than usual. Into his mind popped something he'd heard as a child and internalized: "Be sure your sin will find you out."†

Dear God, how can life change in an instant? Everything that grounded your world—gone. In a heartbeat!

Charmaine was still coming toward him.

Smiling.

Dimpled.

Expectant and beautiful.

His mind reeled. His heart beat double-time. *God, rewind this day. Please. I beg You. Go back. Back to before the phone rang. Let this not be happening.*

There was no answer.

His wife leaned down and greeted him with a kiss. Pulling her onto his lap, he hugged her tightly and held on for dear life.

Pastor Al amused baby Jessica as he waited for his wife to join him on the living room couch. This was his favorite part of the day, when he and his small family could turn their attention to God and seek wisdom and comfort. Judith walked into the room looking a bit dopey.

"Bad night?" he asked.

"Look at her. You would not believe that she was up at 5:00 a.m. Not hungry, mind you, because I tried to nurse her. Madam only wanted to play," Judith informed her husband as she tightened the belt of her pink robe.

Pastor Al smiled indulgently at his little love. "Did you keep Mommy up, my sweet?"

Baby Jess beamed at Daddy. At 3 months old, she was quickly learning the power of her charming smile. Judith felt her mother's heart fill with pride and thanksgiving. Despite her constant lack of sleep, she would not trade a moment of this time with her daughter for anything in the world. And seeing that soft look overtaking her face, Andrew reached for her hand and pulled her down beside him.

"I wish I could stay here this morning and watch Jess so you could catch a few extra winks, but I have to go to the church. We need to get ready for tomorrow, and I have the program to take to Sister Steele."

"I thought Sister Paulie was doing bulletins this quarter."

"She is. However, she's working today, so she arranged for Sister Steele to do the funeral program."

Stifling a yawn, Judith said, "Don't worry about me. I'll catch a few minutes of shut-eye when our princess goes down for her morning nap. Poor Lenore. And Brian and Samantha. They must be devastated."

"Lenore's not shed a single tear throughout this whole weekend. It's as if she's shell-shocked. I'm worried about her," remarked Andrew.

"Give her time. The wound is raw, and her adrenaline's still pumping. Sometime soon she'll wake up and see the gaping hole. Then the pain will hit big-time. Let's continue to lift them up in prayer."

"I'm reminded of the apostle Paul's statement 'Give thanks in all circumstances, for this is God's will for you in Christ Jesus.'‡ At times like these, it is not easy to be a believer. My spirit rebels against the idea of being thankful for this death." He shook his head. "But I'll give that rebellion to God and thank Him for the gift of Robert's influence, even though I will miss him a lot. I am . . ." Andrew's voice grew husky, and he made swallowing motions against the lump trying to block his throat.

Sensing his struggle, Judith put her arms around him and started to pray.

"O heavenly Father, our maker, creator, and life-sustainer, You know the plans You have for us, Lord, but we don't. Here we are walking through the valley of the shadow of death. Robert Baptiste, our friend, a husband, father, but most of all, Your child, is gone from us, and our hearts are broken with grief. Help us not to faint. Uphold us as we stumble beneath the burden of this loss. Tomorrow we bury him, and we are not ready. O God, we are not ready. So today we ask You to help us consider the sparrows. Just as You take care of them, You will take care of us. We cannot get through this pain on our own, and so we claim Your strength. Please comfort Lenore and Brian and Samantha. Comfort the extended family. Lord, we look forward to seeing Robert with You in heaven. Until then, please keep us trusting even when it is difficult to fathom Your ways. We ask in the name of Jesus. Amen."

"Amen," echoed Andrew. Placing his index finger under his wife's chin, he lifted her face to his. His soulful eyes met hers, and he declared over his daughter's babble, "I love you, Judith Edwards-Simms. You always know what to say to get the wind back under my wings. God must love me very much to give you to me to love."

He saw she was moved close to tears, so he drew her even closer to him and kissed her forehead, as if pronouncing a benediction. He felt her unspoken words of affirmation in the tight hug and the closer snuggle of her body against his.

Pastor Al reached for his Bible, from which he'd draw additional strength and get direction for this day.

♦ ♦ ♦ ♦ ♦

Charmaine returned Scott's tight hug, then relaxed her hold. "H'mm," she murmured softly. "That was a nice hug." Eyes on the clock, she straightened the collar of his crisp blue shirt, kissed him lightly on the lips, and made to rise. Scott's arms tightened briefly, then released her. She slid into the chair next to him and, per their weekday morning custom, picked up her Bible, located her text for the day, and waited for Scott to do the same.

They had made a pact to read the Bible through within the year. And each morning before they headed off to work, each would share a text from their respective readings that they found personally meaningful.

Scott's Bible, however, lay untouched.

Nudging him, Charmaine prompted, "Earth to Scott. Come in."
"Huh?"

"For someone who was so chipper early this morning, you look quite deflated. You peak way too early in the day," Charmaine joked. "You need to take it slow and easy the way I do. Then you can peak later in the day."

The hint of a smile upturned one corner of Scott's mouth. "Sorry, love." Making no move to reach for his Bible, he said, "You start with your text."

Charmaine looked at him quizzically, but decided to proceed. "All right. My selection today comes from Isaiah 43, verses 5 to 7. 'Do not be afraid, for I am with you; I will bring your children from the east and gather you from the west. I will say to the north, "Give them up!" and to the south, "Do not hold them back." Bring my sons from afar and my daughters from the ends of the earth—everyone who is called by my name, whom I created for my glory, whom I formed and made.' "

She turned to Scott to explain why the text appealed to her, but her husband's dark-brown skin had gone ashen. He pushed away from the table and rushed to the bathroom.

Alarmed, Charmaine rushed after him. What could be the matter! Scott was hardly ever sick.

She found him bent doubled over the sink, frantically splashing cold water onto his face.

"Honey, what's the matter?" she asked, rubbing his back. "You obviously have an upset stomach. Do you think it was something you ate at the Baptistes'?"

Scott's hand stilled its splashing motions. He mumbled something inaudible.

Charmaine's alarm intensified. "Honey, tell me what's wrong so I can help you. Do you need me to call an ambulance?"

He managed to grind out the words "upset stomach" before his body heaved again.

Nothing came up.

His stomach heaved again, arching his back while his mouth involuntarily opened wide.

Nothing.

Scott groaned.

Frantic, Charmaine said, "I'll go make you some ginger tea. That should help to settle things."

Scott held up his dripping right hand to stop her, but she was gone. He rested his head on the side of the sink. The cold enamel soothed his cheek, and the spray from the still-running tap misted his face. But his brain remained hot, crazily firing off in all directions.

Dear God, please. Please. Please.

Suddenly the urge to retch returned, now stronger than before. Scott's chest felt on fire, but he was helpless against the total conspiracy of his body parts working in unison to rid him of its bile. His stomach started to expel mouthfuls of mucus and acid, leaving him with no alternative but to grab on to the edges of the counter and hold on tight.

In the kitchen Charmaine ignored the kettle for the speed of the microwave. In three minutes flat she was stirring a spoonful of honey into the mug of ginger tea and hanging up the telephone. Hurrying back, she was relieved to hear Scott finally expelling whatever was ailing his stomach. Making a quick dash to the bedroom, she placed the mug of tea on the bedside table, retrieved a facecloth from the linen closet, and rushed into the bathroom to help.

His face was beaded with sweat, and damp patches on his blue shirt clung against his skin. Wetting the cloth, she lovingly wiped his face and neck.

When it seemed as if his stomach had stopped its heaving, she gently propelled him toward the bedroom.

"Let's get you back to bed, mister. You're in no shape to be going into the office today."

"But . . ."

"No arguments, Scott. I've already called your office. Your manager assures me that everything will be taken care of. Today you need to rest. It's been a stressful weekend, and with tomorrow's funeral, you need time to recuperate. Now take a few sips of this tea, and see if the tummy rebels."

Scott lifted the mug with shaking hands. Charmaine steadied his hands with hers and guided the mug to his lips. He sipped and waited. The stomach did not rebel. He sipped again. The stomach stayed calm. Then he drank it all.

The last thing he remembered as he drifted off to sleep was his wife stacking pillows behind his back and tucking the comforter under his arms.

---

* See Eph. 3:20.
† Num. 32:23, KJV.
‡ 1 Thess. 5:18.

Chapter Twelve

Pain, Pain, Go Away

At 10:00 sharp Lenore and Gwen arrived at the funeral home. It had been a quiet ride. Taking a deep breath, Len got out of the car. "OK, friend, let's go do battle with monster number one for today."

They were greeted promptly by a solemn-looking middle-aged man. Good morning, ladies, and welcome to Brown's. I am Reginald Brown the third. How can we be of assistance to you today?"

Len was fascinated. The man's lips did not seem to be moving at all, yet she could hear him quite clearly.

"Mrs.—?" prompted Reginald Brown. The third.

Focus, Lenore!

"My husband, Robert Baptiste, is here. I have brought the clothes for him to be dressed in."

"Oh, yes. Yes. Your husband's funeral is tomorrow. At Brown's we do everything we can to make this difficult time as stress-free as possible. Please let us know everything you need, and we will move mountains to make it happen." He paused and waited expectantly.

"Thank you. I will keep that in mind," replied Lenore, hoping she'd given the right answer.

His solemn countenance shifted into a beam. She had obviously given the perfect answer.

"You also have a viewing this evening from 7:00 to 9:00. Correct?"

Lenore nodded. "That's right. I mean, that's correct." She felt her body becoming tight.

"And which of the three caskets did you finally decide on, Mrs. Baptiste?" the funeral director asked through closed lips.

How does he do that? Len wondered, staring at his mouth.

"Mrs. Baptiste?" prompted Reginald Brown the third.

Seeing Lenore's frozen stare, Gwen took charge. "Could you please remind us of the ones under consideration?"

"Most certainly. Just give me a moment to review your file. Ah, yes. This way, please." He led them down the hallway to a large room containing dozens of caskets of all sizes. Gwen guided Lenore back to her functioning self.

Walking over to a lacquer-finished black box with brass handles and burgundy-cushioned interior, Reginald Brown the third said, "This was one that you liked, then over there by the wall, that honey-colored one was another option, and finally the white immediately to your right."

Gwen looked to Lenore. "What will it be, Len?"

Pulling herself together with obvious effort, Lenore decided. "Let's get him the honey-colored one. It looks warm. Robert likes to work with that color of wood."

"Excellent choice, Mrs. Baptiste! Just excellent! That is one of our best selections. Now, don't worry your head about a thing. All is in order, so we can proceed with due alacrity. Now, if you don't need anything else, I will get our staff working to put things in place for later this evening and tomorrow. Remember, 'Call on Brown. We'll never let you down.' It's a pleasure to be of service to you." Reginald bowed deeply from the waist. After he straightened up, he briskly escorted them to the front door and, giving a final wave, disappeared back into the building.

Outside the funeral home Gwen looked with concern at her friend. Lenore looked . . . strange. "Are you OK?"

"Say 'alacrity,'" replied Lenore.

"What!"

"Say 'alacrity.'"

"OK." Gwen eyed her friend skeptically. "Alacrity."

"Your lips move."

"Yes. And that is a problem?"

"His lips did not move the whole time he spoke. How can you say 'alacrity' and not have your lips move?"

"Maybe he can throw his voice. He could have been a ventriloquist prior to becoming Reginald Brown the third," responded Gwen in sepulchral tones.

"'Call on Brown. We never let you down,'" sang Lenore.

"We'll take your bodies and put them in the ground," responded Gwen, grinning wickedly.

Lenore bent double, weeping tears of laughter. She choked out, "And when you get to heaven, you can claim your crown."

Gwen howled. "That is precious. Stop. Please. "There must be something in the etiquette book of Reginald—"

"—Brown the third," joined in Lenore.

Gwen shrieked with glee and tried to whisper "—that says the way we're behaving is inappropriate for the premises of a funeral home."

Lenore's laughter dried up suddenly as her heart remembered its loss. Feeling the strength leaving her legs, she leaned against the porch pillar for support.

"Oh, Robert! Robert. You can't be gone!" Bleak eyes implored the heavens, empty of tears and full of pain.

Gwen, feeling her own throat closing up, hugged Lenore. "I know, my friend. Death is hard stuff for the living. Yet in the midst of this very difficult morning, God granted us a little reprieve of laughter. Come on. Let's go tackle monster number two. Shopping."

Brian reluctantly pushed himself out from under the covers. He looked at the clock. Past 10:00. He needed to call the college to let them know he wouldn't be around this week. Dragging his tired body off the bed, he padded to the bathroom and splashed cold water on his face. He needed to wake up. He felt drugged. He thought he could sleep for a month.

Peering through the window, he saw a day lit up with sunshine. Spring was everywhere. A shower. He needed to shower. He turned on the faucet and stepped under the spray. Tiny needle-pricks of water bit into his back, chest, and face and ran down to his feet. He worked to empty his aching mind and almost succeeded except for the chant that had started the moment he recovered from his faint in the driveway on Friday night.

Pain, pain, go away. Come again another day. Pain, pain, go away. Come again another day. Pain, pain . . .

A knock on the door snapped his eyes open.

"Brian?" It was his sister.

"Yeah."

"Are you going to school today?"

"No."

"Should I go?"

"No."

"OK."

He heard her footsteps retreating. "Sam," he called.

"Yes."

"You OK?"

"I don't know . . . I suppose so . . . I guess not."

"I'll be out in a few minutes, OK?"

"OK."

"Mom back yet?"

"I don't think so. She went with Sis Bolski."

"OK."

Oh, dear God, she sounded so lost. Brian turned off the hot tap and gasped as the cold water hit his chest. He added just enough hot to make the cold bearable.

Pain, pain, go away . . .

* * *

Pulling into the mall parking lot, Gwen switched off the ignition and turned to Len. "Which store will it be, Len? Max's or Hortensia's?"

"Let's go to Hortensia's. They usually have a good selection of formal occasion dresses. Robert always liked the dresses I bought here."

"So did Stephan. Our men had excellent taste in clothes."

"Yeah. But yours left, and mine is gone," Lenore said flatly.

In the silence the women acknowledged the truth of the statement, and then Gwen softly reminded them, "Despite the losses, God remains."

Lenore drew strength from that. "Yes, He does. Constant as always."

The women left the car and walked with purpose toward Hortensia's.

* * *

When Scott awoke again, it was past noon.

"Hey there, sleepyhead! Feeling better?"

His eyes focused on Charmaine sitting on a chair beside the bed. "You didn't go to work?"

"Nope," she said, walking over to him.

"But—"

"I took a personal day off. I couldn't leave when I didn't know how this bug would behave in your body. I'm glad you slept even though you were mumbling a lot initially. I sponged your face, but you kept moving your head rom side to side, calling my name and saying 'No, no.' When I assured you that I was here, you calmed down and relaxed."

"Thanks, honey. You're the best."

"Ah, shucks. What's a girl to do when her guy's sick?"

Straightening up to a sitting position against the pillows, Scott reached for her hand and pulled her down on the bed beside him. After looking deeply into her eyes, he closed his in a quick prayer. Opening them again, he said, "Charmaine, we need to talk."

"That sounds ominous."

He did not smile.

Trying to inject a degree of levity into the moment, Charmaine clapped one hand against her cheek, batted her eyelids and twanged Southern-style, "Pray tell me, deah? What evah can it be that's gotten you in such a solemn mood?"

Scott remained unsmiling.

Tugging on his fingers, she sobered. "What is it, love?"

"I'm not sick, Charmaine."

Charmaine swatted at him. "You're something else, Scott Henry! You get me all worked up over whatever you have to tell me, and then say this. Obviously your brain is addled. I was here this morning, remember? When you were heaving up gross-looking stuff into the bathroom sink. That was 'sick' in my book."

"I don't mean I wasn't sick. I mean that I'm not sick, sick."

"Scott!"

He closed his eyes and gathered his thoughts. "I'm not saying this right, but hear me out, Charmaine. I was perfectly fine when I woke up this morning. I really was. Then the phone rang. Do you remember that the phone rang?"

"Yeah."

"That phone call was what made me sick."

Charmaine's face was a study in puzzlement. "What? How?"

"Do you remember the woman who called for me on Saturday?"
Charmaine nodded.

"Well, she called again this morning. Said she had some difficult news. I don't mean the news was in itself difficult, but it was hard to hear. At least for me. Well, maybe for her, too. I don't know. But it's . . . it will be . . . difficult. For us."

"Scott, you're scaring me!"

Scott plowed on unevenly. "She told me that her daughter died a few weeks ago from cancer. Before she died, she made her mother—this Lana—promise to locate the father of her child."

Charmaine leaned forward, shoulders hunched. Puzzled. "Yeah, so?"

"She said that I am the father of the child, Charmaine. That I have a daughter."

"What!"

Charmaine flew off the bed and eyeballed her husband.

"Say that again, Scott. I'm sure I heard you wrong. Did you just tell me that you have a child? That . . . that . . . *you* are a father? You're kidding me! Right? This is some kind of sick joke."

Scott said nothing.

"Who is this woman accusing you of such a thing?" demanded Charmaine, fists clenched tightly against her side.

"Lana Turner is Emily's mom."

"Who is Emily?" she barked.

"Emily, or Emelia, is a girl I used to date. Remember, I told you about her yesterday."

Out of Charmaine's right clenched fist popped an accusing finger that lifted her hand from her side. Making stabbing motions to emphasize her point, she laid into him. "But you dismissed her as just a girl from your past. Someone you once dated, but you moved on because she was ready to be serious and you weren't! You told me that it was nothing for me to concern myself about. You told me that I was the only woman for you. If you 'just dated her,' how come she's accusing you of fathering her child? How long ago was this? When did you date this woman?" Charmaine couldn't stop the slew of questions being flung out by her brain.

Scott rested his head in his hands. It felt so heavy. All of him was heavy.

Charmaine pressed on, fear making her harsh. "Scott, answer me! I need you to answer me. When did you date this woman?" She stopped with a gasp, a new—obvious—thought slammed into her brain.

"For her to accuse you of being the father of her child, you must have . . . you . . . you had sex with her, Scott?"

"Yes."

"How many times?"

"How many times does it take?" Scott heard himself yell. He forced his voice into calm. "This all happened a long time ago, Charmaine. A long time ago when I had no sense."

"Well, this has to be a mistake. You can't just take this woman's word for it. There are tests, you know. DNA tests to clear your name. To prove that this can't be happening, to prove—O God, wake me up from this nightmare. This can't be happening. Scott, please tell me this isn't happening."

Scott reached for his wife and pulled her back down beside him, cradling her in his arms.

Oh, my love.

Her body was stiff. He rubbed her back, hoping for some pliancy.

Look what I've done.

And the saying came back to him: "Be sure your sin will find you out."

This wasn't a nightmare.

This was hell.

"Scott?" Charmaine's choked whisper was against his ear.

"H'mm."

"What do we do?"

"The grandmother wants me to meet the child."

Charmaine's head snapped up, crashing into his chin. Tears watered his eyes.

Absently rubbing her head where it had connected with his chin, she raged, "Meet her? Meet her? Meet her when?"

"As soon as possible. It seems the grandmother is also ailing and is in no condition to take care of the child for long."

"Well, when are you going? Where do they live?" Charmaine sprung out of Scott's arms and off the bed, and begun a frenetic pacing around the room. "This is a nightmare." She slapped herself on the cheeks. "Wake up, girl. Wake up!"

Scott looked on helplessly, not knowing what to do. Charmaine's pacing came to a sudden stop beside him. She opened her mouth to say something, changed her mind, and closed it. She gave him a long, hard look and then quietly left the room.

He heard the bathroom door close, the click of the lock, then silence.

This is not hell, thought Scott. *This is double hell.*

Chapter Thirteen

We'll Be OK

H ey, Candice, wait up!"
Turning, Candice saw the tall lanky figure of Sammy Watson running toward her. Even though she was a year older and in her final year at Emerson Christian Academy, she and Sammy shared some of the same classes. He was that bright. He slowed to a walk as he caught up to her. "Headed for the caf?"

"Yeah. But I think it's the dreaded burnt pizza today. My fault. I slept in this morning and had no time to make a decent lunch. So how ya doing?"

"All right, I guess."

"Yeah. That's about true for me, too. Merely all right. Between Bro Baptiste's death, school, and the Easter play (which is still on, by the way—I noticed you were missing from rehearsal last night), I feel as though I'm just barely coping."

"Sorry about last night. A few of us guys went with Scott over to the Baptistes'. I should have called you."

"Yeah, you should have called, but I understand. You're the least of my worries about the program. You already have your Pilate role down pat. However, I do need the whole cast for Thursday's rehearsal. Friday night's and Saturday's performances have got to be as near perfect as possible. Plus, Pastor Al told me that quite a number of community members have called to say they'll be coming. No pressure there!"

Spying a table about to be vacated, Candice shot away to grab it. Sammy hustled to catch up to her.

"That was some quick footwork!" he secured a chair with his backpack and asked, "What would you like? One or two slices of the burnt pizza with cheese? My treat."

"One, please. That way I won't have double the heartburn later. But you don't have to buy me lunch."

She dug into her knapsack for her wallet. "Here's some money." Looking up to hand the money over, she noticed that Sammy was already at the counter. She made a mental note to treat him next time. While she waited, she pulled out her trusted notepad and started a new 'Things to Do for the Easter Play' list.

Sammy returned to find Candice deep in concentration and writing furiously. When his eyes caught the page title, he waited for her to finish the item she was writing, then nipped the pen from her fingers.

"Hey, why'd you do that? I was on a roll."

"Eat, Candice. The list will still be there 15 minutes from now. This bad pizza will taste 10 times worse in that same amount of time."

He handed her a slice on a paper plate along with a bottle of fruit punch, then uncovered two delicious-looking slices of chocolate cake.

"Where did you get that?" Candice hissed. "Hide it quick before we attract too many friends." Not waiting for him to act, she grabbed the container, re-covered it with a napkin, and stuck it under her chair.

"Candice, what are you doing?" questioned a puzzled Sammy.

"Sammy Watson, I know that my friend Sam thinks you are the sweetest guy to walk the face of the earth, but if she didn't like you, I would fall in love with you right here, right now."

Comprehension dawned in Sammy's eyes. "Ah! The cake! Why, Candice, I didn't know you were a fellow addict. However, much as I admire you, I would not suggest falling for me. You'd only be loving me for my cake-producing abilities and not because of my unlimited charm. That, my friend, is no basis for a relationship!"

"Aw, shucks!" Reaching for her pizza, Candice asked, "Where did you get the cake?"

"I made it."

"Yeah, right. Really, where did you get it? I can't wait to taste it, but I have to get through this pizza first. Parental programming kicking in. Dessert must follow main meal."

Sammy raised an eyebrow. "You're not suggesting that I am incapable of making a cake, are you? And you wouldn't be implying that the reason that I am incapable is that I am a man, would you?" Not waiting for her response, he continued, "'Cause then, I would have to draw the conclusion that despite your objections, in the deepest part of you, you are sexist."

"You made it?" Candice's look was full of awe. "A thousand and one pardons!"

She tossed her remaining bit of pizza onto the plate and reached under her chair. "This I gotta taste. Oh, it looks so good. Yum! I need a fork!"

Sammy produced two, wrapped in napkins.

Candice's eyes widened. "Oh, you really made it. You even brought forks!"

Sammy watched as she speared a piece of the cake and placed it reverently in her mouth. Her eyelids dropped shut, and a look of pure pleasure rippled across her face. When she opened her eyes, she squinted at Sammy and demanded:

"OK, who do you want me to kill? What secrets do you want me to reveal for this piece of rapture? Just name it. I will do it. Sammy! This is worthy of a standing ovation. This is the best, and I mean the very best, chocolate cake I have ever tasted. When did you learn to bake like this? And when did you do this, by the way? Didn't you say that you were at the Baptistes' last night?

"Whoa! One question at a time. You know I like to write, right?"

Candice nodded. "The bestseller by the time you turn 25."

Sammy beamed at her, pleased that she remembered. "Well, sometimes when I'm stuck in my writing, I get this craving for something sweet. I tried eating the store-bought cookies Mom usually buys, but they were always too dry or the cake available was too crumbly. So I started to experiment with baking. Chocolate in particular. I love chocolate. Last night after I got back from the Baptistes', I was trying to compose a poem, and it just wouldn't come out the way I wanted it to. So at 10:30 I decided to bake this. By the time it was in the oven, my muse and I reconnected, resulting in fresh inspiration for my poem. After I grabbed a shower, I frosted the cake and went to bed. A perfect ending to an almost-perfect day."

Candice stood up and bowed. "May the imaginary gods of chocolate and all of life's pleasures continue to inspire you in your writing and baking. And may I continue to be a recipient of your mental-block productions." Sitting back down, she held up her palm in a gesture for silence. "Now please, do not speak to me until I finish this bit of heaven."

Sammy watched in awe as she demolished not just the one but both pieces of cake. Reaching for the lid, she covered the now-empty container, eased back in her seat, closed her eyes, and sighed out her contentment. Suddenly her body became rigid with attention, her eyes widened in shock, and her hand flew up to cover her mouth.

"Oh, Sammy! I ate all the cake!"

"Umm-mm," murmured an amused Sammy.

"Why didn't you stop me?" Cupping her flushed and burning cheeks, she moaned. "I'm mortified. This is so embarrassing. Brother Baptiste's death must be taking more of a toll on me than I thought. I've never, ever done anything like this before."

Sammy felt a laugh coming from deep in his belly. She looked so funny, a smudge of frosting staining one corner of her mouth, face gone pink, full of shock and horror. He bit down on the laugh that still found a way to emerge in the shape of a grin.

"It gives a cook great pleasure to see his work being truly appreciated. Don't worry—I have more at home. My family's not big on chocolate, so there'll be some when I get home. Does that make you feel better?"

Somewhat mollified, Candice relaxed. "Thanks, Sammy. You're a good sport."

"About those secrets you promised to divulge, however—" Sammy grinned at her wickedly. "I have a small request."

Candice groaned. "Every pleasure must be paid for." Straightening as if for an inquisition, she asked, "What do you want to know?"

"Earlier I think I heard you mention something about Samantha. About her thinking I am sweet, or something to that effect?"

Candice groaned again. "Did I say that?"

Sammy nodded.

"Out loud?" she questioned.

Sammy nodded.

"Sam is going to kill me," she stated.

Barely managing to hold on to his cool, Sammy asked, "So you—I mean— you think she likes me?"

Reluctantly Candice owned up. "Yes, she likes you."

"Yes!" Sammy's arm shot up in the air, his face all smiles.

Her earlier embarrassment gone, Candice glared at him. "If you so much as hint to her that I told you, Sammy Watson, I promise that I will arrange for the scaffolding to come crashing down in the middle of your Pilate's balcony scene."

Unperturbed, the Sammy Watson in question got up from the table, returned the empty cake container to his backpack, gathered their garbage, and said in his best Jamaican imitation, "No problem, mon. My lips are sealed, and my heart is healed. See you latah." Then he headed toward the garbage receptacle to make his deposit. As he neared the exit, he turned and blew Candice a kiss and strutted out of the room like a peacock on display.

Shaking her head at his antics, Candice picked up her pen and completed her list, glad for the short vacation from the heaviness in her heart.

Lenore, Samantha, and Brian had little to say to each other en route to the funeral home. After Lenore had completed her morning activities, she'd returned home to find that her children had thoroughly cleaned up the house and were sitting together in the recreation room watching television.

They must have had a talk during her absence, because they demonstrated a kind of solicitude toward her that was quite unlike their typical teenage self-absorption.

When she'd returned from her errands with Gwen, Brian had greeted her at the door, taken her bags, and deposited them in her room. Samantha had taken her by the hand to the kitchen table and offered her tea and toast. It had been so touching she'd felt her eyes sting. *God, I had prayed for us to be closer to each other, but was this the only way?*

Brian had brought a list to the table and, after conferring with Samantha, he'd said, "Well, Mom, it's been a very difficult weekend, but Sam and I have agreed that we need to work together. I've told her that if she needs to cry it's OK with me, and I won't yell." Turning to his sister, he'd said, "Sorry I yelled at you last night. I'll try not to let it happen again."

At which she'd responded, "It's OK. I'll try not to be such a crybaby."

To which he'd replied, "Cry if you want to, Sam. I just feel like breaking things. Or running. Yesterday's run made me feel a bit better."

Lenore had stared at her children as if they'd descended from another planet.

Referring back to the list in his hand, Brian had continued, "Mom, for your information, we have notified both our schools that we will be away for the week. We've confirmed with Pastor Al that the funeral program will be ready today and called back Sister Murdock. She wanted to know how many out-of-town guests we were expecting for the funeral. We told her 25 to 30. She wanted us to tell you not to worry about any foodstuff, because the church's catering committee is taking care of it. We've picked out our clothes for both this evening and tomorrow and have confirmed all the pall-bearers. And Sam has decided that she will sing."

Lenore had looked across at her daughter, "You're sure you're feeling up to it, Sam?"

Giving her mom a tremulous smile, Sam had nodded.

Taking charge again, Brian had continued, "The only thing we need you to tell us, unless you have additional chores for us to do at the moment, is what to expect this evening at the funeral home. Will we have some time with Dad before the actual viewing starts?"

Heart swelling with love for her children and gratitude to God, Len had said, "Brian and Samantha, I didn't think I could love you more than I already do. Yet you have done this mother's heart a world of good today. Thank you for your help, but most of all for your caring." Reaching across the table to Brian and beside her to Sam, she'd held on to their hands. "We'll get through this. Oh, God is so good!"

She'd felt Brian shift at the mention of God, but he'd squeezed her fingers and begged her with his eyes to not get emotional.

Recalling the question on the table, Lenore had assured them that they would have some time alone with their dad before the guests came. She'd also explained as best as she could what to expect at the viewing service. They'd asked a few questions, and then tried to shepherd her upstairs to get some rest. When she'd protested, they'd compromised on the rec room, and to ensure she obeyed, Brian had sat her down on the couch, with him and Sam as sentries on either side of her.

One hour later she'd awakened to find them both fast asleep at her side.

Thank You, God, that in this craziest of days You gave us an interlude of peace. The resumed ringing of the telephone had brought an end to the interlude.

Now on the way to the viewing, there was little left to be said. Brian, wearing gray pants, black turtleneck, and blazer, looked the picture of Robert as he maneuvered the car into the funeral home parking lot. Sam, sitting in the back seat, stared out the window. She looked lost.

Brian parked the car in the section reserved for them and, after undoing his seat belt, reached across to open his mother's door and back for Sam's.

With the chirpy voice of nervousness, he rallied the women. "Let's do it."

Reginald Brown the third was there in person to greet the trio and guide them to the viewing room. On seeing him, Lenore again felt the urge to giggle, but cleared her throat instead. Entering the room, she saw that about 50 chairs were arranged in auditorium-style, separated by a center aisle leading to the front of the room. Soft music played, and a hush was in the air.

Reginald led them slowly toward the central piece of furniture in the room, the honey-colored casket. Straightening her spine, Lenore anchored her children on either side of her, creating a horizontal line. Supporting each other thus, they took step after slow step to the place of reckoning, eyes fixed frontward.

Halfway up the aisle, Lenore felt Samantha stall in the procession. Lenore's grip on her daughter tightened, and the procession stopped. Brian circled around and closed them in a tight triangle.

They stayed like that for a few minutes.

Breathing.

Waiting.

Drawing and giving strength to each other.

At Samantha's nod, Brian opened up the triangle to reform the horizontal line, and the procession resumed.

At the front of the room Reginald Brown the third waited for them with patient understanding.

As the casket loomed closer, Lenore could feel her chest growing tight.

You can do this!

Ten more steps.

Nine.

Breathe!

Eight.

Seven.

Inhale. Exhale.

Six.

The sweet, spicy scent of flowers was heavy in the air. Their steps echoed in the quiet.

Five.

Lenore could make out the shape of Robert's nose.

Four.

His lips. Those lips that had kissed her to sleep every night for the past 27 years.

Three.

Ah! There was his face. All of it. His chest where used to beat a heart that loved her dearly. Sleeping. Soon to wake up and smile at her.

Two!

Samantha broke away and rushed to the casket. Lenore froze, Brian still glued to her side.

"Daddy! Wake up. Daddy, please wake up!" coaxed Samantha in a strangled whisper. She touched his face and quickly pulled back her hand. "Mom, he's so cold."

Cold as death.

One.

Lenore's heart floated the rest of her body to the honey-colored casket where lay her beloved, his face now stilled. She memorized every pore, straightened his bushy brows, and adjusted his tie. He hated it being too tight on his neck. So handsome, her Robert.

"Hey, darling."

Lenore waited for a response she knew was irrational to expect. Her husband was dead, yet she persevered, undeterred.

"I'll see you tomorrow."

Kissing her two middle fingers, she gently laid them on his too-cold lips, waiting for the heat from her touch to warm them.

Standing alone, one step away from his dad, Brian stared and would not believe.

Dad!

He wanted to shake his dad's hand. Wanted to hug him. Wanted to thank him for all he had done. But his dad's hands were closed across his chest, and he couldn't bring himself to disturb them.

Brian would insist later that at the moment he stood staring at his dad, he felt a cold draft enter the room. The cold circled around his feet and started to crawl up and under the leg of his pants, all the way up, shivering his chest,

goose-bumping his neck, and chattering his teeth. When it had fully en-
gulfed his whole face and head, he felt something hot and salty sliding out
from one of his eyes, making a path down his cheek, before seeping into the
corner of his mouth. This was followed by another and another from the
other eye, sliding down the busy playground of his cheeks. More and more
heat, warming his face, burning it up, till he couldn't feel any cold at all.

He felt a familiar hand steady him. And then a smaller one on the other
side of him.

He ignored them.

He wanted this time.

More time.

The hands fell away, but he could still sense them close by.

"Goodbye, Dad." His voice wavered, then grew strong. "I'll take care of
everything. Don't worry. I learned from the best."

Backing up two steps from the casket, he called his body to attention and
gave his dad his best-ever Pathfinder's salute.

Holding the salute for a long minute, he finally rested, as if ordered to
stand at ease. Stand easy.

Reaching out blindly for the waiting hands, he drew his mother and sister to his side and convinced himself, "We'll be OK."

No one knew when Reginald Brown the third left the room.

Tuesday

Chapter Fourteen

God's Aching Heart

B y 10:30 a.m. on this early April morning, a full half hour before the service was scheduled to begin, the church was packed to capacity. Funeral flowers in great abundance lined the front of the sanctuary, creating a picturesque backdrop to the honey-colored box that held the remains of Robert Baptiste. The somber tones of the organ labored to create a cushion of peace, but despite the silent cheerleading of the floral squad, the air was thick with the scent of sorrow.

One by one the members of New Haven Ministries and friends had walked up the long middle aisle to the front of the church to pay their respects and say goodbye. The procession up the aisle was still attracting newcomers. In the relative quiet of the church, after viewing the body, some people wept openly, their grief bare for all to see. Others returned to their seats with jaws locked and grief bottled.

It was getting warm inside the church, and the ceiling fans had been called into service. At the gentle stirring of the air, one yellow petal from the central floral arrangement began to lose its tenuous connection to the stem. It teetered then lost its grip, falling silently without a bounce against the burgundy carpet. No one noticed the fall.

Samantha, in a simple aquamarine dress that was a favorite of her father's, sat with her mom, brother, and other relatives on the middle front pew, receiving hugs without words, and many messages of encouragement. Already feeling the weight of too many smiles given in response to words of comfort, she experienced a sudden tension of memory as she watched a father walk up, clutching the hand of his little girl.

The father stood in front of the casket and looked at Robert, then hung his head. Samantha and those nearby saw the little girl tugging on her dad's hand and heard her quite clearly in her best approximation of a church whisper.

"I want to see too, Daddy. Pick me up, please."

Her dad picked her up.

Both of them stared at Robert for a while, and then the little one asked, "Why is Mifter Baptist sleeping in his nice clothes, Daddy? He's going to get them all crushed."

The dad answered, "He's going to have a long nap, honey, and when he wakes up, the first person he's going to see is Jesus. Mr. Baptiste wants to make sure that when he sees Jesus, he looks his best. On the outside as well as on the inside."

The little one's eyes widened. "Is he all dressed up on the inside, too?"

"Mr. Baptiste was one of the best-dressed men I've ever known, sweetheart. You see, when you're dressed up real nice on the inside, it makes you look very good on the outside, too."

Becoming aware that the queue was backlogged behind him, the father, after saying a few words to the Baptiste family, set his daughter down and turned to walk back to their seats. But the little one stopped and looked up at her daddy.

"Am I dressed nice on my insides, Daddy?"

The dad reached down, picked her up again, and kissed her cheek. "Yes, honey. Inside, you look like an angel."

Samantha felt the first sting of tears for the day and prayed for strength to hold it together until after she did her song for her daddy.

Seated five pews behind the Baptiste family, Scott reread the notes he'd put on the scrap of paper. Thoughts of Robert. Memories to share. His heart thudding in his ears. Beside him sat Charmaine. Two inches separated their bodies, but it felt like an ocean. He longed to hold her hand, but was afraid of . . .

Braving the elements, he reached across the ocean, took her hand, and brought it to his lap. Her fingers gripped his once, then lay moist and limp in his. Looking straight ahead, he tightened his grip.

Back in the vestry Pastor Al conferred with the members of the platform party about the order of the program. Soon it would be time to start the service. He felt a grip on his shoulder and jumped, startled.

Robert!

It was Brian. Come to see that everything was in order. Making himself do anything but more sitting, greeting, and waiting.

Understanding, Pastor Al sent him off to inform the funeral director that they could close the casket in five minutes and to tell the audio team to ensure the platform microphones were on and ready to go.

Judith came in at that minute to give him her usual pre-presentation hug. She called it her hug of support. He felt it as a hug of faith.

Somewhere between Scott's reach across the two-inch barrier separating him and Charmaine and the first few items of the funeral service, he came to a decision. Bowing his head to ask God's guidance, he felt a quiet reassurance that he'd made the right choice. Instead of the notes he'd written, he would sing a simple ballad, one written way back in the days following his conversion when his guitar was his best friend, providing him with a musical detox to his break with the past.

The program was proceeding unannounced. So far, everyone was holding it together. A few tears here and there, some babies fussing, but no major meltdown. He released Charmaine's hand, put it back on her lap, and quietly exited with the seniors who'd just completed their tribute.

Outside in the parking lot the sun shone brightly, but the air was a mite nippy. He retrieved his guitar from its case in the car's trunk, closed the trunk, leaned against the car, and strummed a few chords. With one eye on his watch, he quickly tuned the instrument. Then he hummed the first few bars of the song.

He was ready.

Reentering the sanctuary, Scott discovered that his tribute was the next item on the program. Checking in with God again, he received the same quiet assurance that he should proceed. Hearing a hearty round of amens, he squared his shoulders and walked confidently to the podium. After adjusting the microphone to his height, he began to speak.

"Robert Baptiste was a man of faith. If he had days of doubt before he grew into his unswerving faith, I never knew about them. But I do know that for faith to grow strong it has to be tested and tried and get daily exercise. So what do I say about a man of faith? A man who was a great husband, a father to emulate, and a brother to us all? I say nothing, because Robert's life said everything. So what I'll do is sing this song for you, for me, for those of us who might be experiencing a crisis of faith today."

Securing the strap of the guitar more snugly across his chest, Scott plucked a simple melody into life. The babies stopped their fussing. The hush was expectant. Then when a feather drop could be heard, Scott's rich tenor filled the room.

> *As I stand here in this quiet hour, listening to the silence,*
> *My mind goes back to the days gone past.*
> *Unfiltered scenes now seem so vast.*
> *Speak to me now through Your Spirit as I lift my heart heavenward.*
> *Lord, I have a question to ask of You.*
>
> *How can You sit in Your lofty abode?*
> *Watch these children that You fashioned from birth?*
> *How can You watch them hurt like this,*
> *When You say You're a tower of strength?*
> *How can You bear their pain, my God, as You watch them?*
> *Don't You ache to be their friend?*
> *Tell me, Lord, is Your heart made of stone?*

The chords, plucked with intensity and rage, shattered the silence of the church. Some members of the congregation looked bewildered. This was not a funeral song. Whatever had come over young Brother Scott?

The melody and words gained strength as Scott moved on to the second verse.

> *See them as they gallantly go, some stumbling and some fighting.*
> *Watch that one as she moves, see behind the smiling face,*
> *And watch that child as he gropes in the darkness for a friend.*
> *Tell me, Lord, is Your heart made of stone?*

Scott swung the song back to the questioning chorus. *How can You sit in Your lofty abode . . . ?*

Brian could not believe that this was happening at his dad's funeral. Scott was actually singing about how he, Brian, felt. The injustice of his dad's death. Yes! Yes! How can there be a God who allows things like this to happen? A God who claims to love! "No good thing will he withhold from them that walk uprightly."* Ha! Tell that to another fool. His dad was good. The very best. Yet God took him. Bully for you, Scott. This must be a stone-hearted God!

The song transitioned through a riff and then slowed to the kind of reflection that precedes acceptance.

Yet I think again,
If I as one of those children that You fashioned from birth,
If I can watch and feel their pain so intensely that I hurt,
Then how much more is Your pain, my God?
For so much greater is Your love.
How much more is Your hurt, because You're God?

That's why You can sit in Your lofty abode
And watch these children that You fashioned from birth.
You can watch them hurt so much,
Knowing You can be their tower of strength.
You can bear our pain, my God, and sustain us
And be our never-failing friend.
You and You alone,
Because You're God.
Yes, You and You alone,
Because You're God.

The final notes from the guitar seemed to meander down through the aisles and pause for several heartbeats. Then the silence returned.

The bewildered believers relaxed. Paradise was not lost after all. Brother Scott had reminded them that God hurts when they hurt. Lovely young man that Scott Henry.

But Brian was having none of it.

No! No! I will not accept this. He does not care. He cannot.

His chest was on fire, but he sat quietly between his mother and his sister—rebellious, yet bravely holding the family together.

Lenore stood in front of the microphone and faced her friends and her family. She was unaware of the full hearts that watched her, the hands waiting and eager to catch her, and the prayers that bombarded heaven's gate to sustain her. Dry-eyed, she conversed with her listeners.

"'Here we grow again.' That's what Robert used to say to me when difficulties came our way. He would square his shoulders as if gearing up for battle and say, 'Here we grow again, love.' You see, my husband firmly believed that pain, though unpleasant, was necessary for our growth. That if we didn't experience difficulties, hardships, bad times, and bad stuff, we would stalemate—or was it stagnate? But you get the idea.

"So here we grow again. But I hadn't counted on growing on so soon without my Robert." Her eyes looked bleak. "The suddenness of his death has left us completely bereft. I turn to say something to him, and he's not there. I feel a gentle touch on my shoulder, and it's just a phantom. And I find myself without tears at the funeral of the love of my life."

Lenore spoke to the face of Sister Agnes. "Why is that? Why can I not cry for the man who wooed me with gentle romance? who secured my world with his quiet strength and loved our children with boundaries, hugs, and time?"

Her eyes found Gwen's. "You know me. I cry when babies are born. I get choked up when a child hugs a dog. I've cried buckets of tears at every wedding, funeral, graduation, and sad or happy story. Why can't I weep for my beloved?"

The lost look in Lenore's eyes, the plea for the release of tears along with the puzzlement on her face, strained the heartstrings of the congregation. But most of them held it together.

Samantha, however, lost her fight and quietly wept for herself and her mother. Brian's chest exploded with grief, but his eyes rapidly blinked the waiting tears into recession. And Lenore remained dry-eyed, looking perplexed—curious, even—as she continued to converse with her friends.

"I'm not without hope, you know. I know I will see my Robert again in heaven. I believe what God says, that He will make all things new one day.† I trust Him because I cannot do otherwise. Yet it hurts so much. We hurt so much."

Lenore's face relaxed into a small smile. "But during this week every single time my steps faltered, God sent an angel with the face, voice, or arms of one of you to sustain me. Isn't our God an awesome God?"

Wet praises rang out from the congregation.

She continued, her body unmoving but her face doing the gesturing. "So let us not be defeated by this hard thing that's come upon us. Help me. Help

Brian. Help Samantha. Pray for us and our family. God will see us through."

Lenore moved away from behind the podium, walked down the four steps to stand at the apex of the aisle by the box where lay the body of her husband. She had no microphone, but her voice carried to every corner of the sanctuary.

"Dear Robert. I know you can't hear me now. But thank you for a love like no other. Thank you for a heart as big as your hands. Thank you for romance and for Friday night candles. Thank you for being a true example of priesthood and for modeling God to our children every day of your life. I don't know how I'll walk on without you. But I will not let this growth opportunity be wasted. I will hunt day and night for the pearl in this sea of grief your death has left us in. Before God and these witnesses today, I reaffirm my faith and consecrate myself again to God till I have finished the course."

Lenore's words stopped. She just stood beside the casket and stared, feet rooted to the carpet.

As the silence became large, Brian began to rise, to go to her, to stand with her, but a less-confident voice wobbled back into action, and he made himself sit back, on standby.

"But sweetheart, despite what I say, I don't want to go home to the empty house and the empty room and the empty bed without you. I don't want to watch the sunset on Victoria Day without you. How will I fly—without you?"

Brian came off standby and went to stand beside his mother. She did not even look up. She only paused, listening, and then nodded her head as if God had answered her question.

"Yes. I know. God will send His angels."

Placing her right hand on the polished wooden box, she remembered her vows. "'I, Lenore Elaine Baptiste, took thee, Robert Abraham Baptiste, to be my wedded husband. To love and to cherish, in sickness and health, when things were easy and especially when they were difficult, till death did us part.' And for ever and ever and ever, Robert, I will hold you close to my heart. Rest in Jesus, sweetheart. I love you."

Lenore then kissed her two middle fingers and placed them reverently on the covered casket, right at the spot where Robert's head lay beneath.

It seemed as if the congregation drew in a shuddering collective breath, and the heartstrings, which were already strained beyond endurance, snapped, catapulting even the most stalwart over the edge and into an abyss of tears.

Niagara fell.

Amid the biggest meltdown ever at New Haven, Samantha, not knowing the source of strength in her legs, walked steadily to the podium. Removing a cordless microphone from a nearby stand, she positioned herself on the other side of her mother, joining with Brian to again form the horizontal line of support.

Nodding to the audio operator, she closed her eyes and waited for the introductory strains of "We Shall Behold Him."

She sang as she had never sung before. Amid the weeping in the room, the grief and pain, she became a finely tuned instrument conducted by a master musician. Sustained by family hands and angel wings, she sermonized with conviction:

"The angels shall sound the shout of His coming,
The sleeping shall rise from their slumbering place.
And those who remain shall be changed in a moment,
And we shall behold Him then face to face."‡

As she advanced toward the last note of the song, the congregation advanced with her.

And when her voice hit that last high note, clear and true, they sprang to their feet in praise and jubilation, faces still raining tears, clapping, cheering, hoping, and believing that death was not the end.

It is but a sleep.

Pastor Al brought the service to a close with a few more words of comfort, and at the peal of the organ, the staff of Brown's came to take Robert away to his final earthly resting place, accompanied by an entourage fit for a king.

Later, at the graveside, Charmaine waited in the long line to offer her words of encouragement to Lenore and the kids. On reaching them, she hugged first Brian, then Samantha, and finally Lenore. She understood a little of their loss. Yesterday afternoon something precious of hers had also died. But she had no one to mourn with her. No one to comfort her.

She'd listened to her husband sing earlier about a crisis of faith and moving on to acceptance. She'd tried to tongue-tap around the sore spot in her heart to gauge the depth of the hurt, but the sharp pain that lashed out at her probing told her it was too soon and too fresh. So she hung on to those needing comfort, drawing from them some for herself.

Dust to dust. Ashes to ashes.

---

* Ps. 84:11, KJV.
† See Rev. 21:4, 5.
‡ "We Shall Behold Him," by Dottie Rambo. Copyright 1980 John T. Benson Publishing Co. (ASCAP). All rights reserved. Used by permission.

Wednesday

Chapter Fifteen

Mr. Perfect Has Feet of Clay

The days immediately following a burial can take on a surreal quality. Lives of friends placed on hold during the heat of a crisis start clamoring for attention. So back they go to those things put on hold, because life insists on going on.

People also begin to pull away, because the days after a burial are awkward days. There is nothing to plan. No distraction of preparation. Just emptiness and deep pockets of silence when words are not enough. Awkward, because folks do not know how to help the bereaved with the healing, the hard times, and the coming to terms. Especially the coming to terms, which is a personal matter with its own timetable.

On Wednesday morning Charmaine kissed her husband with cold lips and departed for her daily walk to the subway station and work. She felt awful. Actually, truth be told, she did not know what she felt. Since Monday afternoon she had alternated between periods of pure anger, denial, defeatism, and unfathomable hurt. Now she just felt shell-shocked.

Her husband a father? Of a 10-year-old?

She would not be the only mother of his children or the only one to experience the joy of bringing his children into the world. Why had she not thought to ask? She knew he had not always been a follower of Christ, even though he'd grown up in the church. But to come face to face with the sins of his past! To know that he had been so intimate with another woman! Had been so irresponsible to have unprotected sex with her, and now had an almost-grown child whose mother was dead! What was she to do? God could not really expect her to accept this, this . . .

"Ma'am, are you planning to deposit that token and board the train today? You're holding up traffic." The impatient-sounding voice came from right behind Charmaine's ear.

She came to attention to find her fingers poised over the ticket box, clutching her subway token. When did she get here? A line about six deep, including her questioner, waited impatiently behind her. She could not recall her walk to the subway station.

"I'm sorry. Sorry. I was distracted."

A large woman pushed past her, deposited her ticket, and snapped, "Make up your mind, lady. Even Moses holding up his walking stick at the Red River didn't dawdle about hitting the rock. Some of us have to work for a living."

Quickly dropping her token in the box, Charmaine pushed against the turnstile and headed down the stairs. She must remember that one to share with Scott tonight.

And then it all came back. The pain. There would be no sharing with Scott tonight. He was going to leave straight from work to drive to Montreal to meet his child.

But you could have gone with him. Didn't he beg you to? And you refused. You just . . .

■ ■ ■ ■ ■

Tuesday Night

"Honey, please talk to me. I know it's asking a lot of you, but please, Charmaine, help me through this. I did not plan it. I didn't know that this would happen and mess up our lives like this. You must believe me when I say that I love you and have loved no other human being the way I love you, Charmaine. I'm sorry that because of my mistakes you have to be hurt like this. But I can't ignore the fact that there is a child, honey. A child that I am responsible for bringing into this world. I can't ignore her, Charmaine."

Still fully dressed from Robert's funeral, Scott had sat her down on the bed beside him and started his plea. She sat stiffly, unmoved by his words. She did not want to be hard, but this was too raw, and already it seemed as if he had embraced the idea of his fatherhood. At least he wasn't referring to the child as his daughter.

Tugging on her fingers, he begged, "Speak to me, Charmaine. Yell. Cry. Throw something! React in some other way than this stony silence. I can't deal with the silence, honey. Please tell me how you feel about all this."

Finally she said, "*This* changes everything."

"What do you mean by 'everything'?"

"I don't know how I feel about things anymore. I feel cheated. As if I'm second-best. As I said, it changes everything."

"Maybe this is our storm. Maybe this was sent to test us," Scott reflected.

Charmaine rounded on him with a snort. "This might be our storm, but *you* brought it on! You brought it right into our home, Scott. So don't sermonize to me. I'm not one of your boys. I did not ask for this, and I want no part of it."

"You can't mean that, Charmaine. You're making it sound as if I planned this to hurt you. I—"

"Don't you get it?" she interrupted. "That's what you needed to tell your guys last Friday night! Sex comes with consequences! Babies can get made when you have sex. That's why God wants it within marriage, Scott. But no, you had to go mess around with some girl and then walk away, not knowing that the consequences of your . . . your . . . seed planting would come back to haunt you 10 years later. I, on the other hand, waited for you. Waited for marriage to have my first sexual encounter, and now *I* have to live with *your* past. And you have the audacity to sit here and babble foolishness to me about this being our storm! You have some nerve!"

Scott was defeated. He had no rebuttals. Nothing with which to defend himself. She was right. That's what he had told Brian on Friday. Those early decisions to love them and leave them were the worst mistakes of his life. However, mistakes have to be dealt with, and he had to deal with his.

"You're right, Charmaine. Every single thing you say is correct. I brought this storm into our lives. The last thing I ever wanted to do was to cause you pain, yet that's wht I've done."

He saw her brush a tear from her face. *Heaven help us!*

"Can you find it in your heart to forgive me? Knowing that I love you next to God and need you in my life like I need to breathe?"

Charmaine's heart was breaking. She loved this man. She couldn't stand to see him so defeated, so humbled. Clasping his hands, she softened.

"Oh, Scott! Scott! What are we going to do?"

He had gathered her to him, laying his face against her own. His tears mingled with hers.

"Come with me tomorrow to meet them. If we leave right after work, we can get there by 9:00. I promised the grandmother yesterday. But I can't face this without you by my side. Please come with me to meet this daughter of mine and—"

Charmaine jerked back, her voice dead.

"Your *daughter*. I see you've come to terms with things quite nicely. Excuse me. I need to go to the bathroom."

When she came out much, much later, she had silently undressed, donned her nightgown, took a pillow and blanket, and gone to sleep on the couch in the living room. Oceans apart again.

▰ ▰ ▰ ▰ ▰

That was yesterday. So you reeled from the shock of him saying the word 'daughter.' Today is a new day. Don't you think you could have left him some hope this morning? something to take with him on the lonely drive to Montreal? Some Christian you are, Charmaine O'Dell Henry. Some Christian!

Charmaine reached for the peace that passes all understanding and found none. Like an automaton, she boarded the train, still arguing with her inner voices.

▰ ▰ ▰ ▰ ▰

Pastor Al could hear the phone ringing insistently as he approached his office on Wednesday morning. Before he had a chance to grab it, the voice message system clicked on.

"Pastor Al, Andrew, this is Scott. I don't know how busy your schedule is today, but if you can spare some time to see me this morning, I'd really appreciate it. I won't be going in to work, so you can call me back at home."

Pastor Al wrote down Scott's number and stared at the paper. Scott called him Andrew only when talking to him as a friend. All other times it was Pastor Al. Scott insisted that it was an important sign of respect for the office of the pastorate.

Stowing his briefcase under his desk, Pastor Al checked his appointment calendar and saw that he could fit Scott in at 11:00. He dialed the number.

"Hello," Scott answered.

"Scott, this is Andrew. How are you doing?"

"Not great right now. I need to talk to you today if you can fit me in."

"I have an unbooked slot at 11:00. Will that do?"

"That would be perfect. I'll see you then."

"Is there anything—" Andrew started to ask, but Scott had hung up. He'd have to wait and see.

Turning to review the messages that had piled up over the past few days, Andrew prepared for a busy Wednesday. One call was from a mother needing help for a son who no longer wanted to come to church. There were several messages from folks who wanted prayer or visitation or encouragement as they faced surgery, looked for work, or dealt with family crises. Robert's death seemed to have precipitated a lot of revived pain for some. Andrew bowed his head, and the words of Scott's song at yesterday's funeral came back to him. *How can You bear their pain, my God, as You watch them?* . . .

He couldn't remember the rest of the words, but he knew beyond the shadow of a doubt that God could meet all the needs that he'd copied onto the writing pad. Bowing his head, he exercised his faith and asked for the guidance of his heavenly Father to be an instrument in helping to meet those needs. He prayed for the Baptiste family. He prayed also for Scott and whatever the problem was that he'd hear about soon. And he prayed for himself, that God would keep his faith strong and use him today and always.

On his drive to the church Scott wondered at the brain's capacity to compartmentalize. After a night spent more in mental turmoil and prayer than in sleep, he'd watched his wife walk away this morning. When the front door closed, he felt a chapter in his life close too.

He opened another door in his mind called work and realized that he could not do that today. Sounding quite calm to his own ears, he'd talked for a long time with his manager and arranged to have the rest of the week off—to attend to some personal issues. Then he'd called the pastor, showered, and managed to get himself to his car and on his way to church with only a very tiny part of his working brain in operation.

Well, well, look what we have here. Mr. Perfect with feet of clay. You certainly got your comeuppance, Mr. Henry! Oh, yes, you were going to be a role model for the guys. A mentor. Someone they can talk to about stuff. Now look at you! Just another deadbeat dad with a past.

Scott made a halfhearted attempt to stifle the voice in his head. It had to be the devil. But feeling a greater need for some kind of penance, he allowed the voice to flail him, ripping bits of grace from his redeemed life. He deserved every stripe.

Steering the car into the parking lot, he turned off the ignition and rested his head on the steering wheel. *God, please help me. I know You said that You will not give us more than we can bear, but this one is breaking my back. Of course, this wasn't Your doing. It was mine. Yet I ask that You sustain me, please. Today and always, please hold me up.*

And in the middle of the turmoil, he clearly heard the reassurance of the Spirit. *My grace is sufficient for you.**

Buoyed by that promise, he opened the door and went to meet his pastor and friend.

■ ◢ ◢ ◢ ■

"And Charmaine? How is she taking this?" Andrew asked after he'd quietly listened to Scott's story.

"Not good at all. I asked her to come with me to Montreal to meet the child and the grandmother, and she reacted as if I'd slapped her. But I can't ignore this, Andrew. I have seen too many deadbeat dads around. I had one myself. Even though I just found out about this, I can't go on knowing that a child I fathered is growing up without my influence in her life."

Nodding, Pastor Al answered, "I hear you on that. However, how do you know that this child is yours? that this is not just some woman's desire to pin the child on a dad, and you got picked?"

Scott stared at the carpet. "Believe me, I thought about that. Charmaine asked the same question. But . . . but Emily is not the kind of person to do something like that. You see, even in my wild days, I made a point not to go out with girls in the church, or any Christian girl, for that matter. Emily—her actual name is Emelia—was an exception. She challenged my male ego."

Grimacing as if the memories hurt, Scott admitted in a small voice, "I'm ashamed, Pastor Al. I became determined to see if I could crack her resolve to stay a virgin until marriage, and I promised her the moon. I told her I loved her. Romanced her. Even went to church with her a couple of times. I convinced her with the argument that it's OK to do it if you love each other."

"I guess you did," commented Pastor Al.

Scott, looking up with dreary eyes, said nothing. He didn't need to.

"What happened after that?"

"I left. Not right away, but pretty soon after. She'd started to get nesting instincts, and at the time that was the last thing I wanted."

"You had no idea she was pregnant?"

"None whatsoever. But the ironic thing is that even though I got her to compromise her values, after I dumped her I felt sick, like the lowest kind of scum. After Emelia, I lost all desire to be a stud. Without knowing it, she sent me back to God. All that stuff I learned growing up in church came back to haunt me. And so I told my mom that I needed to find myself, and left Montreal. Spent the summer working odd jobs on farms for room and board, or living in my beaten-up Civic. Sometime during that summer I bought a guitar and taught myself how to play it. With the guitar and nature, and my Bible, I found my way back to the Father. Soon after that, I ended up in Toronto, applied to college, and have been here ever since. But now I have to go back."

"I'll come with you."

"What?"

"I said I'll come with you. Personally, I think this is too much to ask of Charmaine right now. But if, as you say, the grandmother is ailing, then time is of the essence. So let me call Judith and rearrange the rest of my day, and I'll accompany you to Montreal."

"You can't do that, Andrew! Judith and baby Jess need you. And tonight is prayer meeting. You have to be here for that."

But Andrew was already on the phone. In no time he had arranged for Lenore to stay with Judith. His instinct that the distraction would be good for Lenore was well founded when she responded as if a lifeline had been handed her. She even offered to prepare dinner and create a family-affair kind of evening.

Judith, while curious about the reason for his impromptu leave, was glad to be able to spend some time with Lenore, Brian, and Samantha. She had not been able to do much during the past few days.

Next, Pastor Al called the prayer ministries coordinator and asked if she could lead out in the prayer meeting that night. Her yes was equally enthusiastic. He hung up the phone with a smile on his face. He continually marveled about how God can work when we let Him.

"All's well. I have a few phone calls to return, which should take me about an hour or so, and then I need to run home and grab some clothes. After that, I'm all yours. When would you like to leave?"

Scott, feeling his voice choking up again for the umpteenth time during the past few days, looked at this friend and pastor, gratitude mingled with relief on his face. "Andrew, I wish I could find it within me to convince you not to do this, but I need a friend today. Thank you, man. This will not be forgotten." Looking at his watch, he said, "How about 2:30 or 3:00? I'll pick you up at your place. First, though, I'll call the grandmother and tell her to expect us about 8:00. Then I'll book a hotel room for us to stay for the night. Plus, I want to let Charmaine know what's going on. I really appreciate this, Andrew. God bless you, man."

Andrew got up from behind the desk and slapped Scott on the back. "That's what God put us here for. To be a comfort and help to each other. Plus, I know if the tables were reversed, you'd do the very same thing for me."

"Yeah, I guess I would. But I wouldn't wish this reversal of tables on my worst enemy, let alone my very good friend. Thanks again. I'll see you in a couple hours."

---

* 2 Cor. 12:9.

Chapter Sixteen

What Tomorrow Brings . . .

There You go again, God. Just when I thought I couldn't stand the silence anymore, You sent me another help. Lenore's planning brain ticked off the many things she could make to take over to the Simmses for dinner. They would have a feast. Apple pie for dessert, lasagna, spinach mandarin salad sprinkled with almonds and served with raspberry vinaigrette. She would bake the pie and lasagna from home. Then prepare the salad once she got to Judith's house.

Not used to being at home on a weekday, Samantha did not know what to do with herself. Reminded again of the reason for her being at home, she went in search of her brother. She knocked on his closed bedroom door. No answer. Opening it, she peered in to find the bed empty and neatly made.

Wandering downstairs, she searched the kitchen, then the rec room. Still no Brian.

"Brian, are you here?" she called.

She heard his muffled voice. "I'm in here."

Following the sound of the voice, she noticed that the door to their dad's space was ajar. Pushing it open, she found her brother sitting at their dad's desk.

"How come you're here?"

Checking to make sure she wasn't trying to pick a fight with him, Brian saw only curiosity. He understood her question. When they had moved into this house, their dad had allocated for himself this room off the rec room. It served as his den. Unless invited, they learned to stay clear of the space, referring to it not as a den, but as Dad's space. The door always remained slightly open, except when Dad was in a private meeting. And definitely no one went into the space when Dad wasn't there—even though the door was never locked.

Brian wasn't sure how to answer his sister's question, but he remembered his promise to be patient with her.

"I felt restless," he said. "I didn't really plan to come in here, but ended up by the door. Then I had to come in."

"How long have you been here? Does Mom know you're here?"

Despite his best intentions, he felt impatience creep into his voice. "I don't know, Sam," he said. "What difference does it make?"

Sam, suddenly remembering her promise, was quick to intervene. "I wasn't accusing you of anything. It's just weird to see you sitting there. I didn't realize before how much you look like Dad."

The muscles worked in Brian's jaw. Afraid that the wrong words spoken might spin them off into another quarrel, which was a far easier way to deflect their grief, he made himself ask softly, "Was there something that you wanted me to do?"

Sam eased herself more fully into the room. Walking over to the bookshelf, she picked up a photo of her dad with half of his head cut off. Her first attempt at photography. She carefully placed the photo back on the shelf and answered her brother's question.

"Not really. I think I should go back to school. The house feels weird, and I don't know how to be in it. I don't really know what to do with myself." Sam paused to search for words to describe how she was feeling, then continued: "Remember the time I fell off my bike and hit my face on the edge of the pavement?"

Brian was quick to recall. "Yeah. You came running into the house dripping blood all over the place. Mom was so scared."

"I'd broken a tooth. That's what had caused all the bleeding. They had to take the tooth out, but for days afterward, my tongue would keep looking for the spot where the tooth was. It's as if it didn't know what to do with the space." Anchoring her body against the bookshelf, Sam spoke to the room. "That's how I'm feeling right now. As if I don't know what to do with the space Dad has left. Nothing fits anymore."

Brian stared at his sister. When did she grow up to be so smart? That was exactly how he felt. Trying to navigate around a space that used to be filled, but was now empty.

Lenore came downstairs later to find them both in their dad's space, sharing the big chair, heads together, leafing through memories of days gone by. She withdrew to the kitchen to prepare her feast.

Todd decided that he'd put off calling Brian for too long. Sure, he'd been there for him at the funeral. Been one of the pallbearers even, but still he felt that he needed to connect with Brian. One-to-one. He'd been too quiet. Too locked up. Not like Brian at all. So this evening he would drop by. No more excuses.

Charmaine returned from lunch to find that she'd missed Scott's call. She called his work, only to hear the recorded message on his voicemail that he would be out of the office for the rest of the week. How come he hadn't told her that this morning? She dialed his cell phone and received a prompt to leave a message. Finally she called home. Knowing that the messaging system would activate after four rings, she was just about to hang up when Scott answered. The voice messaging came on at the same time.

"Hold on a moment."

She heard him deactivate the system. She pictured him tucking the phone between his ear and right shoulder in his typical way, and missed him already.

But the phone was not tucked comfortably in its usual place between Scott's ear and right shoulder. Recognizing Charmaine's voice, he stood erect and formal. Prepared for a barrage of questions and accusations—his just deserts for messing up their happy home.

"Hi," he said cautiously.

"Hi," she said.

"How are you doing?" he asked.

"OK, I guess," she replied.

This was so wrong. They had never been this formal with each other before. Never!

"Not working today?" she asked.

"I asked for the rest of the week off," he answered.

"Oh," she said.

"Charmaine—" he started.

"Yes?" she interrupted.

"I'm going to Montreal this afternoon. When you get home, I won't be here. I'm sorry that I tried to pressure you last night into coming with me. That wasn't fair. I talked to Andrew about the situation, and he volunteered to accompany me. We're going to leave around 3:00, but I'll call you later on. OK?" His voice caught in his throat. "Just remember that I love you."

"OK."

Say something else! This is your other chance. Tell him that you love him. Reassure him. He needs your support now, Charmaine. 'For better or for worse.' You promised him 'for better or for worse.' Extend grace to your husband, Charmaine. The same grace God daily extends to you.

She heard Scott waiting, but could not find the words. Heard his sigh, but could not summon any comfort from within her misery.

"'Bye. I'll call you later. Pray for me, love," he closed.

"OK."

Pause.

Pause.

Pause.

Pause.

She counted them. Four silent beseeches. She opened her mouth to say nothing, but the connection was severed.

Oh, what a wretch I am. God, You have to help me. I'm drowning. I can't do this swim. You promised that when we walk through the water You will be with us. That the flames would not overpower us, but here I am failing You, Father. So easy to preach grace. So hard to live it.

"Charmaine, call for you on line 3." The voice of Marie, her coworker, interrupted her reverie. Thinking this was her second chance, she quickly picked up the receiver.

"Scott!"

"Hello, is this Mrs. Henry?"

Heart flip-flopping in panic, she answered, "Yes. Who is calling, please?" *O God, let him not be dead.*

"This is Sears calling. Your catalog order is ready for pickup."

"What!"

"Your order is ready for pickup," said the patient voice.

"Oh. My order. Yes. I remember. I mean, I will remember. Thanks." Charmaine hung up the phone before she made more of an idiot of herself.

"You OK? Was that person who died a relative?" Marie asked.

"Not a blood relative, but we were very close," replied Charmaine.

Marie nodded her head in understanding. "Sometimes the death of friends is harder to deal with than the death of relatives. At least you have your faith to help you deal with it."

Charmaine felt her head nodding yes to a lie.

At 6:00 Lenore called Samantha and Brian to get ready for their visit to the Simmses.

"Take along some extra clothes. Pastor Al had to go out of town, and we're staying the night with Judith and Jess."

Brian and Sam entered the kitchen together.

"Mom, if you don't mind, I'll pass on the sleepover," Brian said. "Todd called earlier to say he'd be dropping by around 8:00. I could ask him to pick me up there or take the car and pick up you and Sam in the morning. Besides, I don't feel very sociable right now. I think I can manage dinner, but that's it." He didn't mention that Sister Simms' constant need to pray over people would drive him crazy.

Lenore said, "Oh." Turning to her daughter, she asked, "How about you?"

"I'm OK with sleeping over. I love Jess. She's so cute. But I want to go to school tomorrow. Maybe not for the whole day, but I need to get out of the house. Start doing something normal again. So I don't mind sleeping over if Brian can pick me up about 8:30. My first class isn't until 10:00."

"Are you sure you're ready?" questioned the mother in Lenore.

"No. But as Daddy used to say, 'every journey begins with a single step.' I'll go put my things together."

Lenore gaped at her daughter as she left the room. Brian answered her unspoken question.

"Yes. I was thinking the very same thing earlier. When did she grow up?"

Charmaine inserted the key in the door of her apartment, and for the first time since getting married, she did not look forward to going in. She entered anyway. The space that until now had seemed so cozy and homey reeked of pleasures past. She noticed that Scott had removed the pillow and bedding she'd left on the couch.

Their bedroom was neat as a pin. No outward sign that all was not well in paradise. Weary beyond words, she sat on the bed and, missing her husband terribly, reached across for his pillow and inhaled him close to her.

She wished she could talk to someone, but this was too private. And maybe it would all turn out to be a bad case of mistaken identity. Then her life could return to normal.

That chapter is closed, honey. There is no going back. There is only going forward.

How true! Even if this turned out to be a case of mistaken identity, she felt that she'd failed God and her husband in some intangible way. She had not been equal to the test.

"It's not enough to be your best, dear. You have to be better than your best."

Her mother's words came back to her as if Lucinda O'Dell was right there in the room. She wished she could call her and just talk. Maybe she would have something nice to say. Maybe this time she would not make her feel like she was not good enough. Maybe . . .

"Maybe does not a pie make." Another of her mom's sayings.

Oh, Mom, I need you to be a mother today.

Charmaine jumped when the phone rang. Wanting desperately to speak with her husband, she picked it up.

It was Lucinda O'Dell. "What exactly is the matter with you now? You have been on my mind all day." The no-nonsense voice of her mother leaped through the instrument.

Charmaine's greeting to her mother was laden with respectful disappointment. "Hello, Mother. I was just thinking about you. How are you?"

"Forget the pleasantries. Nothing is the matter with me. I called to see how you are doing. Ever since you were born, Charmaine, I could always tell when something was bugging you. I thought now that you're grown it would go away, but there it was, waking me up this morning. I tried to ignore it the whole day long, but I know I won't get a wink of sleep until I call you, so you might as well put me out of my misery."

Charmaine felt her hackles rise. Her mother could create that reaction in her in a mad minute. "I'm perfectly—"

"Charmaine Elizabeth O'Dell Henry," Lucinda interrupted, "if you are gearing up to tell me that you're perfectly fine, I am going to be very cross. Do you hear me? I do not like having feelings I cannot understand govern my life. I've learned to live with these feelings when it comes to you because I have never been wrong before. But I do not like having them. So please do not insult me with the 'I'm perfectly fine' line."

"OK, Mom. I'm sorry. I am not perfectly fine."

"Well, what is it?"

"I can't talk about it."

"What you mean is that you will not tell your mother. What secret do you have that you think I've never heard before? Tell me! What agony do you think you're experiencing that I have not been through?"

Charmaine prayed for forbearance. "Mom, I didn't mean it that way. It's just that Scott and I are going through a rough patch right now, and we just need to work through it. OK?"

Undeterred, Lucinda pressed on. "What kind of rough patch could you be going through with that nice young man? If he had to, Scott would find a way to walk on water for you. He loves you that much. Are you allowing those pesky feelings of insecurity to mess up your marriage?"

"Mom, it's not like that at all."

Like a brilliant surgeon with a bad bedside manner, Lucinda cut and separated. "OK, don't tell me. Let me guess. I think I know my child pretty well to guess what kind of things would rock her world. So humor me. Scott is having an affair with another woman?"

"No, Mother."

"Good. That narrows down the choices pretty much." Speaking as if to herself, Lucinda continued. "If it is not an affair, not that I believed that for a moment, then it must be something from his past." One word tumbled after the other, then suddenly: "Does he have a child?"

Hearing Charmaine's quick intake of breath, Lucinda crowed. "Jackpot!"

Charmaine felt as if she'd been stripped naked. She hugged Scott's pillow tight to her middle to stop the shaking that had taken over her body. As though from a long distance she heard a voice.

"Charmaine? Answer me, Charmaine."

She was furious. "I'm so happy to have assisted you once more in your quest to be right, Mother."

"Don't talk foolishness, child. I am your mother. I care what happens to you."

Charmaine was shouting now. "Well, you have a very interesting way of showing it. Right at this moment I could have done with a hug or some words of comfort, but your need to be right is far more important than my need to be comforted. Why can't you ever put my needs ahead of your own? What did I ever do to have you be so hard on me?"

For once, no reply.

Silence on the line.

Moments later a somewhat softer Lucinda asked, "Is that really how you feel? how you have always felt?"

"Yes, Mother. Always. But I'm sorry for yelling at you. It just all tumbled out."

"But why didn't you say something before?" Her voice was almost contrite. "I don't read minds, you know."

Searching for a first step toward reparation, Charmaine said gently, "Just the heart of grieving daughters."

"One daughter, Charmaine. You're all I've had since your dad ..."

"I know, Mother. You're all I have too."

Needing to get back to the heart of her daughter's grief, Lucinda asked, "So what if he has a child? He still loves you. Doesn't he?"

"Yes, Mama. He does. And he begged me to go with him to go meet this child. This 10-year-old daughter." Her voice shook at the words. "But I couldn't. I just couldn't. What am I going to do with a 10-year-old child? The mother is dead. He's gone there now to meet the grandmother and child and ... and I think I'm going to lose my mind."

Uncharacteristically, Lucinda had no comeback. Her daughter called her 'Mama' only when she was scared.

"That is a tough one."

Charmaine did not need to agree with her.

Lucinda probed some more. "Tell me what you are most afraid will happen."

"Pardon me?"

"What are you most afraid will happen?"

No response.

"Charmaine, are you there?"

"Well, I'm not very good at sharing," confessed Charmaine.

Lucinda dismissed that. "Curse of the only child. What else?"

Another long silence.

"I wanted to be the mother of his children."

"Did you specify to God that the children had to be yours by birth?

"No . . ."

"Then you can still do that. Be mother to his child, and mother to your children, too. What else, Charmaine? Tell me all of it. There's nobody I will be telling my child's secrets to, so get it all out."

"I feel as though I've failed him, Mom. I call myself a Christian, but I am so *angry* with him. For messing up our home. Our security. And once the news gets out, everyone will know and talk about us. And worst of all, pity us. The perfect couple gone to hell. The boys he works with will lose another male role model, and that will mess them up. And maybe . . ."

"Say it."

"Maybe . . . well . . . maybe in trying to make up for the years he has lost," she said with a sob, "maybe he will love this child more than he loves me."

Lucinda's practical heart ached for her daughter. Not knowing how to offer nurturing by words, she said, "Do you want to come home for a bit?"

Charmaine removed the pillow from against her middle and breathed. The shaking had mysteriously gone away.

"Not right now, Mom. I'll wait and see what tomorrow brings, but thanks for the offer."

"You're going to be OK, you know," Lucinda said bracingly. "We O'Dell women may fall, but we never stay down."

"I hope you're right, Mom. Thanks for listening to your beacon and calling me. I actually feel a little bit better."

"Like I always say, 'A problem shared . . .'" started Lucinda.

"'. . . is a problem halved,'" completed Charmaine.

"I'm going to hang up now. Call if you need me. 'Bye."

"'Bye, Mom."

So what if there were no prayers and lifting of each other up to God? Her mother was her mother. Doing the job the best she knew. A churchgoer but not a Christian, Lucinda had taken Charmaine to church as a child and later sent her because she thought the institution to be a good influence, providing some of the nurturing she could not supply.

Another soul I am failing to influence for God.

Chapter Seventeen

A Ram in the Bushes

The sign read "Welcome to Montreal."

"Are you ready for this?" Andrew asked Scott.

"No."

"We have some time. Let's check into the hotel first and get rid of our luggage. We can freshen up and then be on our way."

"Sounds good to me. I think we turn right here to get to the hotel. It's the Holiday Inn."

"Looks posh. So this is how the laity lives," teased Andrew.

"Not really. But we have a points system with them from work. I hope you don't mind, but I booked only one room. It has two beds. If you want your own room, we can ask—"

"Relax, Scott. Haven't we bunked together many times before?"

"Yeah. I just thought . . ."

"I'll forgive you. Your brain is a bit taxed at the moment."

"I hope they have short-term parking. Finding any kind of parking in downtown Montreal is tough."

"God will provide. How far do we have to go from here to get to your . . . the house? Is it within walking distance?"

"No. They're on the South Shore in Brossard. About a 15-minute drive."

"No Holiday Inn there, I take it?"

"Can't recall. Charmaine and I have stayed at this one before."

In less time than he wanted it to take, they were processed and checked in. Their room on the fourteenth floor gave them a panoramic view of the downtown core of the city. Antsy, Scott paced around the room, then stopped suddenly.

"I'll go grab a shower."

"You do that," Andrew replied, adding, "and even though this is a hotel, try to leave some hot water for the rest of us."

Scott flung a towel at him. "Funny guy!"

' Andrew used the time to call home to check in with Judith.

"Simms residence," answered Judith. He could hear from her voice that she had been eating.

"Hey, honey."

"Andrew!" Her glad greeting put a smile on his face.

"The one and only. How are things?"

"We're fine. Just fine. You will not believe this woman called Lenore Baptiste. She came over here loaded with food. Spinich mandarin salad, green beans, apple pie, and the best melt-in-your-mouth lasagna I have ever tasted. We were just finishing up our long lazy dinner when the phone rang. Samantha is off entertaining Jess, and I am actually having an adult conversation over dinner. Is this paradise or what?"

Feeling great that their evening was going well, Andrew could not, however, resist teasing her. "So what are you trying to imply, honey?"

Amused that every time she fell for the bait of his teasing, Andrew predicted her next question.

"Imply about what?" she asked innocently

"You don't have adult conversations with me?"

"Oh, you! You know that's not what I mean. I am just having a great evening and . . ."

Andrew delivered her. "And I am just teasing. How is Lenore?"

"About the same as usual. Brian left just a little while ago. Says he's going to meet up with Todd. By the way, you'll never believe this. Jess sat with Brian the entire evening. She reached out her little baby arms to him and smiled at him all during dinner. Our daughter, who does not go to any male but you!"

"Wow! That is unbelievable!"

"I know. At first Brian looked shocked that she wanted him, and then was pleased as punch. Said something about the touch of the Baptiste men. Insufferable little egomaniac."

"Honey! You didn't call him that to his face."

"Yes, I did. He knows I'm teasing, but he really played it up."

" 'Sister Pastor'—that's what he calls me—'you wound me. Such words coming from the Mother Teresa of New Haven.' " That's exactly what he said. Called me the Mother Teresa of New Haven. Oh, Andrew, it was such a treat to see him smiling again. After the funeral I thought his face was going to break from clenching his jaw so hard."

"God is full of surprises, isn't He? He can take the most unusual of circumstance and make out of it something excellent. Kiss baby Jess for me and give my love to Lenore and Samantha. Tell them I'll call when I get back in town tomorrow. And you, ma'am, I hope you get a long sleep tonight. We're about to head out now to that meeting I told you about. Pray for us, OK?"

"You know I will. I love you, Andrew."

"I love you too, Judith. Good night."

Scott opened the bathroom door in time to hear Andrew's declaration of love to his wife and felt a great longing for his own.

"Henry, your bathroom time is up!" Andrew bellowed, replacing the phone on its cradle.

"Cool your jets. I'm done." Opening the door wider, Scott asked, "Did anyone ever tell you that you act like a sergeant major?"

"Yes. You. Many times. So get over yourself." Grabbing a change of clothes, Andrew headed for the shower.

Scott saluted the door. "Yes, sir!"

"I heard that," yelled Andrew from behind the closed door.

▰ ▰ ▰ ▰ ▰

Scott sat in the car, eyeing the house they were about to enter.

"Are you ready now?" asked Andrew.

"Readier."

"Is that a word?"

"Too bad! It will have to do."

"Let us talk to the Father."

"Good idea. Should have thought of that."

"Relax, Scott. God knew from the day He created you that this day would come. He knew how it would affect you and what you would need. He even knew I would be here with you. He will guide you through it no matter how difficult it gets. Remember that."

Exhaling air he didn't realize he'd been holding, Scott allowed his shoulders to loosen. In less than a minute he would walk into that house, and everything would change. He exhaled again as Andrew began to pray.

"Dearest of Fathers, we appeal to You tonight as our Father because it is wisdom we now seek. You know what is about to unfold just as You know the end from the beginning. You have been preparing us for this moment when a change would come. In that house is a little girl who has lost her mom and is soon to lose a grandmother. So much loss in one little life. And You have brought us here for such a time as this. If that child is indeed Scott's, give him a father's wisdom to know what to do. Relax his tense nerves. Calm his fears. Give him the confidence of the faithful to believe that he can do all things through Christ who strengthens him.* We claim Your promises, Father. We ask in faith knowing that You will see us through. Go before us to that door. Let Your presence enter every room and touch everyone there, leaving a trail of peace. In Jesus' name we ask. Amen."

"Are you ready?"

"Yes."

"Good. Let's go."

Inside the walls of the brick bungalow Lana Turner puttered. Making busy when she should be sitting still. Even though Emelia had prepared Celeste for this moment, Lana wasn't quite sure how much the child had taken in. Her vague memories of that young man Emelia had dated were not good ones. Thought too highly of himself, he did. But he certainly had charm. The bad boy kind of charm that lures good women to their own demise. And to think that was the man she had to trust to care for her grandchild. *God, help us!*

She heard a car door slam. Then another. Could that be him? Did he come bringing his wife? Her ears perked to catch the fall of footsteps on the creaky stair of the porch.

Nothing.

She relaxed. *Not yet.*

"Grandmother, when is the man who's my father going to get here?"

"Soon, Celeste. Maybe in the next 10 minutes or so. He called to say they were on their way. Be patient," Lana counseled as she slowly paced.

"Is he going to be a good father, Grandmother?"

The doorbell rang. Lana felt her sick heart flutter far too rapidly for its own good. She prayed. *Please give me some time, God. Just a little bit more time.*

"I'll get it, Grandmother. You sit." Lana did not even try to stop her. *She's too old already for her 10 years.*

Voices in the hallway told Lana that at least two people had come, and the too-old voice of her grandchild was inviting the guests in.

Two men entered her living room looking less nervous than she felt. Neither one resembling the macho man of days gone by. The taller and slimmer of the two stepped forward and identified himself.

"Mrs. Turner, I'm Scott. Scott Henry."

Oh! Good eyes and a strong chin. Let the rest of him be good, God.

"Hello, Scott," replied Lana, nodding in his direction. She willed her face to deliver a smile of greeting. *Help me, Jesus.*

Turning to the girl, Scott said, "And you must be . . ."

Lana watched the young man blanch. She could tell he was searching his mind frantically for her granddaughter's name. Did she tell him when they spoke? She couldn't recall.

Celeste rescued him. "I'm Celeste. Celeste Fernandez. French and Spanish names all mixed together. Would you and your friend like to have a seat? Grandmother and I made some refreshments in case you were hungry from your long trip."

"That was very nice of you both. And yes, we would be very pleased to take a seat," replied Scott.

Celeste walked the few steps to a three-seater sofa decorated with white crocheted doilies along the back and beckoned them to sit. She waited as Scott's friend took the right corner of the sofa and Scott the center cushion. Then she sat down beside Scott.

"My mother told me all about you. When she discovered that her cancer was back, she told me that she would try to get in touch with you so you could know about me. But soon after that, we found out about Grandmother's heart, and so she made Grandmother promise that if she, my mother, died first, Grandmother should get in touch with you as soon as possible afterward. So Grandmother did, and here you are."

Looking past Scott toward Andrew, the girl asked, "Are you my father's brother or his friend?"

"I am his friend," answered Andrew.

"Why did you come?"

"Because that's what friends do."

Celeste considered this for a moment then turned candid eyes on Scott. "Were you scared about meeting me?" She did not allow him to answer. "I did not sleep well last night. I had a bad dream, so I went to Grandmother's room. Since she was not having a good sleep either, we talked to God about the problem and tried not to worry too much about it."

Seeing that the men were completely floored by her outspoken but guileless grandchild, Lana asked Celeste to go and fetch them all something to drink.

"Sure, Grandmother." Then to the two men: "I'll be back as soon as I can. I do need to be careful with Grandmother's things."

Looking after her with love in her eyes, Lana remarked, "She tries hard to please. But she is a sweetheart." She stopped herself from saying more lest they think she was trying to make a sale of her grandchild's best features. Turning her full attention to the men in the room, she brought her gaze to rest on Scott.

"Now, Mr. Scott, for the record, I want to let you know that I did not approve of your treatment of my daughter way back then. That is now water under the bridge, however, but I pray that you have changed for the better. Emelia insisted that you not be told of the pregnancy or the child. You were never to know.

"Of course, when she was diagnosed with cancer, and knowing that my own ticker could tick its last tock any time, Emelia relented. She decided that if she could not stay in remission, you were to be contacted—but only after her death. So as I feel my own time running out, please tell me that God has worked a miracle in your life and you are a new man."

Seeing Scott squirm, Andrew interceded. "I can answer that question for you, Mrs. Turner."

"Who exactly are you again?" asked Lana. "I don't think we were formally introduced."

"My name is Andrew Leonardo Simms. I am the pastor of New Haven Ministries in Toronto. Scott is one of my parishioners and also a very dear friend."

Lana's brows furrowed and smoothed. "I've heard of you. You're the one with that celebration-style church in Toronto, aren't you?"

"Everything we preach and do is based solidly on Bible principles," defended Andrew.

"Did I say otherwise? You young people are too sensitive. You need to relax more and not take everything so personally. I have copies of a few of your programs," she added, motioning toward a small desk, "and applaud what you are doing. You have found a way to stay true to the Bible and yet be a youth-friendly church. Something a lot of these do-gooder geriatric churches could learn from. So what can you tell me about this young man to whom I will soon be forced to leave my grandchild to raise?"

Scott leaned forward. "Pardon me, Mrs. Turner, but I really would prefer to speak for myself," he interjected.

The half smile Lana sent toward him did not console him. "Have no fear, young man. I will hear from you in time. Right now, however, I want to hear from the man of God himself. Why don't you go and see what's taking my dear Celeste so long in the kitchen? It's right through that door. She might have a few questions for you herself."

Recognizing that he had been summarily dismissed, Scott rose and headed in the direction of Lana's pointed finger, all the while reminding himself that he had committed this strangest of nights into the hands of his heavenly Father. Pushing gently against the swinging door, he spoke softly so as not to startle his—the child.

"Hey. It's me. Scott. Your grandmother sent me to see how you're faring."

Celeste had arranged four drinking glasses on a tray and was in the process of carefully measuring out what looked like fruit punch into each glass, her face a picture of intense concentration. Before turning to Scott, she finished filling up the glass she'd started and replaced the jug on the counter.

"I think she just wanted to talk to your friend about you without you being there. I don't need any help. I do this for Grandmother's guests all the time. Whenever she gets really ill, I even prepare her meals. I'm pretty reliable that way."

"Oh," said a bemused Scott.

"You can sit if you want," she said, indicating a stool by the kitchen counter. "We can talk in here till Grandmother is ready for us. When she is, she'll send your friend to come and get you."

"Is that right?"

"Trust me. You'll see."

"I'll trust you. So . . . what can we do to pass the time?"

"Well, I am very curious about you and would really like to ask you a lot of questions, but Mamasita would consider that behavior impolite."

"I see. And who is Mamasita? Is that your name for your mom?"

"Yes, that's what I've always called her." Tilting her head to one side, she asked, "Since you asked me two questions—even though they were really the same question—can I ask you two in exchange? I think that would be fair and not too impolite. It would be like we are trading information."

"Ask me anything you want, Celeste," Scott said, taking the previously proffered seat.

"Did you love my mom?"

Anything except that!

Scott searched for words that were honest and appropriate. "Well, I met your mom when we were both very young. I thought I was, how should I say it—?

Celeste supplied, "'All that?' 'The cat's meow?' That would be what Grandmother would say."

"Both will do. I liked her a lot, though, but we made some decisions that were not very smart."

"You had sex," Celeste deadpanned as if she were talking about the latest Nancy Drew book she'd read. Scott's shocked look caused her to reassure him.

"Mamasita told me. She likes for me to know the truth about things."

Scott reached madly for more words. Better words. "Not . . . I mean, there's nothing wrong with"—somehow he couldn't repeat her frank words—"but it was very wrong for us to do it without being married and committed to each other."

Later Scott would marvel at the first full conversation he ended up having with this child—his, his daughter. She did not look anything like him. What if Charmaine was right? What if she really wasn't his? *Dear God, what am I doing here?*

A soundless voice soothed his soul. *My grace is sufficient for you.*

"And that's how I came to be," Celeste stated again matter-of-factly with no hint of rebuke.

Scott sighed. "I'm sorry, Celeste. I did not know you existed until a few days ago when your grandmother called. I would not have ignored you had I known. I would have tried to be here for you the best way I could."

"Mamasita said it was for the best that you did not know. She said you might have returned to us because you had to, not because you wanted to. She said that relationships work best when people love each other and choose to be together."

"Your mother was very smart. I liked that about her."

"Except when it came to you," replied Celeste in her nonjudgmental tone.

"Touché!"

"So do you think you can be a good father, Scott?" The child's voice begged for assurance. "Grandmother is going to be gone soon, and even though I'm trying very, very hard to be brave, I get scared about what's going to happen to me. Mamasita and Grandmother tell me that God will provide for me just as He provided that ram for Abraham so that he didn't have to kill his son. But why did God take my mommy and will soon take my nana? Doesn't He know that they're all I have, and that I will miss them so much? Why is He being so mean? Sometimes, sometimes I just want to yell, 'Hey, You, God! Go pick on someone else. I'm just a little kid, and it's not fair that I have to—' "

Suddenly Celeste's eyes flew open in disbelief. She'd actually said out loud those terrible things about God. And to a stranger! Her father! Ashamed, she covered her face with her hands, but soon a tear forced its way out between the creases of her fingers.

Without stopping to think about it, Scott hurried to offer comfort. He knelt in front of her, gently held her by the shoulders, and spoke quietly.

"Oh, honey, honey. Don't be so upset. You're right—sometimes God does seem mean. I too wonder why He does some of the things that He does or why He allows some things to happen." He stopped, weighted by guilt and responsibility. "You've had to deal with so much in such a short time, little one, so it's OK to be scared. It's even OK to be mad. The Bible is full of a lot of people who got mad at God for things they thought He should have done but didn't."

The creased fingers opened up in one section. "It is?"

"Yes, it is. People like David, Jeremiah, Hosea, Mary, and Martha. God doesn't mind if you get mad at Him. He understands everything we feel, and He wants us to talk to Him about those feelings. He just wants us to talk to Him, period."

Celeste pulled back slightly, but said nothing for a few seconds. Then she nodded as if coming to a momentous decision. "OK. I will try that. Starting tonight, I will talk to God about everything." She stuck out her tear-dampened right hand and shook Scott's. "Thank you, Scott. I am not a usually a crybaby, you know."

Still gripping her small hand, Scott looked at her solemnly. "Someone much wiser than me said that tears are the safety valves for heavy hearts. Every once in a while you need to cry just to make sure those safety valves get the exercise they need. So promise me that you will keep them in good shape. OK?"

"Well, since you put it that way, I will." Celeste reached for a paper towel, dampened it, and dabbed at her eyes. Then after blinking a few times, she turned to Scott, "Do I look presentable enough to go back to Grandmother and your friend?"

Bowing deeply from the waist, Scott said, "Yes, my lady. You look the picture of fortitude." She giggled. Just like a 10-year-old should.

Only then did Scott feel his eyes sting.

Oh, Charmaine, this child who looks nothing like me has just taken a piece of my heart.

Outwardly, however, he continued the butler charade. Picking up the tray of drinks, he said, "Allow me to take these for you, milady. And by the way, we are ready to go out, and your grandmother has not called for us as you predicted she would. So there!"

Turning with the tray, he almost collided into Andrew. "I've been sent to fetch young Scott and Lady Celeste."

Scott made a face at Celeste, but she held her head high and preceded him out of the room. As she passed him she whispered, "Maybe you are my ram in the bushes."

---

* See Phil. 4:13.

Thursday

Chapter Eighteen

Not OK—but Acting As if It Is

Lenore slowly surfaced from sleep to the clear cry of a baby. For a while she was disoriented, trying to figure out why there was a baby at her house. Then she remembered where she was and hurried out of bed to see what was ailing baby Jess. She had just scooped the young one into her arms when Samantha came into the room, stifling a yawn.

"Oh, you're here. I heard her crying too." Reaching for Jess's hand, she cooed, "What's the matter with you? Had a bad dream?" Jess's face broke into smiles while the tears still clung to her lashes.

Lenore sat in the rocking chair and started to sing a lullaby. Jess nestled her head against Lenore's bosom as if all were well with her world.

"Is that all you needed? Some company? Your bum feels dry, and you're not acting hungry. Did something scare baby Jess?" Jess's only response was to smile some more around the thumb that had found its way into her mouth.

Samantha plopped down on the floor beside the rocker. "Isn't she the cutest thing?"

Lenore smiled. "Just like you were."

Samantha was affronted. "You don't think I'm cute anymore?"

"Nope. Definitely not!"

"Mom!"

"I think my daughter is a very beautiful young woman who makes me feel very honored to be her mother."

Jess made a noise that Lenore was sure sounded like "Yes!"

Feeling embarrassed but very pleased, Samantha rested her head against her mother's knee. Eventually she asked, "So how are you really doing, Mom?"

Lenore sighed. "I really don't know. Until you asked just now, I had forgotten that I was hurting. I don't believe I've taken it all in. I know your father is dead, but it's as if it's too much for my brain. I find I drift off into these limbo moments, when it feels as if he is still at work or gone to run an errand and will be back soon. Then it all comes crashing back that he's never coming back from work or that errand, and my brain goes into shock again."

"But Mom, you haven't cried. You and Dad were so close. I know your heart must be broken. Why can't you cry?"

Voice heavy with feeling, Lenore said, "I don't know, but I think one day I will. Probably enough tears to drown us all."

"That's me already. I think I've cried enough tears for you and Brian. But you know what, Mom? Something happened to me at the funeral on Tuesday. As I was singing that song, for the first time I felt the words to be real for me. That when Jesus comes again, and the dead in Christ wake up, we shall all be changed. Daddy won't be dead anymore. He will rise to meet us in the air to be with Jesus forever. Even though I miss him so much, I have a kind of soft confidence that I will see him again. I don't know if I'm explaining it right, but even though I'm crying because I miss him, I am not in deep despair."

"Oh, honey. I'm so glad. That's what Christians call the blessed assurance. That's one of the many joys of being a believer. We grieve, but are not hopeless."

Jess chose that moment to expel a loud burp, shocking both herself and the women in conversation. Her frightened look sent Lenore and Samantha into fits of giggles. Jess soon recovered, crowed, and babbled in delight, reveling in the entertainment effect she was having.

And that's how Judith found them when she entered the room. Arms akimbo, she scolded, "Here you all are having a party in my house without so much as an invitation to the homeowner."

Still smiling, Samantha replied, "We were summoned by the homeowner." Pointing to Jess, she said, "This one right here."

"She doesn't count," said Judith. "She does not have a job."

"Well, she definitely is an entertaining host," said Lenore. "She joined in the conversation, smiled when appropriate, and burped loudly to show her appreciation of her guests."

Not missing a beat, Judith responded, "The first two qualities she got from me. The burping, of course, must be from her father."

At this juncture Jess decided that she wanted only her mom for company and reached out her baby arms for transfer. Judith's face softened with mother love. Sam drew a bit closer to Lenore, who responded with a gentle massage of her daughter's shoulders.

Tucking Jess in the crook of her arm, Judith slid down along the wall until she was seated on the floor. "I have so enjoyed having you here with me for a visit. God knew exactly what I needed. You two and Brian have been a great blessing to me and to Jess. Thank you."

Lenore indicated to Sam that she was about to rise. "Thank you for helping us to get through another day, Judith. I was starting to go stir-crazy yesterday when Andrew called. God knew I too needed a lifeline."

"Thanks for me too," said Sam. "I think I'll go back to school today. I'm going to call Brian to see if he can drop me there."

"Are you sure, Sam?" asked Lenore.

"Well, it's either today or Monday. There won't be much difference in a few days, but if it gets too much, I'll leave early. At least the first day back will be out of the way."

"All right, love. Go call your brother. I'll hang around with Judith and Jess until Pastor Al comes home. Tell Brian that I'll call when I'm ready to be picked up. Tell him to take my cell phone. I can never remember his number."

Judith snapped into host mode. "School! Breakfast. You need breakfast."

Lenore shooed her out of the room. "Your job this morning, after you've fed and bathed Jess, is to give her to me and go have a long soak in the bath. At least for a half hour. I'll take care of breakfast if you allow me to take over your kitchen."

"Never look a gift horse in the mouth. I'll take it," replied Judith.

Mumbling out loud about being referred to as a horse, Lenore exited the room, her narrowed eyes directed toward Judith. Judith grinned at Samantha.

Yep. A baby step, but a step nonetheless toward the future.

Thursday morning for Charmaine started out even more difficult than Wednesday. Scott had called late Wednesday night. Even though she had worked hard to be more open than she was the day before, she'd still found it difficult to bring back the warmth to her voice. Probably feeling her reticence and trying to make up for it, he had talked nonstop about the child. Charmaine thought that even a fool couldn't miss the dampened excitement in his voice. She knew it! He had started to have feelings for the child. The love affair had begun. After he'd bid her good night, she had tried to pray for peace, but it had eluded her.

Now on the morning of the day he was to return, she found herself questioning her loyalty, her faith, her Christianity, her love, and most of all, her sanity. Still she persevered in prayer. But no answers jumped out of the sky or came to her, even in a still small voice.

This was not going to be easy. For all she knew, this might be the beginning of the end. She felt unequal to the task and considered the option of backing out before it completely overwhelmed her. Much as she drilled for it, she couldn't find the forgiveness she needed to give to her husband. She didn't know if it existed in her psyche. She, Charmaine O'Dell Henry, was proving to be a hypocrite to all that she had previously professed and believed in. And that was the ultimate betrayal.

Maybe going home to mother for a little while might not be a bad idea.

"How did you sleep?" asked Andrew, eyeing Scott from behind the pages of his Bible.

Scott sat up in bed, propped the two pillows against the headboard, and leaned his back into them. "Not very well. My head was too full of stuff."

Placing the Bible on his bedside table, Andrew asked, "Anything you want to talk about? You didn't say much last night after we left the house."

"I know. But my brain was too busy trying to process everything. To me, the whole evening was weird and sad and exciting and . . . I feel as if I've been flattened. Completely run over."

"I hear you. The evening definitely had all those elements. That little girl is something else. You can't help loving her. She's a young-old one. Wise and childlike at the same time. Her grandmother is pretty shrewd too."

"Tell me about it. After my stint with her, I felt as if I'd been raked over with gloved nails," replied Scott.

"Wouldn't you do the same if you were dying and your motherless grandchild, a mere 10 years old, was going to be left alone in the world in the care of a stranger-father?"

Letting out a frustrated breath, Scott said, "I'd probably be more ruthless.

But Andrew, what is this going to do to my marriage? Charmaine is not handling this well at all. Last night when I called her she sounded so remote. I think I'm losing her. At the same time, I can't ignore this child if I am her father."

"What do you mean if? You don't believe she's yours?" asked Andrew sharply.

"I don't know what to believe. She looks nothing like me. The problem is culpability. I could be her father because I slept with her mother." A pause. "More than once," he added softly. "But how can I be sure? Charmaine will take one look at the child and dismiss this whole thing as a major conspiracy. And the child would be left alone again. I couldn't do that to her, Andrew. She thinks I'm her ram in the bushes."

"She said that?"

"Yeah, last night as we were leaving the kitchen, when you came to get us. She'd been crying. Feeling as if God didn't love her. Saying that if God did, He wouldn't be asking her to say goodbye to both her mother and her grandmother. Man, it just about broke my heart. Then after a few minutes she dried up her eyes and asked me if she looked presentable. Why should a 10-year-old kid have to go through that?"

"Trouble happens. That's the long and short of it. It plays no favorites. But how did you leave things with the grandmother? After she dismissed me and Celeste to the den to 'show the young pastor the books'? Was she pushing for some kind of resolution? Asking you to take the child by a certain date?"

Scott pondered the question. "I guess to a certain extent she was. Problem is that she could be around for another six months or she could go in a moment. She wants things settled for Celeste sooner than later. I told her that I would need to talk things over with my wife, and optimistically explained that the news will take us a little time to get used to. But Charmaine seems to be in lockdown mode, man. I can't get through to her."

Gently Andrew probed around the tender feelings of his friend. "Do you know exactly what you want to get through to Charmaine?"

Scott leaped off the bed. "I want her to accept this! I want her to be with me 100 percent. I want her not to hate me for something that happened so long ago. She's my life, Andrew! Without her I'd be lost!"

Taking time to catch his breath, Scott continued more calmly. "Before you call me an idiot and a fool, I'm not completely self-absorbed. I know this news is hard to take in. It completely changes our lives. I'm reeling myself, so I can imagine a little bit of what she's going through. She'll probably always see this child as a competitor for my attention. Think I'll love her less. Worry about all the things people will say when they find out, and worst of all, feel as though I have completely failed in her ideal of what a husband should be—one that does not bring a surprise child into a marriage."

"I could talk with Charmaine if you want," Andrew offered.

Seeing hope leap into Scott's eyes, he was quick to caution, "Not that I can guarantee it will do any good. But I could invite her to talk to me about how she's feeling. Maybe that would help her get a better handle on the situation and objectify it a bit for her."

"I'd really appreciate it, Andrew. Man, I feel as though I'm already asking so much of you. You dropped everything to come here with me, and now this."

"Say another word of thanks, Scott, and I'm going to have to slug you. Hard."

Scott held up his hands in surrender. "OK. I'll shut up!"

"By the way, what's in the envelope the grandmother gave you?"

"Probably ID papers for Celeste. That's all I need. Charmaine will take one look at it and assume I've decided to keep the child without discussing it with her. How can life suddenly become so complicated?"

"You're forgetting that God is always in the equation."

"No. I'm not forgetting. But I'm pretty upset right now. Scared, even. But being 'touched with our frailties,' He understands how I'm feeling. Anyway, nothing is going to get solved sitting here. I'm going to grab a shower, and then we need to hit the road."

"Just leave me some . . . "

"Shut up, Simms. There's enough hot water for all the guests. Plus, you can always go first if you wish."

"And lose my opportunity to heckle you? You must be kidding!"

"You're a mean man, Pastor Simms. Way beyond redemption."

"Only through men's eyes, Henry. Never through God's."

Scott's grimace told Andrew he'd succeeded in having the last word.

* * *

"Sam, is that you?"

Samantha paused in her second attempt to recall the combination to her locker, and turned to meet a pair of concerned eyes. "Hi, Sammy."

"What are you doing here?"

"I go to school here, remember!"

"But you should be at home. Isn't it too soon?"

Samantha was touched by Sammy's concern. "I figured that whether I came back today or Monday, it wouldn't make much of a difference. Besides, I needed to get out of the house."

Sammy nodded in understanding. "I hear you. You have a class now?"

"No, actually. I had history, but Sir is sick, and apparently there wasn't enough time for them to arrange for a substitute. So for the next hour I'm a free woman."

Sammy could hear tiredness in her voice. "Want to go to the caf for a bite?"

"Only if you're OK with my poor company," she replied. "Maybe something on the menu will entice me to—" Sam slapped her head. "What am I saying? Hardly anything on that cafeteria menu entices. Some days I think the food here is part of a major experiment, with us as the guinea pigs. And by the way, shouldn't you be in class?"

"I should, but since I am naturally brilliant and can make a strong case for needing to comfort a grieving friend . . . "

Samantha laughed and conceded a temporary victory to the lock. "You're something else, Sammy Watson."

A voice echoed from behind. "Yeah! Definitely something else!"

"Candy!" Samantha cried, bumping Sammy out of the way to hug her friend.

"The one and only," replied Candice, hugging her back. Stepping back to appraise Samantha, she demanded, "And pray tell me, Miss Thing, what are you doing here?"

"Very same question I asked her," interjected Sammy, rubbing a supposedly bruised shoulder. "Except I didn't get any great big hug. All I got was a massive shove. I'm sure I'm maimed for life."

Samantha gave the offended shoulder a rub and said, "There. Feel better now? Sorry I ran you down."

Looking as if he'd died and gone to heaven, Sammy let his eyes roll back in his head and purred, "No problem. Anytime. Run me over anytime."

Eyeing him in mock disgust, Candice said, "This is nauseating. However, before I was so rudely interrupted by Mr. Romeo here, I was asking what you were doing at school, Samantha Baptiste. I don't recall receiving an answer."

"Ladies and gentlemen, here speaks our dictator, I mean director, Candice Attila Hitler!" Samantha took a step backward and bowed to Candice while Sammy clapped and whistled.

Candice's eyes filled up with tears. "Oh, Sam. It's so good to have you back taking potshots at me. Are you sure you're OK?"

Samantha sobered. "No, I'm not OK, but I have to start acting as if."

"Well, if you need anything—to talk or cry or anything—promise you'll let me know. As you can see, I don't need a lot of motivation lately to cry," Candice added, dabbing at her eyes. "At the funeral, when you got up to sing for your dad—are you OK if I talk about it?"

Samantha assured her that it was OK.

"Good! As I was saying, when you got up to sing, I was so nervous for you. Your mother already had me weeping buckets, but then it was as though something happened to you, Sam. You should have seen yourself. You . . . I don't even know how to describe it. It's as if you were transported someplace beautiful, and took all of us along with you."

Samantha smiled shyly and admitted, "I know. I felt as if I were riding above the pain and I could see heaven. Since then I haven't felt so bad about things. It's as though God gave me peace. I'm sad, but I'm not strung out with grief, as I was before."

"That must be the peace that passes understanding mentioned in the Bible,"* commented Sammy, propping his elbow on a nearby locker.

"God is carrying you, Sam. Sometimes I think He just picks us up and carries us."

"And since He's carrying me," said Samantha, "you can count on me to be at rehearsals tonight. I have a feeling that something extra-special is going to happen this Easter."

Candice squeezed Samantha's arm. "I sure hope so. We could all do with something special this year." Turning to Sammy, Candice said, "I'll see you later as well. Gotta run to my next class." Looking at her watch, she yelped. "Yikes, I'm 10 minutes late already! See you tonight, guys."

"So about that snack offer, Sammy Watson? Is it still on?"

Sammy's grin answered before he did. "You bet!" He offered the crook of his arm, which Samantha took, and they headed down the hallway to the cafeteria.

Brian was driving aimlessly around the area of Sam's school when his mom's cell phone began ringing. Pulling off to the side of the road, he flipped it open.

"Ready for pickup, Mom?"

"Is that you, Brian?"

"Yes."

"This is Mrs. Price. I thought I was calling Lenore's phone."

"You did. I am just answering it for her."

"Oh. Where is . . . can I talk to your mother? Oh, dear. I hate to do this with everything that's happened, but . . ."

"Is everything OK, Mrs. Price? Do you need me to come?"

"That's so like your dad. He would have said those very words. Yes, I'm OK. I'm fine. It's just that Mr. Singh passed away this morning. His son came by a few minutes ago to let me know. Why are so many sad things happening all of a sudden? It is so hard to deal with. I just don't know what to do."

"Mrs. Price, Mom is visiting a friend at the moment, but I'll call her, and then we'll come by as soon as we can, OK?"

"Thank you, Robert."

Brian started to correct her, but she'd hung up.

He called the Simms house and, after saying a few words of greeting to Judith, spoke with his mother. She took the news more calmly than he'd expected. But then again, his mom had a lot of faith. More faith than he would ever have or need.

Lenore kissed Judith goodbye and thanked her again for a lovely visit.

Brother Singh is finally gone. Be with the family, Lord. Sustain them as You are sustaining us.

In no time Brian had Lenore back at their house and had left to pick up Samantha from school. She stowed the overnight bag she'd brought to Judith's in the front closet and rushed across the street to see Emily—outspoken, eccentric, and faithful Emily.

Ever since they'd moved into the neighborhood, Emily Price had adopted first Robert and then the rest of the family. Robert remained her favorite.

He was the one who made sure her snow was shoveled in the winter and her grass mowed in the summer.

When the Baptistes planted flowers in the springtime, Lenore and Robert assisted Emily with her planting as well. Her baking was always a welcome addition to the Baptistes' table. She made the most delectable desserts, showing a strong preference for coffee cakes.

They all loved her, and over time she so adopted them as her family that she saw nothing wrong with scolding them when she thought they'd misbehaved. Not that she ever scolded Robert. In her eyes, he was perfect—except for his belief in this God business. But at least he wasn't too chatty about it. In Emily's opinion he was what a Christian should be. Doing good deeds and not just preaching about doing good. Robert lived his sermons.

She must have been watching from the window, because the door opened before Lenore could ring the bell.

With distress written all over her face, Emily said, "Dear Lenore, I am so sorry that I had to call you, but it all felt too much for me. This is all too much!"

Lenore gathered the frail frame close to her. "There, there. Don't distress yourself too much. He is at peace now. The pain is all gone."

"But it's too much death. When my Thomas died, I thought I would not be able to bear it, but I toughed it out. Death is not normal, Lenore. There's something about it that makes me want to scream. Yes, me! Scream, I tell you. Life should not have to be interrupted by death. It feels wrong!" Pulling away from Lenore's embrace, she said, "You probably think these are the ramblings of a scared old woman."

Keeping one arm around Emily, Lenore closed the door and guided her friend into the house and toward the kitchen, Emily's favorite room. "First, I don't think I've ever heard you ramble. And I completely agree that the notion of death, the cessation of life, is something to rebel at."

Emily sat down on one of the many straight-backed chairs in the kitchen. "I suppose this is where you tell me that your God can fix death. Well, He's taking a lot of centuries to do so. That young man who sang at Robert's funeral had it right. Your God's heart must be made of stone!"

"Oh, Emily, but that's the reason He died! That's why we celebrate Easter. To remind us that even our biggest enemy—death—can be, and has been, conquered."

Emily sniffed. "Your notion of conquer must be different from mine. You're a sensible woman, Lenore. Look around you. People are still dying every single day. Nothing has been conquered. If anything, things are getting worse. Deaths from AIDS, natural disasters, wars, and all kinds of new diseases. As far as I see it, death is having a field day with humanity."

Lenore pulled up a chair and sat knee to knee in front of Emily. Taking her hands, she began to explain.

"What Easter demonstrated, Emily, is that God is bigger than death. Death could not contain Jesus in the grave. His tomb is empty. He is the resurrection. He is life. And He tells us that if we believe in Him, we will never die—that death is, in actuality, just a sleep. And after God has given everyone repeated opportunities to discover and accept Him as Lord of their lives, He will come again and eradicate death forever, taking us to live with Him in an earth made new."

"Poppycock!" Emily snorted, pulling her hands away. "Pure poppycock!"

Reminding herself that spiritual things required spiritual discernment, Lenore searched for a point of agreement.

"You know, you're right," she said. "It is foolishness. Left unexamined, it is foolishness. However, it's your responsibility to examine it for yourself, Emily. Examine all of it with an open mind. God wants no one believing in Him without having a reason for their belief. Actually, He encourages us with the command 'Come now, let us reason together.'"†

Pausing to gauge Emily's reaction, Lenore continued. "Here's what will happen at the end of your open-minded examination: You will have very strong evidence for believing and equally strong reasons for not believing. Either one of these options will require a leap of faith, because both choices leave questions unanswered and unexplained."

"What do you mean by leap of faith?" Emily asked.

"Well, it's like this. In my opinion, the problem of pain and suffering is one of the strongest reasons for not believing. How can there be a God who loves us and yet allows His creation to suffer unspeakable pain? On the other hand, to me the awesome beauty of a sunset or the intricate detail painted into the petal of a flower are strong reasons for believing. If there's nobody out there, why bother to add beauty to things that are perishable? So it's a matter of which option you will choose to guide your life."

Seeing that Emily was still listening, Len said, "I choose to believe in God because it makes sense to my soul. Not always to my mind, but in the innermost part of me, it makes sense that I am created by a loving God. It makes sense, when I look at the design in the human body and in nature, how things that I pretty much take for granted are kept in such perfect balance that the earth stays in motion.

"What boggles my mind, however, is that this Creator-God that I believe in designed me with the ability to choose *not* to be a part of Him. This God of the universe wants to have a love relationship with me. Me! No matter how badly I've treated Him or how much I spurn His attention—nothing I do or can do will stop Him from loving me. Nothing! It drives me nuts sometimes, Emily! But then, it could only be a Supreme Being who could do that. Because I surely couldn't. So I believe and continue to believe, because I cannot resist a love like that! When strong arguments and unanswered questions overwhelm my ability to provide reasoned answers, and my mind wavers to 'poppycock,' my soul just won't let me."

Reaching again for Emily's hands, Lenore said, "That's what He did at Easter, Emily. He demonstrated that He can lay down His life and take it up again. But don't take my word for it. Every person needs to come to that faith for herself. Just know that whatever your choice, whatever your decision, God will respect it. That's just the way He is. He desires love that is given freely."

Emily gently touched Lenore's face. "And you still believe after Robert? After everything?"

"Yes, I do."

"And what if this God takes Samantha, and Brian, too and then gives you a lingering and painful disease? Will you still believe?"

"You ask tough questions, Emily. Those would be very tough things to deal with. But God has demonstrated that even when He's silent, when our cries seem to not reach heaven, He will show us His power. So yes, my desire would be to still stay with Him though I lose everything I now hold precious."

Emily patted Lenore's cheek. "You're a good woman, Lenore. I will think about what you said."

"Why don't you come with us tomorrow night to see the Easter pageant? Samantha is singing, and it's usually pretty good. I will take personal responsibility for keeping all those God-talking people away from you."

"It's just a play, right? No preaching?"

"No preaching. Just music and drama. Pastor Al usually says a few words at the beginning and end of the program, but they are words of introduction and thanks. Will that do?"

"I'll consider it. God knows somebody needs to see to you now that Robert is gone. How I miss him."

Emily's words caused Lenore's body to remember its pain.

Robert! Dear Robert! First you, and now Mr. Singh. Sustain me, Father God. I can't do this by myself. Carry me today, please.

Seeing the bleak look return to Lenore's eyes, Emily mentally kicked herself. "Oh, Len. Some friend I am. Here you are with your own grief, and I'm adding to it. You need to cry, Lenore. I am very worried about you. You are going to make yourself sick if you don't cry."

Lenore's sad smile pulled at Emily's heartstrings. Making a sudden decision, she said, "OK. I'll come to your program tomorrow night. I see I'm going to have to take you in hand, young lady. Now, let's have a cup of tea and some of those scones I made this morning. Then we can walk across to visit with the Singhs. You think you can handle that?"

"I'll have some tea with you, but then I need to run home. Sam and Brian will be coming home shortly, and I want to check in with Brian. He's trying to hide it, but my boy is very angry right now. I think later this evening would be a better time to visit the Singhs."

"I noticed that," said Emily, referring to Brian. "Who is he angry with?"

Sighing, Lenore answered. "I suppose God, life, death. Everything that's making him hurt."

---

* Isa. 1:18.

I Can't Do This, God!

After Brian collected Samantha from school, he drove straight home. Turning the car into the driveway, he switched off the ignition and remained seated.

"You're not coming in?" asked Samantha, opening her door.

"In a while."

"You OK, Bry?"

"I'll be fine," he said, staring out past the windshield. "Just go on in. See how Mom's doing. I just need a few minutes."

Brian could see that his sister did not quite believe him. Her face mirrored both her desire to say more and her decision to honor his wish to be left alone. Seeing pools of water begin to gather in her eyes, his voice roughened.

"Sam! Just go inside. Leave me alone for a while. If I'm not there in 10 minutes, you can come and drag me out of the car. Deal?"

"Fine!" She flounced off.

Great, Brian! Now you've gotten her upset after promising that you would take care of her. Big talker you are.

But Brian's mind had moved past Samantha. He wondered who he was kidding. He would never be all right again. He could still see the ambulance pulling away from the curb, see his mother's broken-up face. He still felt the urge to run away from the pain or run after whatever had taken his dad.

Bring him back! I still need him. I can't fill your shoes, Dad. I don't know how to help them. Pain, pain go away . . . pain, pain, go away . . .

The more Brian thought about his loss, the more he felt something building up inside. It started with a tingling in his toes and soon consumed his whole body. It took a few moments for him to recognize it as rage. That shook him, but steadied his focus. He'd never felt such clarity of thought. Such undiluted anger.

"How could You take him? How could You!"

Trust in Me, My child.

"Ah, you've decided to answer me now!" He spit the words aloud. "Too late, Mr. Good God! My trust in You died last Friday night. You don't care about anyone but Yourself. So go worship Yourself."

My son, give Me your pain. Give Me your heart.

"Heart? What heart? I have no heart left for You."

Brian, don't shut Him out, son. Don't shut out the voice of the Spirit.

Brian could hear his dad's voice in his head as if he were sitting next to him in the car. But his father's voice eased neither the pain nor the Spirit's voice Brian was determined to tune out.

He had to get out or hit something. Anything!

Run, boy. Move!

Forgetting his promise to Sam, Brian flicked the engine to life and backed crazily out of the driveway, burning rubber as the car took the first corner down the street. Faster and faster he went, startling pedestrians.

Where are you going, Brian? Things getting too much for you?

"Shut up!" he yelled to the current voice in his head. "Just shut the—" His brain slammed shut the door that would have let the swearword out.

His foot eased up on the gas. "No!" he said through gritted teeth. "I won't do that."

He never swore. Not since he was 5 years old and Jeffery Underhill had taught him a word. He had used it on Samantha, and then Daddy had found out, and well, he'd had the long talk about the many other choices of words within the English language that did not hurt or annoy, but could better express feelings.

Ever since, he'd never sworn again.

But that was close, wasn't it, Brian? If you thought it, it's just about as good as saying it, huh? After all, you're upset. Who wouldn't be? To lose a father who was so good, so perfect, so loved? And here you are trying to fill his shoes. You're only 19 years old. What do you know about taking care of a family? You need to take care of you. C'mon, get some of the pressure off your shoulders. It will kill you.

"No swearing," Brian spoke to the voice in his head. "I will not swear."

*"Resist the devil, and he will flee from you."** The Spirit voice was back, but the other one was not prepared to cede his prey.

OK. OK. Take a chill pill. You don't want to swear. Stupid, but I can live with that. What you really need is a little something to help you with the pain. You're not going to make it without something to help you cope.

As the battle for supremacy raged in Brian's mind, his speed picked up again. He could not go fast enough. Down side streets and up lanes. Running nowhere fast!

Run, boy. Run like the wind!

He screeched to a halt at a red traffic light.

"Come on!" Brian hurried the light. As he revved the engine impatiently, his fingers drummed out a staccato rhythm on the steering wheel.

"Come on, stupid light!"

Straight ahead a billboard arrested his attention. It showed a young executive kicking back after a seemingly heavy day at work, holding a glass of lemon-garnished liquid. The caption read "Even Mr. Responsibility needs some downtime."

That's exactly what I need. Some downtime, Brian thought bitterly.

Now you're getting the picture. A little relaxation. A little edge off the pain. You know you deserve it. Relax.

Brian! The Spirit's voice was urgent. *Think! Every journey begins with a single step. Don't go there, Brian. God wants better for you. He desires . . .*

"YOU shut up! I'm not interested in hearing anything about what God desires. He knows nothing about what's good for me! If He did, He wouldn't have taken my father."

But God . . .

The sudden loud honk of a truck horn indicating the change in traffic light caused Brian's foot to spasm on the clutch and stall the car. Furious, he double-turned the key in the ignition, grimaced at the rebelling engine, and smoked away from the intersection.

Somebody needs a little relaxation, I'm thinking!

But the Spirit voice continued to console: *My peace I leave with you. My peace I give unto you. Not as the world gives do I give. Let not your . . . †*

"No more! Both of you just shut up. Leave me alone."

Through an act of will, Brian silenced all the voices in his head—except for the one singing the continued refrain.

Pain, pain, go away. Come again another day. Pain . . .

Charmaine looked at the clock on her computer screen for the sixth time in the past five minutes. She willed the time to creep slowly toward 4:30, when she could leave the office. So far, it was cooperating with her.

Scott had called this morning. Said he and Andrew were going to be leaving Montreal no later than 10:00 a.m. If they'd had no major traffic holdups, he should be home by now. Her heart was desperate to see him, to hug him, but her mind was not in sync.

She'd promised Candice and Sis Bolski that she'd help with the wardrobe, and see to it that the pageant participants were appropriately outfitted, so she needed to go home, change, and gather her labeling equipment, measuring tape, and other paraphernalia. She also needed to face her husband, and she was afraid.

Her heart cried out. *I can't do this, God. You picked the wrong girl for this test. You picked a failure.*

You can do all things through Christ, the voice assured.[‡]

Charmaine was not unfamiliar with the voice of the Spirit. They'd had many talks in the past when things were good. Daily she had tried to practice putting her mind in the presence of God, and some days she could hear Him quite clearly talking to her.

Before, when life was manageable and her foundation secure, she'd asked God to do whatever it would take to make her more like Him. Foolish woman— to make such a request. Now she felt that God was answering her prayer.

"My yoke is easy."

"Easy! God, you don't know what You're asking of me. I cannot do this test. Give me another. Let this be a nightmare and please wake me up."

"My burden is light."[§]

"You don't understand. It's not that I don't want to do the right thing. I just can't. I want to be there for my husband. I want to be supportive, but . . . Father, I am too hurt.

I am the Great Physician. I am the Balm in Gilead. I AM.

"OK, Lord. I will try. I will go home and try again."

Don't try, My daughter. Trust.

It was 4:35.

* * *

Scott, who had been counting down the minutes, heard her key in the door and felt the urge to run to open it for his wife. But his body froze in place at the kitchen's entry—about eight feet from the front door. He could see her as soon as she came in, and she him.

How can it be possible, he thought, *that I now question everything I want to do or say to her?* He knew his love for her had not wavered one iota. Yet that love now tied his hands and bound his feet. He was afraid that the wrong thing said or done within the next few minutes would drive her away from him. So he waited for her to come in. Tense with anticipation. Praying for a miracle.

She came through the door with her posture bowed, despondency sitting on her shoulders. Then she looked across the room and saw him. Joy flashed past her face for a moment and then disappeared.

"Hey there." Her voice was husky with feeling.

"Hey there." His softened with longing.

The refrigerator hummed.

The clocked ticked.

The door slowly swung back on its hinges and clicked shut.

Scott swallowed. His wife hung in front of the closed door clutching her handbag, looking unsure. Looking lost.

Somebody needed to move, to speak, to break the growing silence before it took over the room.

Scott took a few steps forward.

"How was your day?" he asked.

Charmaine rested her handbag at her feet.

"All right, I guess. Yours?"

"Have I told you lately how much I love you?"

Charmaine's head snapped up.

In three quick steps Scott was directly in front of her.

He did not touch her.

"My day became all right when you walked through that door, Charmaine. That's what you do to me. What you mean to me. No matter what we have to go through, I want you to know that my days are not bearable without your love."

Charmaine could not move. His words were undoing her.

"Oh, Scott."

On its own volition, she felt her head turning from side to side.

"Oh, Scott!"

Frantic that the turning of the head meant her denial of his love, Scott uttered a soft demand.

"Look at me, Charmaine."

163

Her head halted in its sideways motion.

He riveted her with his eyes and held her complete attention. She could not look away. And then she really looked at him as he proceeded to undress his soul to her through his eyes.

Going beyond words, he showed her everything.

All he had to offer.

His full, complete, and total commitment.

All he stood to lose.

Deep need and delicate vulnerabilities were displayed for her eyes only.

And finally, he showed her his heart.

When Scott was sure she had seen everything, he slowly closed his eyes.

"Kiss me, Charmaine. Kiss the man who loves you next to God."

He waited.

Eyes closed, he waited.

He heard her shallow breathing.

He could feel her mental fight.

God, help her take that step to me. Help her . . .

He felt the touch of five fingers against the side of his cheek.

He dared not breathe.

The fingers were joined by five more on the other side of his face.

He felt a thumb move softly over his lips.

Scott released a ragged breath but stood firm. Eyes shut tight.

He felt her heat drawing closer before her body fitted itself against him.

Then heaven came down when she kissed his lips, mingling salty tears in her surrender.

His aching arms reached around to draw her even closer to him.

Then they ached no more.

Mom, has Brian come in yet?" asked Samantha, coming into the kitchen.

"I don't think so." Her hands in yellow mitts, Lenore lifted a covered dish from the oven. "You need him?"

"I was hoping he'd drive me to rehearsal. I don't think I have enough time to catch the bus," Sam said, glancing at her watch. "I'll check the drive. He said he needed some time alone, so he's probably still there."

"For more than an hour?" her mom questioned. "I'm sure I heard the car leave a while back."

Samantha pulled out a chair and dropped into it. "Great! Now how will I get to practice?"

"Call his cell, Sam. No sense stewing over the fact that he's not here."

Sam was reaching for the phone when the front door opened and Brian walked in.

"Hey, Mom."

"Hi, son. Your sister was just about to call you. Went for a drive?"

"Yeah." Brian took off his jacket and threw it on the back of a chair. "Anything to eat?"

"Why don't you two go wash up, and I'll have some supper on the table in about five minutes."

"Thanks, Mom. Sorry I didn't let you know I was going back out. Just needed to get away for a while."

"You OK, son?" Lenore wished she could ease the pain she knew he was experiencing. Unlike Samantha, he refused to talk about how he was feeling.

"No. But I guess OK will come one day."

Lenore nodded.

Samantha followed her brother out of the kitchen. She watched him go slowly up the stairs and wished she could do something to help him. But he was locked up so tight.

"Brian."

He stopped in midflight, not turning around. "Yes, Sam."

"I didn't come back out to call you because I wanted you to have that time alone you asked for. I hope it helped."

Was it just her imagination, or did he flinch? Samantha wondered.

"Thanks." He turned and gave her a weak version of a smile, a snapshot of the ghost of Brian past.

⬛ ⬛ ⬛ ⬛ ⬛

In a few minutes brother and sister returned to the kitchen and helped their mother put the meal together. They had not dined together as a family since last Friday night. By unspoken consensus they ate in the kitchen, knowing that the dining room would be screaming Robert's absence. Their small talk helped to fill the emptiness. After a while Brian pushed away his half-eaten supper and focused on his mother.

"How are we doing, Mom?"

Lenore placed her empty fork along with the unused knife in the closed position. Samantha followed suit.

"How do you mean, Brian?"

His tone all business, Brian elaborated. "Finances. What's our money situation? What things have to be seen to? Will you have to get a job? Can we afford my school fees and Samantha's and still pay our bills?"

Lenore held up her hand. "Whoa! Slow down, son. I think we're fine, at least for a while. Your dad purchased a funeral plan quite a few years back. You know your father. He wanted to make sure everything was taken care of, just in case." Lenore closed her eyes when she felt the burning in her throat. "Anyway, that took care of the funeral arrangements. Plus, we have his life insurance—another thing your daddy insisted on. I suppose I should call them to let them know, but . . ."

"I'll take care of it, Mom," said Brian.

"I'll help too," chimed in Samantha.

Lenore reached across the table and clasped the hand of her son and daughter. "Thank you, children. How about we take care of it together? I've been meaning to get around to it, but I just can't seem to rally the energy." She looked at Brian. "We really are OK for a while."

"What about the house and the car?" he persisted. "Are they paid for? I can work construction over the summer. The pay is pretty good, and that would help take care of some of the bills."

"I can teach swimming at the recreation center," Samantha added.

"No, son. Go ahead and apply for that internship you wanted. And Sam, if you want to work at the rec center over the summer, do so. But we are not in a desperate situation. The insurance settlement should be enough to allow us to proceed with the plans that your father and I have for you both. So while I appreciate your willingness to help out, let's make no changes to things unless we talk about them together first. OK?"

Both Sam and Brian nodded. Brian felt some of the weight he was carrying fall from his back. He wished the stone in his heart could be fixed as easily.

Lenore got up suddenly and began to gather the half-empty dinner plates. Brian was about to assist when Samantha tapped his foot under the table and gave him the eye.

"Brian, can you give me a ride to practice? I've missed the bus."

He frowned at her but said nothing. Rising from the table, he reached for his jacket. "Do you want to come along for the ride, Mom?"

"No, no. You two go ahead. Emily and I are going to visit with the Singhs later. And I don't want to know too much about the program. Tomorrow your dad and I will be able to enjoy it fully without any preconceptions."

Brian and Samantha made eye contact, but neither could find it within them to correct their mother.

"OK, Mom. We won't stay out too late." They quickly washed their hands, kissed her, and headed out the door.

In the car Brian questioned Samantha, "What was the meaning of that toe tap under the table? I was only trying to help."

"I know you were. But if you did, it would be one less thing she had to do. Right now Mom needs to keep herself busy. It's her way of dealing with the pain. It doesn't mean that we should never help, but since we were going out, clearing the table and washing the dishes would occupy her till it is time to go to the Singhs."

"Oh," said Brian. "But busyness isn't going to cure the pain. I mean, she still hasn't cried. I'm starting to worry about her. What if she cracks?"

Not having an answer, Samantha said, "Then I guess we'll have to ask God to make her cry."

"As if He'd care," Brian snorted.

"Brian! How can you say that?" Samantha retorted. "God is—"

"Save it, Sam." Brian turned on the radio and focused on the road ahead, while his sister closed her mouth and eyes. One to stop herself from arguing with her brother, and the other to focus on the silent prayer directed to God the Father.

---

* James 4:7, KJV.
† See John 14:27.
‡ See Phil. 4:13.
§ Matt. 11:30.

Good Friday

Chapter Twenty

The Kingdom of Grace

Pastor Al woke up to the happy babble of baby Jess in her room next door. Judith stirred beside him.

"The princess of the castle is awake, Your Majesty," Judith said.

"I heard. However, it sounds as if she's busy conducting the royal orchestra and does not need our immediate presence, which leaves me with the opportunity to have some quality time with my queen."

Smiling regally at her husband, Queen Judith asked, "And what is it that would please the king this morning?"

"I have a rather unusual request."

"Oh? And what, pray tell, is your request, sire?"

"I need both your ears."

"But Your Highness, these are the only two ears I have. If I gave them to you, I'd be less able to attend to the needs of the princess and the king."

"My queen misunderstands. I do not wish to physically remove her ears. I desire to have them listen to me for a few minutes, and at the end of my discourse I would be most appreciative of a word from my trusted advisor."

"In that case, your wish is granted. I will lend you my ears."

Andrew smiled at her, and she smiled back. He loved such moments as this, when they could completely relax with each other. This is what Scott felt he was in danger of losing with Charmaine. This camaraderie. This joy of living. This unconditional love. Could something like that happen to him and Judith? Would he be capable of extending forgiveness to her if he discovered some great sin from her past? Could she forgive him anything?

"Earth to King Andrew. Come in!"

Andrew focused. In a few strokes he gave her a shortened version of Scott's story, starting with the office visit followed by the trip to Montreal, the little girl, and where things stood currently. He had no qualms about sharing the situation with his wife, because she not only was his partner in ministry, but also totally understood the importance of confidentiality in their vocation.

When he finished, she softly said, "Wow. Satan must be high-fiving his minions round about now."

Andrew nodded. "I'm sure he is."

"The child, what did you say her name was?"

"Celeste. Boy, she's something else."

"How do you mean?"

"I'm not sure how to explain it. She's wise beyond her years. An old soul and a little girl blended in a child's body. Scott told me that she thinks he's her 'ram in the bushes.'"

"As in Abraham and Isaac?"

"You got it."

"So she knows about God then?"

"Yes. Both she and her grandmother are fellow believers. The grandmother told me she'd heard of our church. Gave me quite the grilling, too. Talk about someone who knows her Bible!"

"So what is it that you want my advice on?"

"Charmaine, first of all. Then the young men that Scott's been working with—how is this going to affect them? Scott was telling me that some of them were struggling with morality issues, especially about sex. He didn't mention any names, but this news could have a big impact on our church family."

Judith quoted, "'Sufficient unto the day is the evil thereof.'* I can't recall who should get credit for that statement, but I've always taken it to mean that we should not borrow tomorrow's trouble today. First we put the matter in God's hands and trust that He will turn this thing that could become a nasty business into a blessing. Charmaine is somewhat reserved, and even though I don't know her as well as I'd like, I think this is something she and Scott have to work out on their own. I'd be the first to agree that it is a bit of a bombshell. It will take time, and Scott has to be patient. I do know, however, that Charmaine loves Scott a lot. Her whole demeanor lights up when he walks into a room. I think our job right now is to lift them up daily in prayer."

Andrew sighed. "I already told Scott that I would invite Charmaine to talk with me about how she is feeling. He looked so hopeful when I suggested it, but you're right. They need to come to grips with this for themselves." Andrew took Judith's hand. "What would you suggest for the guys?"

"As for the guys, let's hope Scott speaks with them about it before they hear it through the grapevine. And if, as you say, the grandmother is ailing, the reality of the child coming here may happen sooner than later. Does she look anything like Scott?"

"That's the kicker," Andrew told her. "She looks nothing at all like him."

"I guess having her the spitting image of him would make this too easy and not require as much faith. Would he consider a paternity test?" asked Judith.

"Well, it's a bit more complicated than that. The child literally has no one else in the world but her grandmother. Scott says that even if she's not his, he couldn't abandon her now. Accepting that she's his without evidence at least leaves him with the belief that he's her father."

"But that makes it more difficult for Charmaine," wailed Judith. "From her perspective, why would he not want to do the test? After all, if the child is his, the test would clear up all doubts right at the outset. If she's not his, and given that she has no one else, they could apply to become her foster or adoptive parents. Then Charmaine would feel that she at least had some choice in the decision. She has a soft heart for lost souls."

Andrew looked thoughtful. "Lots to think about. Thanks for listening, honey. We will turn it over to God and ask Him to show us how and when to help."

Judith laughed. "Speaking of help, it sounds as though our princess is finished with the orchestra and needs her breakfast."

"I'll get her," said Andrew, rising from the bed. "While she's nursing, I can give thanks to our Father for His many blessings on this Good Friday. Then I need to go to the church to see that all is in order for tonight's program."

6:30 p.m.

In the converted communal costume room, Gwen felt anxiety-tinged excitement rolling off the cast members. Used to the pre-performance jitters, she did what she could to calm them by ensuring that the costume of each was one thing less to worry about.

Candice bounced into the dressing room clad in her director's garb—black pants and black tee. She kept a more formal jacket close by, in case she was called upon to make an up-front appearance after the program. However, now minutes before curtain, she needed the full attention of her crew.

"Listen up, everyone." The buzz in the room continued unabated.

The shrill of a whistle caused everyone to jump, Gwen included.

Candice grinned. "Sorry for the rude awakening, but I need your attention. We have 30 minutes before the curtain rises. At 6:45 I want every single cast member to be in this room. I repeat: 6:45 p.m. At that time I will be giving last-minute instructions, and Pastor Al will be here to pray with all of us. No one in costume should be seen anywhere but backstage. Is that clear?"

Those in the room yelled "Clear."

"Samantha, I need to speak with you for a minute, please." As Sam joined Candice, the buzz returned to the pre-announcement din. Gwen smiled. The Easter pre-trial was now playing.

6:50 p.m.

Pastor Al looked around at the small crowd of cast members and crew. Already the auditorium upstairs was 90 percent full. He stood on a chair, held up his right hand, and waited for the place to quiet.

"If you could see what I see when I look at you, your hearts would be bursting with pride, just as mine is right now. We're going to have a very packed house tonight."

"I think I'm going to be sick," someone said.

Pastor Al turned to the sound of the voice, but a retired nurse was already on the task.

"As I was saying, upstairs in the audience are a lot of people who have come out to see and hear the Easter story. This annual program has captured the attention of the community as well as members of our congregation. Tonight we have an opportunity to talk about the kingdom of grace to people who may not listen during the rest of the year. I'm saying that not to scare you, but to let you know the enormous potential this has for ministry."

Pastor Al had everyone's full attention. "I feel that God is about to do something grand this weekend. It's been a rough week, full of trials and pain. But God can and will work all things for our good."

Making eye contact with as many of the cast members as he could, Pastor Al implored, "Be God's instrument tonight. Every one of you. No matter how small your part, be an instrument for God. Let Him use you to bring home the Easter message: God loves us. That's it in a nutshell. God loves us so much that He gave up everything and endured all kinds of awful things so that we could be restored to Him."

Then Pastor Al bowed his head and lifted his hands toward heaven and began to pray.

"God of all people, we come asking You to use our hands, our feet, our voices, and our expressions to make clear the message that You are love. In comparison to Your omnipotence, we are such inadequate vessels, but we offer up these vessels to You tonight. Starting with Mary's anointing, into the garden, through Your struggle of submission, the arrest, the beatings, the trials, the conviction, the road to the cross, those cursed nails, Your feelings of abandonment, the jeering, and the commendation of Your Spirit to the Father, please let Your ultimate sacrifice receive a heaven-inspired depiction tonight. May lost and hurting souls discover or rediscover You as we submit ourselves to Your leading. Amen."

After the prayer, Pastor Al raised his head, gave his typical lopsided grin, and stepped down from the chair. Before the noise and the mad rush could take over the room, Candice climbed onto the chair.

"Thank you, Pastor Al. Well, folks, I don't have much else to add but this: You know your lines. You've done your preparation. Remember the words of Pastor Al's prayer. Be an instrument for God tonight. And thank you for allowing me the privilege of working with you. Now listen up! Band members, stagehands, lighting and audio crew, please go now to your positions. As usual, Pastor Al will say a few words of welcome to the audience. After that, the band will play one verse of 'Were You There?' Sam, you will join in afterward with the words of the song. Take the audience back to that time when—" Candice's head swiveled.

"Where's Samantha? Somebody find Samantha now! Smoke machine team, not too early with the smoke, OK? Let's go, people. Curtain in five."

Jumping down from the chair, Candice dashed out of the room, brown curls flying in the wind. "Samantha!"

6:55 p.m.

Judith was in the washroom giving Jess a hurried diaper change. She had not yet given Andrew his customary hug. Even though he was not preaching tonight, she liked to be there for him just before he went to the podium. But Jess was being her most wiggly self and wanted to play. In Judith's haste the Velcro on one side of the diaper snapped. *Oh, no! Not today!* As she was frantically doing a one-hand search for a replacement diaper, she heard the sound of someone being sick in the stall across from the change table.

Resting her hand on Jess's middle, she called out, "Hello. This is Judith Simms. Are you OK?"

The question was answered by a splash and a moan. Quickly securing the new diaper, she finished dressing the baby and, picking her up, hurried to the stall door. The moaning stopped, and the door opened.

A chalk-faced Samantha emerged.

"Samantha, honey, what's the matter? Upset stomach?"

The girl did not answer, but bent over the sink to rinse her mouth. She looked awful.

"Has anybody seen Sam?" Candice burst into the washroom looking wild-eyed. "Sam! You need to be on stage! Pastor Al is beginning his welcome."

"I can't, Candy." Sam bolted back into the stall and locked the door.

Candice's mind refused to function. She was not prepared for this. Samantha playing the role of Mary Magdalene was the musical glue that tied together all the elements of tonight's performance. She could not be sick.

Seeing the stumped look on Candice's face, Judith intervened.

"Candice."

Candice's mouth moved soundlessly. Judith tapped her urgently on her arm. "Candice!"

She was relieved to see the focus return to Candice's eyes.

"Tell me. What does Samantha need to do tonight? More precisely, what does she need to do in the next few minutes?"

"She needs to sing the first verse of 'Were You There?' after the band has played it through once."

"And after that?" prompted Judith.

"The smoke comes on, and once it starts to clear, the scene opens at Simon's house. The Easter story is being told by Sam, I mean Mary Magdalene. She's come to the present to take us back to the past. It was at Simon's house that she anointed Jesus' feet with the expensive oil, so she sings about the oil in her alabaster box."

174

"Is the costume the same for both appearances?"

"No, just the headpiece. We set it up that way so that the audience can keep track of her."

"What key is the song in?"

"I don't remember!" Candice felt the panic returning. "I can't believe this is happening!"

The stall door opened again, and a shaky Samantha reemerged. She gave Candice a look full of apology.

"I'm so sorry, Candy. Just stall things for a little bit longer. I need a few more minutes."

As Samantha bent to rerinse her mouth, Judith said, "Give me your shawl, Sam."

"Why?" asked a puzzled Candice.

"Sam and I are about the same size. I'll sing the first song, and by the time I'm done, we're going to need a miracle to make Samantha better."

Desperate to try anything, the shawl was quickly transferred from Samantha to Judith. It was providential that she was wearing a long black skirt and black turtleneck and also had the voice of an angel.

"Candice, are you in here?" asked Gwen, poking her head through the washroom entrance. "The band is playing, and there is no . . . Samantha."

"Gwen, take Jess and stay with Sam. Run, Candice! I'm right behind you. Tell the band to play the first verse of the song again. I'll come in the second time through. Yikes! I need a microphone."

"There's a drop mike right over the spot where you'll be singing. Stand on the spot marked with an electrical-taped X. Stage right, a bit to the front."

Out in the hallway, Candice and Judith separated. Through her headset Candice called in the change to the band leader as she ran to the back of the stage to cue the person who was in charge of the smoke machine. *God, please help us!*

Judith forced her mind to be calm. *Work through me, Lord. Before the beginning of time You knew this moment would come. Set the stage, Lord. Use me.*

She stood on the X and felt peace envelop her despite her shaky knees. She bowed her head as the violin led out the second time around, on the first two lines of the song. By the third line, the bass guitar was adding some heartbeats and the drummer was brush-stroking the cymbals. Haunting and sweet, the pianist added a bit of soul to the keys, causing the hairs on her arms to stand. And just like that, she was transported back there.

7:05 p.m.

Pastor Al had expected to see Judith before he made his way to the front to do the welcome, but assumed she was delayed by Jess. After he finished, he went in search of her. He'd noticed before the house lights dimmed that she was not in her usual seat. In the hallway he ran into Samantha and Gwen, who was holding Jess.

"Where's Judith?"

"She should be singing right about . . . now." Pastor Al's confusion was comical to watch as he listened to the sound of his wife's voice coming through the hall system.

"How?

Gwen filled him in. "Short version. Samantha got sick. Judith is singing. Samantha is better now and will continue from here on. Here is your beautiful daughter. Please find a seat somewhere and enjoy the rare luxury of sitting together with your wife and child in church."

"I doubt that very much. We have no empty seats in there. The ushers were bringing in extra chairs even as I was welcoming our guests."

As Pastor Al was finishing his sentence, Candice burst around the corner and screeched to a halt beside them, body bouncing with tension and excitement.

"How are you, Sam?"

"I think I'm ready. I'm getting that feeling again."

"You're going to be sick?"

"No. I think I'll be fine. It's the—"

Candice eyes brightened as she caught on. "The 'God is holding you up' feeling?"

Samantha nodded.

Turning to Pastor Al, Candice softly squealed. "Did you hear that, Pastor Al? Did you hear that?"

Gwen answered. "The message is coming through loud and clear. In case we might be of the opinion that we are doing any of this in our own power, God is letting us know right at the start of this performance that He can take any circumstance and work it out in ways far beyond what we could dream of."

"Come on, Sam," urged Candice. "Let's get you backstage."

Pastor Al was gazing slack-jawed after the two departing young women when Gwen snagged his attention. "We'd better fasten our seat belts, Pastor. It looks as though God is up to some awesome business tonight."

On that note Gwen gave her pastor's arm a squeeze and hurried upstairs to restore some order to the costume room. For now the closed-circuit television in the room would have to serve as her connection to the program.

---

* Matt. 6:34, KJV.
† See Rom. 8:28.

Chapter Twenty-one

The Death of a Dream

7:08 p.m.

Her assistance no longer needed with costumes, Charmaine stood at the back of the auditorium. All the seats were filled. Many were occupied by regular members, but she saw an amazing number of new faces in the audience. She wanted to rejoice in the potential for outreach, but her rejoicing could not vent fully because of the heaviness in her heart.

Yes, she'd welcomed her husband home last night. Like someone being rescued from drowning, she'd welcomed his arms around her. How she'd missed him. And then when he had bared his heart to her, she could not resist the love he offered.

But later, as he'd talked about the trip and the child, she'd felt a return of the coldness.

She could tell that Scott already cared for the little girl, but even though she'd tried to talk herself into the "right" kind of feeling, she honestly did not want anything to do with this child. This was not the way she'd planned her life. She knew that others would think her less of a Christian if she did not welcome the child with open arms. Knowing Scott, Charmaine also knew he would not turn his back on his so-called daughter.

Well, too bad! He couldn't have them both.

⬛ ⬛ ⬛ ⬛ ⬛

7:14 p.m.

When Samantha took her place onstage, the feeling of being buoyed up continued as she waited for her cue to sing about the alabaster box. The house lights were off, so as far as she was concerned, she could have been singing to an empty room. Gradually she felt herself being taken over by the music.

Midway during the song when her Mary persona started to make her case for the seeming waste of the expensive oil she'd poured on Jesus' feet and head, Samantha heard Candice's voice from a week ago.

"Pretend that someone dear to you has just died. Sing of death, Samantha."

So as Mary explained what Jesus did for her, how He loved her as no one else ever had, Samantha heard an unplanned wobble in her voice.

Her own daddy was dead. Dead on a Friday, just like Jesus. She wished he was here for her to wash his feet, to tell him how much she loved him, but he was gone. If only she could make them understand what her dad meant to her.

Samantha felt her hands shaking as Mary sang of the loss. A loss that was now her very own. Frantic to get a grip on the feelings that were overpowering her, she clutched the alabaster box tighter. But the music became the message, and she the medium.

How could they know? They weren't there when he wrapped his arms around her, prayed over her, and gently comforted her when she was scared.

Tears streamed down her face, but Samantha did not care. Caught up in her own grief, she thought of all that her father meant to her and all that was now gone.

Flinging out her arms, she gave herself over to the agony. She sang out her pain.

She sang of death.

And that's when the box she was holding fell to the floor, spilling its contents.

Now her grief was inconsolable.

Another precious thing ruined.

Samantha felt her knees buckling and tried to stiffen them. But the knees would not lock and the muscles would not cooperate, and she too, like the box, crumpled to the floor. There she continued to sob out the cost and her loss until the words of the song were no longer intelligible except for the great big heaving sobs that shook her body and communicated her absolute brokenness.

The music stopped.

The sobbing continued a cappella within the silence—a body in the spotlight, shaking with grief.

The musicians looked at each other in the semi-darkness, wondering what to do.

Ever so softly the pianist resumed the melody of the song, adding his signature bass effect to accompany the sobbing going on within the spotlight. Then the violinist, with tears now running down her cheeks, joined her instrument to the mournful cry and took over the melody, bleeding it into a plaintive refrain.

The piano player coaxed his instrument into a gradual retreat, and with Simon's house forming the backdrop, the lone violin wailed while the broken young woman sobbed until finally they became one voice, one pain.

On that pain the lights lowered slowly to black.

Silence, deafening in its completeness, followed. Then a single set of hands started to clap. Soon it was joined by two more and eight more and 50 more and hundreds more, swelling, then spilling over into an avalanche of appreciation. For about five full minutes the clapping continued in the darkness, postponing the start of the second scene.

Emily Price reached in her handbag for a handkerchief. When she had gotten herself under control, she whispered in Lenore's ear.

"Was she acting?"

"I'm not sure. I'd better go check on her. I'll be right back."

"Lenore, before you go, are you by any chance wearing perfume? A crushed rose petal smell?"

Lenore sniffed the air and shook her head. Emily Price's nose twitched.

The play proceeded without intermission. Following the anointing of Jesus by Mary, the audience watched the Last Supper with a sense of impending doom. They followed the procession to the Garden of Gethsemane as Jesus pleaded for His closest friends to watch and pray with Him. They grew restless at the drowsiness that took over the disciples as their Master agonized alone.

A subdued Samantha, teetering on the edge of tears, continued with Mary's story as she took the audience back to Jesus' earlier ministry, His easy rapport with children, His healing of the sick, and even to the resurrection of Lazarus.

The actors who played the Pharisees and Sadducees captured well the spite and jealousy of their historic counterparts, provoking one member of the audience to denounce them outwardly.

Mary showed them Pilate's weak attempt to free Jesus. She sang of Pilate's washing of his hands, and brought the basin that was thrown out afterward when the mob chose the rampant criminal Barabbas over Jesus.

With heaviness of heart, Mary told of the journey to Golgotha. She joined the mourners and spectators as they proceeded far too slowly to the place of death. The whistle of the Roman whip caused the audience to cringe when it felled Jesus to His knees. Surely now they would release Him. But hope was dashed when a man from Africa was ordered to bear the cross and Jesus was dragged along behind.

Mary stepped back from the crowd and sang.
"I was there when they nailed Him to the tree.
I was there when they nailed Him to the tree.
O-o-o-oh.
Sometimes it causes me to tremble, tremble, tremble.
I was there when they nailed Him to the tree."
"Hear the hammer?" Mary asked.
Thuck!
"See His body spasm?"
"Listen to the crowd as they raise the cross:
"'Hee-hee! Some Son of God You are. Come on. Walk off that cross.'
"'The nerve of You, claiming to be God!'
"'Hey, Mister Jesus! I'm God too. See, I can walk, but You can't.'
"'Where is Your power now, big talker?'
"'Look, Jesus. I'm bowing to You. "Hail, King of the Jews."'
"And that's when He said, 'Father, forgive them, for they do not know what they are doing.'* Can you fathom that? What kind of man can do this?
"And then—then He tried to bend back His head to beseech the heavens."
"'My God, my God, why have you forsaken me?'†
"I was there when He said, 'Father, into your hands I commit my spirit.'‡ I was there when His body sagged one final time, then stayed still. I was there when darkness came early that day, and when the earth quaked. I heard that the curtain in the Temple that separated the place where before only the high priest could visit was ripped cleanly in two from top to bottom. It was Friday, right before sunset, when we buried Him. I was there."

The spotlight cut away from Mary as a blue-black light covered the whole church.

Shadows could be seen marching slowly across the stage and up and down the aisles. Someone led, carrying a small light, while the rest of the procession hummed.

Then the leader of the procession sang, "O Lord, Lord."

Someone on the stage answered, "O Lord Jesus, Lord."

The leader called on him again: "O Lord, Lord."

Someone from within the audience answered, "Sweet Jesus."

"Why do You love me so?"

The group asked, "Why, why?"

Over the microphone a voice spoke: " 'For God so loved the world that he gave his one and only Son, that whoever believes in him shall not perish but have eternal life.' "§

Seemingly at random, candles started to flare within the darkness. First from the back, then along the sides and up and down the aisles, until the whole audience was surrounded by light. Mute now, the shadows moved in mournful slowness from their places within the audience to center stage, crisscrossing each other to form the shape of a glowing cross.

Next a few of the shadows shifted to even out the short ends of the cross. The audience gasped as the cross became an X.

The X rotated clockwise three times, then gradually eliminated one of its lines to become a straight line of light, followed by a gap of two spaces and topped off with a single candle, forming the letter I.

Finally the mourners leaned over their candles, allowing their faces for just a moment to be bathed in the light, and then, in one swift motion, blew them out.

Mary stood alone at center stage with the last remaining candle. She seemed loath to relinquish her light. She leaned over her candle, bathing her face in the flickering flame, and then with a sigh of deep reluctance she puckered her lips and blew out the candle, leaving the church in virtual blackness.

That was the undoing of Lenore Baptiste.

Robert! My Robert is dead! You're not here to light the candles with me tonight! No more Friday night candles!

The great wall of defense that had erected itself within Lenore since last Friday night suddenly exploded. The grief it had been containing flew out in all directions, sending shrapnel of pain through every single pore of her body. She felt a small set of arms holding on to her, but flung them off as she tore out of her seat, trampling on strangers' feet and bumping into pews on her desperate run toward the altar—arriving too late to prevent the last candle from being extinguished.

No! No! Let me at least say good night.

But it was too late.

All was black.

Lenore felt a moan building up inside her and locked her jaws.

I must not fall apart. Not here. Please, God. Not now.

But no locking of her jaws could hold it back. A sharp keening rent the silence of the church, arresting her attention. She wondered briefly if someone else was wounded. A small set of arms surrounded her. From a distant place in her mind, she heard voices she somehow knew calling her back, praying over her, and that's when she realized the cry had come out of her own throat, bringing with it a torrent of tears—enough for a baptism.

Once more that night reality bled into the stage story, leaving the audience no room to separate them. Pastor Al, however, came to the rescue. Standing beside the small group that had gathered to mourn with Lenore Baptiste, he asked for the house lights to be brought up to half, and made an appeal.

"Tonight's program is about losses. It was on a Friday night like this that Jesus was killed. Last Friday night Robert Baptiste, a much-loved member of our church family, died suddenly. Tonight marks the one-week anniversary of his death, and the pain is everywhere.

"And because tonight's program is about loss and pain, I am inviting those of you who have experienced a loss this week or this year or sometime in your life—a loss that is still hurting—to come down to the front and tell it to Jesus.

"Jesus knows our sorrows. He knows the things that have hurt us and those that continue to hurt us, and tonight we can come and offer up our pain and losses to Him. So come and join Lenore and her family. Give your pain to the Burden-Bearer. You don't need to tell me what the pain is. Just tell Jesus. Come, and when we have talked to Him about our sorrows, I will end with a prayer of blessing for us all."

Following Pastor Al's words, a number of people rose and made their way to the front. Some were openly crying. Others were holding it together. Barely.

---

* Luke 23:34.
† Mark 15:34.
‡ Luke 23:46.
§ John 3:16.

Chapter Twenty-two

Forsaken

8:47 p.m.

Overwhelmed with the drama unfolding at the front of the stage, Todd decided to make a quick exit. He was surprised how empty the church hallways and corridors were. Everyone was inside watching the more than drama. On his way to the men's room, he came across Brian leaning against a wall.

Reaching out to shake his friend's hand, he greeted, "What's up, Brave? How are you holding up?"

Brian smiled. "I'm cool."

Todd's eyes narrowed. "Say again?"

"What, man? I said I was cool."

And then Todd definitely identified it. "You're drunk!"

"Me? Naw," said Brian, continuing to smile. "I'm not drunk. I'm holding up. See, I can walk a straight line, no problem."

Todd watched with growing horror as Brian put one wobbly foot in front of the other to demonstrate his balance. He needed to act fast.

"That's pretty good, Brian."

"I told you I wasn't drunk. A man's got to be able to hold himself up."

"Yes, he should," agreed Todd. "Hey, since we're missing our meeting tonight, why don't we head over to my place? I could let your mom know."

Todd knew that Mrs. Baptiste would be in no condition to drive home tonight either, but someone else would have to take care of that problem. He needed help, though.

Signaling to Brian, he said, "You know what, the program is just about finished, so wait here while I go catch Sammy. I'll be right back."

Todd had just turned around to head back upstairs when he saw Samantha. Her eyes were red, but the look on her face told Todd that she had witnessed the little exchange between him and her brother.

He signaled for her to follow him. He'd seen enough drama for one night. Mouth agape, she followed.

He found an empty room and waited for her to enter, then closed the door.

"Yes, Samantha. You heard right. Your brother is very drunk. I don't know when or where it happened. I ran into him just a few moments before you came downstairs. I don't think he's in any condition to drive, and given all that just went down inside the church with your mom, I don't think she needs this bit of news right now, wouldn't you agree?"

Samantha nodded.

"So, if you could go backstage and tell Sammy about the situation and have him come by my place later tonight, I would be most appreciative. Just Sammy, Sam. He can be trusted to keep his mouth shut."

Seeing tears start to pool in Samantha's eyes, Todd was quick to reassure. "We will take care of him, Sam. Just tell your mom that Brian is staying with me for the night. OK? Now I need to get back to Brian before the whole church discovers this. If you or your mom need to call, you know my number. Cool?"

Samantha nodded again as Todd gently prodded her out the door.

8:52 p.m.

Samantha hurried to the back of the auditorium, hoping that Sammy was still there. He was, still clad in his Pilate costume. She ran to him.

"Samantha Baptiste! That was some performance you put on tonight! You had the whole cast plus the audience in tears. Not only can you sing, but you can act! Great job! After your scene at Simon's house, I could see the cast getting more serious about their roles. We couldn't mess up following a performance like that. How do you do it? Everyone, behold the great Samantha!"

Whistles, claps, hugs, and backslapping were directed toward Samantha. She smiled and waved distractedly.

"Sammy, I need to talk to you."

Leaning close to Samantha's ear, Sammy whispered, "Lady, when your adoring public cheers you on, you need to bask in it."

Samantha smiled some more and received a few more hugs as she dragged Sammy from the room. "Thanks, everyone. Sammy and I will be back in just a few minutes."

"Sam, hold up. Where's the fire? Give a fella a chance to change before you go dragging him off into the night."

"No time. This is an emergency."

Sammy stopped in his tracks. "What emergency?"

"It's Brian, Sammy."

"What's the matter with Brian? An accident?"

Checking for potential eavesdroppers, Samantha lowered her voice. "He's drunk."

"Drunk!" shouted Sammy.

Seeing Samantha's frantic look, Sammy lowered his voice. "As in alcohol?"

Samantha nodded. "Todd is taking him over to his house and wants to know if you can join them there later. We're trying to keep this hush-hush. My mom has broken down in front of the whole church, and she can't deal with another situation right now, so I need you to help before she finds out."

"Tell Todd I'll be there ASAP. We'll do what we can, Sam. Don't worry— Todd and I will take care of your brother."

"Thanks, Sammy. I really appreciate it. I'll go talk to Todd, and then I need to go check on my mom. I'll call later to see how Brian's doing." Sam waved a quick goodbye and headed downstairs.

"Samantha!" Samantha turned.

Sammy was right on her heels. He wanted to hug her, but stopped himself. "Are you going to be OK?"

"I'll be fine, Sammy. Thanks again. Now go, please."

"I'm on it. I'll talk to you later," said Sammy, hurrying toward the change room.

Samantha had a quick chat with Todd, and hurried back upstairs to see how her mom was doing. On entering the church auditorium, she noticed a group of women clustered around the front pew. Assuming that somewhere in the middle of the cluster was her mom, she headed in that direction.

"Excuse me," a voice close to Samantha said.

Samantha turned. A portly older gentleman beckoned to her.

"You're the young lady who played the role of Mary tonight, aren't you?" he asked.

Before Samantha could acknowledge with a yes, the speaker went on. "Young lady, you are very talented. You got even a hardened man like me to cry tonight. It was a most moving performance."

A passerby overhearing the exchange came and put an arm around Samantha. "Yes, that's our girl. I taught her Bible class in kindergarten and again when she was a junior. I'm Melissa Moore," she greeted the gentleman.

"Preston Thomas," he replied.

To Samantha, Melissa Moore said, "I was so proud of you tonight, honey. This could not have been easy for you to do given the recent loss of your dad."

"It's her dad that the pastor was talking about?" asked Mr. Thomas.

Melissa Moore nodded solemnly. "Shook up the whole church, it did. Brother Baptiste was a man among men. You could have swum a mile in the tears that were shed at his funeral."

Turning to Samantha, Preston Thomas exclaimed, "And after all that you and the rest of your cast were still able to put on such an outstanding performance! It was inspired, I tell you. Inspired!"

Samantha, anxious to get to her mom as well as leave this conversation that was making her uncomfortable, tried to excuse herself without being rude.

"It was all God," she said. "All week long He's been holding me up. I was just a minor instrument tonight, sir. I'm glad you enjoyed the program." Seeing the crowd around her mom starting to disperse, Samantha said, "You'll have to excuse me. I don't mean to be rude, but I need to go see my mom."

"Sure, sure! You do that. The crying is good for her, though. Lets some of the pain out."

Both of them watched Samantha go, her progress stalled frequently by others wanting to tell her they'd been touched by the program.

"Nice young lady," Preston remarked. "Modest, too. I like that."

"Nice family getting knocked around by tragedy," commented Melissa as she followed in Samantha's wake to pay her respects in the form of a hug to Lenore Baptiste.

9:10 p.m.

Scott stood with Pastor Al in the church foyer and shook more hands than he remembered shaking in a long time. Enough could not be said about the evening's program. The ushers were busily collecting cards from both members and visitors, requests for visits and prayers. The buzz in the air finally eased enough for them to look at each other.

"How are the seat belts holding up, Pastor Al?" Andrew did not need to turn around to see who spoke.

"Safe and secure, Sister Bolski. I am without words to describe—"

"Make note of this moment, Sister Gwen," interjected Scott. "This is a first."

"—what happened tonight," continued Andrew, grinning at Scott.

"God happened. That's what," Gwen said.

"When Samantha broke down at the end of the song, I wondered what would happen," Pastor Al continued. "But then when the musicians continued the message without missing a beat as if it had actually been rehearsed, I found tears on my own cheeks. And when that last note of the violin trembled—I'm sure that's what it did—when it trembled and died into the silence and the spotlight narrowed on a sobbing Samantha, I must confess, I did not know which of the women onstage was breaking my heart more—Mary or Samantha."

Scott nodded solemnly. "I suspect that's why the applause was so sustained. The audience was responding to both—even for those who did not know the story within the story." He paused. "By the way, how is Lenore?"

"A few of our seniors have her well in hand," Gwen told him. "I'm just going to get my handbag, and then I'll drive her home. Samantha and Candice will go home together."

"Where's Brian?" Scott asked, looking around. "Come to think of it, I don't recall seeing him tonight."

"Samantha says that he's gone home with Todd. I think he's going to be staying the night," Gwen told him.

"He is? Well, good for Todd. Brian needs that. I'm glad to see he's reaching out to the guys."

Pastor Al and Gwen nodded in agreement. Then Gwen had a thought. "You know what? I think I'll spend the night with Lenore. At times like these one needs friends close. If you don't see us at church tomorrow morning, it will be because of a rough night. Just continue to lift them up in your prayers, gentlemen. Good night."

"God be with you both. Please call me or Judith if we can help in any way," Pastor Al added.

Scott quickly scanned the foyer, then with a huge sigh he said, "I'd better go find Charmaine."

Andrew asked softly, "How are things?"

"I wish I could tell you, Andrew. Just keep us in your prayers. OK?"

Andrew wished he could do something to help. Before he opened his mouth to speak, he remembered Judith's words. So slapping Scott on the back, he said as they separated, "We are, and we will."

9:23 p.m.

Riding home in the back of Lenore's car with Lenore and her friend, Gwen, Emily Price had time to think. After that screech in the church that almost stopped Emily's heart, Lenore had settled into steady crying. By the time they'd gotten her to the car, the tears had become a quiet stream.

Emily, who preferred to shed her tears in private, was uncomfortable with Lenore's breakdown in front of a churchful of people. But that talkative pastor had made it all seem so normal by inviting other hurting people to come and offer up their own hurts to God. And the way those people had surrounded Lenore and comforted her, well, truth be told, Emily was impressed.

She had never experienced a night such as this. Too many emotions, however, were blocking the door of her reason. She wanted them to settle first. Something had happened to her tonight. Something had captured her attention, but she could not quite put her finger on it. For the first time in a long time she felt a . . . quickening in her heart? Why would her mind suggest the word "quickening"?

She'd been to many theatrical performances in her lifetime. Some that had also moved her to tears, but this one . . . Emily shook her head. What exactly was it that was bothering her mind? Was it the music? the singing? the light processional? It had something to do with the light. The absence of light? When that last candle was snuffed out, Emily had felt bereft. That's what it was. She'd experienced a feeling of abandonment.

Emily understood why the blowing out of that last candle had caused Lenore to break down. She knew about Robert and Lenore's Friday night candle ritual. Samantha had put her in the know on a Friday night some years before when Emily had called to talk to her dad. But why should the snuffing out of a candle leave her, Emily, feeling so bereft?

Before she had time to explore her thoughts further, they were in Lenore's driveway—and tears still streamed down Lenore's face. Emily had wanted her friend to cry, but now it seemed as if her tears would never stop.

Gwen helped Lenore from the car and located the house keys. At the door

Lenore mopped up her tears, put on a brave face, and turned to thank them, but Gwen ushered her into the house.

"Don't even think about saying good night to us, Len. We're staying with you."

"That's right," piped up Emily. "Now get upstairs, and if you haven't had a shower by the time I come back, I will personally give you one."

Lenore began to cry again, so Emily quickly amended. "All right, all right. One night without a shower won't kill you. I'm going across to get some clothes, but I'll be right back. We will stay up with you all night if need be. You're not alone. Remember that." Patting Lenore on the shoulder, Emily let herself out the door and hurried across the street.

Lenore started up the stairs toward her room, but midway up, her steps faltered. "Oh, Gwen, I can't do this. I hurt so much. When will the pain end? How will I live without Robert?"

Gwen joined her on the stairs. "One minute at a time, Len. That's the only way."

Lenore lost the strength in her legs and dropped heavily to the step. Pointing toward the upper floor, she cried. "He's not up there, Gwen. Yet he's all over this house. His scent is still on his pillow. His toothbrush is still in the bathroom. The clothes he'd picked out to wear to church last week are still hanging at the front of his closet."

Gwen sat down on the step below Lenore, saying nothing with words but everything with the comfort of her presence. That's how Emily found them some minutes later—two figures a hand-reach from each other. One face still awash with tears and the other full of empathy.

Following the program, Scott and Charmaine had a quiet ride home interspersed by small talk and monosyllabic responses. It was close to 11:00 p.m. On the elevator ride up from the underground garage, Scott took another stab at rescuing their conversational relationship.

"So what did you think of the program tonight?" he asked.

Voice matter-of-fact, Charmaine responded, "I think it went well. The cast and crew did an excellent job."

Well, thought Scott, *at least that was a little better than the one-word answers so far.* Taking that as encouragement, he decided to be expansive.

"Pastor Al's appeal seemed to have tapped into things that a lot of people were feeling," he said. "I was surprised at how many went up. I felt as though I should have gone up there myself, but couldn't understand why. I don't have a loss to offer up or any—"

"I went up." The elevator doors opened, and Charmaine hurried out into the hall, at the same time searching in her bag for the keys. Scott ran to catch up with her.

"You did? Why?"

Charmaine was already opening their apartment door. She waited for Scott to come in, then closed it. Kicking off her shoes directly into the coat closet, she made her way toward their bedroom. Scott, anxious to find out what was going on in her head, followed her.

Charmaine perched on the edge of the bed and faced her husband, who was leaning against the wall close to the bedroom doorway.

"I went up tonight because the appeal was for those who have experienced losses—and *I* have a loss. At least since your news of last Monday, I simply feel that I've lost something. I don't know how to be with you anymore. I don't know what to say to you, and there's nothing I can do to change things back to the way they were before. It's as though we're becoming strangers. But how can that be? I love you." Her voice broke. "I'll never stop loving you." Another pause. "But it does not seem enough anymore."

"What are you saying, Charmaine?"

Her eyes dropped away from Scott's. "I know you, Scott. One of the first things that attracted me to you was your deep caring for people. You can no more turn your back on this little girl in Montreal than you can voluntarily stop breathing. But I don't know how to deal with a child in our life. I am expected to accept her—to have her come live with us—and all that comes with it. I have to live with the mistakes of your past, and even though I know what I should do, I can't do it. I told God that He picked a failure."

Scott leaned his head against the wall and stared at the ceiling. "So what does that mean for us? for our future?"

"I don't know, Scott. I really don't. Tonight I went up front to offer up the loss and the pain to God, but I still feel the same. Even though I love you so much, I can't do this. Scott, I . . . can't . . . do it."

"But Charmaine, this is—" Scott was unable to stop himself from going to her, and he seated himself beside her on the bed. She stiffened, thinking that he was there to accuse her.

"You don't have to say it," she interrupted, her voice flat. "I know it by rote. I promised on our wedding day before God and a number of witnesses that I would love you through thick and thin, when it was easy and even when it was difficult. And here I am telling you that this 'difficult' is too much for me."

"That's not what I was going to say. I was going to say that this is all new both to you and to me. We need to give ourselves time to work through it."

"Scott, do you hear yourself? Time is what we don't seem to have in abundance. From what you've told me, the child's grandmother could die any day. What time do we have?"

Grabbing thin air for a silver lining, Scott replied, "On the other hand, she could live for several months. Maybe more. Come on, Charmaine. Aren't we worth fighting for? Is our relationship so unimportant that you can so easily throw it aside at the first rough patch?"

"This is not a 'patch,' Scott! This is a child who most likely will be around for a long time. Forever, actually . . . if we take her. If this is what you call a patch, then I'd certainly like to hear your definition of a long road. And I didn't say I was leaving you. I just don't want to have to deal with this problem. I can't deal with it . . ."

Scott wondered how many times he would rue the sins of his past, and could not resist the urge to atone again. "Honey, I'm very sorry that my past is causing you pain. But I also can't turn my back on her. She has no one left but her granny, and soon she too will be gone. I couldn't live with myself if I ignored her."

"I know."

"So what would you have me do, Charmaine? How do I save my marriage and still be a father to this child? You cannot doubt that I love you. Tell me you don't doubt that!"

"I don't doubt that you love me, Scott. It's *me*. You have a heart that can love a lot of people. I, on the other hand, can love only a few. I don't know how to share, and . . . I'm not sure I want to."

"So where does that leave us?"

"Nowhere for now."

It was Scott who got up this time and left the room.

Saturday

Chapter Twenty-three

Brian the Not-So-Brave

B rian opened his eyes, then snapped them shut. His head ached, and his mouth seemed filled with ashes. He sensed movement close by and guardedly opened one eye to see who was in his room. Sammy's gleaming white teeth made him close the eye fast.

"What are you doing here, Watson?" he croaked. His throat felt scratchy.

"Keeping you company."

Even Sammy's voice hurt his head. "Yeah, right. Where's Mom?"

"At your house, of course."

Both of Brian's eyes flew open. He winced at the light, but fought against the pain. "What do you mean, at my house? Where am I? Wait a minute—isn't this Todd's room?"

"Uh-huh," said Sammy, rolling up a sleeping bag that lay on the floor.

"What am I doing here?" Brian demanded.

"We brought you here" was Sammy's patient reply.

"Why? And how come I don't remember any of this?"

A soft knock sounded at the door, and Todd entered.

"Morning, Sammy. Hey, Brave. How are you feeling?"

"Lousy! Man, what am I doing in your bed?" barked Brian, trying to sit up.

"What's the last thing you remember, Brian?" asked Todd, closing the door behind him. He pulled out the chair from under his desk and steered it half-way between Sammy's makeshift sleeping bag seat and the bed.

Brian closed his eyes and concentrated. "I remember dropping Mom and Mrs. Price off at the church. I was standing at the back when Samantha started to bawl. Had to get outta there, man. Yes, that's it. That's when I decided to go for a drive. Clear my head."

"And then what?" prompted Todd.

"Well, I remember driving back to the church after . . . 'bout an hour or so, but when I came back the parking lot was full, so I drove across the street to park and wait for the program to finish."

Like a therapist easing a client closer to a moment of truth, Todd pressed gently. "And while you were waiting, what did you do?"

Comprehension dawned on Brian's face. He did not look happy. "Is that why I'm here?"

"Uh-huh," said Todd.

"Bingo!" said Sammy.

"Man, I just needed a little somethin' to help me cope. I'd had it in the car for a while, but last night was the first time, I swear!"

Todd felt himself getting angry, but worked to rein it in. "Well, that little somethin' got you very drunk. What were you thinking, Brian? Do you know what that stuff does to your liver? You know better than that, man!"

"Todd," interjected Sammy, "now might not be a good time."

Brian flung off the sheet and sat up, too infuriated to be dropped by the throbbing pain in his head. "Do you know what it's like to lose a dad, Preacher Boy? No! When you do, come talk to me 'bout what I was thinking!"

Todd got up slowly from the chair and addressed Brian. "You feel like some orange juice?" Not waiting for an answer, he continued. "Good. I'll get some. While I'm gone, I'd suggest a shower. And while you're in the bathroom, help yourself to some toothpaste. That breath of yours is about to peel the paint off the walls. By the way, I suggest we stay home today. We'll continue this discussion later."

Todd quietly walked out of the room and closed the door.

Brian bunched the sheets, slammed them against the wall, and expelled a sharp hiss. "Arrgh! That guy's on a short leash. Where does he come off preaching at me?"

He shot off the bed, immediately grabbing his head and closing his eyes until the room stopped spinning. Through gritted teeth and locked eyelids he demanded, "Get me to the bathroom, Watson."

"No problem. Just rest your hand on my shoulder and step right this way, sir."

Having no strength to do anything else, Brian could only gnash his teeth as Sammy led him out the door.

In the Bolskis' kitchen Candice was feeling strange being home on a Saturday morning without her mom. Usually by now the two of them would be getting ready for church. She was tired. She and Samantha had talked long into the night, but for some reason she could not get herself to sleep in. Her brain was too busy.

It seemed as though everything was spinning out of control. After last night's program, she was in awe of what God could do, but a bit scared about His unpredictability. She would just have to trust that He would work out all things for His good.* Even though it was painful to watch Mrs. Baptiste break down, it was good for her to finally let out some of the bottled-up pain.

Her friend Samantha, who was still sleeping, was, in Candice's estimation, a walking testament of what God could do with wounded but willing people. She'd had a time of it convincing her friend that she did not need to go home, that her mom was in good hands with her two older women friends.

Then there was the problem of Brian. In the wee hours of the morning Samantha had finally opened up to her, and both friends had joined hands, asking God to rescue Brian. With his rejection of God, the alcohol would become a way to numb his pain. In addition to what it was doing to Brian, Mrs. Baptiste did not need this trial on top of everything else.

Todd found his parents in their bedroom, dressed and almost ready for church. His dad was brushing what little was left of his hair, and his mom was having trouble deciding between two black hats. He stood in the doorway watching them perform their regular Saturday morning rituals and smiled. They should have had more children, but alas, as his mom would say, God chose to bless them with only one.

He entered the spacious room, selected one of the black hats, and placed it on his mother's head. She, of course, had to angle it just right. Satisfied with his hair-brushing ministrations, his dad put down the brush and reached for his Bible. That was the cue. He was ready. Todd followed them out of the bedroom.

"Are you coming later with the boys?" his mom asked.

"Actually, we're staying home this morning. Sammy and I are going to keep Brian company. He's too locked up. Maybe we can just get him talking or something."

Mr. and Mrs. Williams nodded in understanding. "That's good of you, son.

Let your mother and I know if there's anything we can do to help. Robert's death is a tough one to deal with."

"Make sure the boys get a good breakfast, honey. There's pancake mix in the cupboard and fresh strawberries in the fridge." Todd's mom gave him a quick peck on the cheek and ran to catch up with his dad, who was already at the front door.

Todd locked the door behind his parents, and was about to go to the kitchen to see what he could rustle up for breakfast when the telephone rang. He thought of ignoring it, but decided to answer just in case it was Samantha or her mom inquiring about Brian.

"Hello."

"Todd, it's Scott. I hear Brian's with you. How is he?"

Assuming that Samantha had made Scott aware of the situation, Todd said, "Except for a sore head, I think he's going to be fine. Stupid thing to have done."

"What do you mean, 'sore head'?"

"His little binge drinking last evening."

"Brian was drunk?"

"Oops. You didn't know? I just assumed that's why you'd called. I had to get him away from church before his mom or someone else found out. That's why he's here. My parents don't even know he was drunk."

"I was afraid something like this would happen. I'll be there as soon as I can."

"We can handle it, Scott."

But Scott had hung up.

Todd clicked the phone off and continued to the kitchen. Deciding against making pancakes, he reached for the bread, added four slices to the toaster, and set the lever to light brown. He was not looking forward to the next few minutes with Brian, but he was not going to sit idly by and allow his friend to start a slide down the wrong side of life. Yet he was the first to admit that Brian was not going to be easy to help.

"Too bad! He's gonna be helped whether he likes it or not."

Just then Sammy strode into the kitchen and, guessing what Todd was referring to, added, "I think I can also be of some assistance."

Todd whirled. "Easy, guy. Don't sneak up on me like that."

"Sorry, man. I assume you're talking about Brian. This is serious. Brian plays brave, but he must be pretty sore to do something stupid like this."

"But we can't let him go there, Sammy. We have to stop him."

"Stop him how? He's just going to put on his attitude and brush this off."

"Then I hope his sore head will remind him not to do anything so stupid again. And just so you know, I don't plan to be gentle with him on this. I hear the smell of scrambled eggs makes people with hangovers want to gag. I might just fry up some eggs when he comes in here."

"You're playing with fire, Todd."

"No, Sammy. He's the one playing with fire, and we need to scare him enough so he won't do it again."

"Then we'd better ask God to show us what to do," said Sammy.

"Best idea you've had all morning. Let's do that."

In the main bathroom, Brian gingerly lowered his face over the sink to rinse the toothpaste from his mouth. He had checked the mirror several times to see if his head had grown, because it felt three times its normal size. He refrained, however, from looking into his eyes.

A knocking on the bathroom door sounded like a stampede on his brain. It was Todd with clothes. "If they're hitched, too bad. That's the best I can do. When you're done, come find us in the kitchen."

Brian slowly cracked open the door and took the clothes. Todd saluted, and left.

A few minutes later Brian entered the kitchen and gingerly lowered himself onto one of the chairs. "Where's that juice you promised?"

Sammy passed him a glass of orange juice.

Brian took a sip. "Don't you have somethin' with a bit more bite?"

"Ever heard that saying about beggars and choosers?" asked Todd.

"Got you," Brian moaned. "I'll keep the orange."

"Atta boy! There's some toast if you want that as well. I'm going to scramble up some eggs for Sammy and myself. Feel up to some of that?"

Brian grimaced. "No thanks."

Todd added some butter to the heating skillet and cracked four eggs into a bowl. After adding a little milk and whisking it, he poured it into the skillet. The smell of butter-fried eggs wafted through the kitchen, sending Brian reeling from the room.

Todd watched him go and called after him. "What's the matter, Brian? Having difficulty holding down your drink?"

Brian did not respond.

"You're an evil man, Todd Williams," remarked Sammy, smiling impishly.

"I know. But I'm being cruel to be kind. What about you? Ready for your eggs?"

"Thought you'd never ask. Where do you keep the jam?"

Todd pointed to the refrigerator, and Sammy helped himself. They both enjoyed a leisurely breakfast knowing that Brian would not be returning anytime soon. Finally Todd pushed away his plate, his face taking on a serious look.

"What do we do now, Sammy? We've known Brian since we were kids. We've watched him doing his thing for the past couple years, and, except for the occasional appeal to his reason, we've done nothing to help him. We've kept his secrets and turned a blind eye while he's done his dirt, and all the while his parents remained in the dark. We can't continue doing that. I don't think we're doing our guy any favors here, man."

"Yeah. Reminds me of Claude," said Sammy.

"And now Claude's on the street, his mind a mess!"

"You know he's going to fight us."

"When does Brian not fight anybody? Our one piece of leverage is our threat to go public—tell his mom and some of the older men he looks up to at church. Brian has so much potential for good. We can't stand by and watch another Claude happen. Poor Mr. Baptiste would turn over in his grave. Plus, I know the earful I'd get from my folks."

"All right. Let's go in for the tackle. Hope there's nothing sharp lying around your living room."

"His tongue is sharp enough as it is. He'll do his damage with that, but we've got to stay on him, Sammy, before this gets any worse. So are you game?"

"I'm with you, bro. Right behind your back."

---

* See Rom. 8:28.

Chapter Twenty-four

A Place to Belong

Dressed in sweat pants and hooded sweatshirt, Scott collected the car keys from the key rack. "I'm heading over to the Williamses' house, Charmaine. Todd and Sammy are with Brian, and I promised them I'd drop by."

"No church today?" she asked, busily wiping down the kitchen counter.

Scott looked at his watch. "I don't think so. After I'm done with the guys, I might go for a drive. I need some time alone with God."

"You just don't want to be around me," accused Charmaine.

Scott looked at her and wondered, *Do you ever really know a person? No matter how much you think you do, there comes a time they seem a stranger.* He decided to be frank.

"Charmaine, I look forward to having you around for the rest of my life. Right now, however, I am completely worn out from talking. I don't have anything more to say to you that I have not already said. I need some time alone to think and pray."

"Fine, then! Go. Obviously your guys are more important than I am."

Scott prayed for patience. "Charmaine, you know that's not true, but I'm not getting into another argument with you, if that's what you're spoiling for." He leaned down to kiss her cheek, but she turned aside. "OK," he said quietly. "I'll see you later, love."

Adding an extra prayer for strength, Scott straightened up and walked out the door.

At the click of the lock, Charmaine flung the dishcloth she'd been using into the sink. Gnashing her teeth in frustration, she stomped her way to the spare room. She needed to do something. Anything. Her eyes fell upon a suitcase stored at the top of the closet.

"That's it. That's what I'll do. I'll show him!"

As she pulled the suitcase toward her, an envelope fell on her shoulder. It was sealed and addressed to Scott Henry and wife. There was no return address.

Despite her churning anger, Charmaine's curiosity was piqued. Setting aside the suitcase, she sat on the floor and tore opened the envelope. Inside were three smaller envelopes—one with Scott's name and one labeled "Celeste's papers." Her eyes widened when she saw that the third envelope was addressed to "Scott's wife."

What?

A feeling of premonition urged her to run from the room, but she didn't. Before her head could evaluate or approve the thought, her fingers tore through the flap of the envelope, revealing two pages of handwritten lines. Despite her trepidation, Charmaine began to read.

Dear Mrs. Henry,

If you are reading this letter, my worst fears have been realized, and both I and probably my mother have died, leaving my precious daughter alone in the world. When I first found out that I had cancer, I prayed earnestly for a miracle. I prayed for healing. When it didn't look as though things were improving, I got so desperate that for days on end I begged God specifically to spare my life for another five years so I could take care of my child a bit longer. I figured that since He had turned back time for King Hezekiah, He might be persuaded to do the same for me.

However, despite my many petitions to God, the cancer is growing very rapidly, and I know that the remaining time I have with my child is very short. So lately I've stopped the prayers of desperation, begging God for what I want, and have been learning to pray the more difficult 'not my will' prayer of submission.

After my devotions this morning, I was strongly impressed to write this letter to you. I had heard through a friend of a friend of a friend that Scott had married. Fortunately, except for my mother, nobody here knows that he is the father of my daughter. I plan to tell Celeste later today, because at some point in the future I suspect she might want to explore her parentage more fully.

I don't know if Scott has made mention of the brief time we dated. It's OK. I came to terms with our past a long time ago, and I really am not bitter. I made some foolish decisions in my youth, but God's grace continues to cover me. Amazing, isn't it? I pray that you too have a wonderful relationship with God. I could not have survived these many years without Him. He can be depended on completely for every single life situation—no matter how tough it gets.

So here is what I must ask of you. Could you find it in your heart to allow my daughter to get to know her father? As God is my witness, I would not be doing this if I had other options. My heart breaks at the thought of her being all alone in the world. I have told her repeatedly the story of Abraham and Isaac, and how God provided a ram in the bushes just at the moment that it looked as if Abraham were going to have to kill his own child to prove his faithfulness to God. She loves that story. Is it possible for you and Scott to be her ram in the bushes?

I know I am asking a lot, but I have no recourse but to throw myself on the mercy of you, a complete stranger, who might be the rescuer of my baby. Could you provide my daughter with a home and a place to belong? Can you give her a place to feel safe and someone to relate to? I dare not ask you to love her, but could you at least find it in your heart not to reject her or abuse her? I ask you because it is the woman in the home who sets the climate. It is you who has the power to give my daughter a good life and not just a tolerable ordeal. Please pray about it and allow God to guide you, and know that I will be praying for you every single day until the breath leaves my body.

In the envelope marked "Celeste's papers" is some important information you should know. For example, you will notice when you meet my daughter (by the way, she really is a sweetheart—so brave during this rough time), she looks nothing like your husband. That's been a blessing, because no one has been able to connect her looks to Scott and recall that we dated for a short time. However, since she looks nothing like him, I assume you will have questions. Is this really Scott's child, or some prank by a dying woman desperate to find a father for her child?

Please, for your peace of mind, a simple blood test will prove that Scott is Celeste's father. Do the test. In the envelope you will find blood type information for both me and Celeste. You can have your physician independently verify these through our family doctor. There are also copies of important documents and instructions to Scott as to where to locate Celeste's banking information. A trust fund has been set up for her through a lawyer here in Montreal that should take care of her expenses up to, and including, university.

I am feeling a lot more at peace since I started to write this letter. It's as though God is telling me that I am on the right track. "Thou wilt keep him in perfect peace, whose mind is stayed on thee: because he trusteth in thee."* So I am trusting in God to take care of this child that He has lent me for a time. I will leave the rest in the hands of my heavenly Father, and in yours.

Sincerely,
Emelia Fernandez

Charmaine sat on the floor, frozen. She literally could not move. If she'd had to name one of the dozen of emotions running through her consciousness, she could not have done so. Her head hurt. Her eyes burned. Her stomach twisted, and her hands shook.

Her shaky fingers carefully refolded the letter along the preformed lines and returned it to the envelope.

Dear Father in heaven, I am so confused. Help me, please. Show me what to do, her heart cried out.

She waited, hoping for a word.

But God was silent.

Emily Price massaged her neck. She was getting too old for couch sleeping, but poor Lenore had needed her, and well, that's what friends were for.

In the wee hours of the morning, exhaustion had taken over, and they'd fallen asleep, Lenore still propped up on the stair, using the upper rung for a pillow, and Gwen on the floor close by.

The brightness of the day indicated late morning.

Emily watched Lenore as she too responded to her body's rebellion at the choice of bed. Once she'd settled into a less-uncomfortable position, Emily saw Lenore's lips moving. Fascinated, Emily watched, wondering what she was dreaming about. Then it dawned on her that Lenore was praying. First thing in the morning?

She saw Lenore's face take on a listening look, followed by a smile. Then a look of peace relaxed her features. What was that all about? Interest piqued, Emily softly inquired.

"Are you OK, Lenore?"

Lenore opened her tired eyes. "I will be," she murmured. "I'm in God's hands."

"I saw your lips moving. I thought at first you were having a nightmare."

"No nightmare. I was praying. Turning all my pain over to God and giving thanks for all that He's done for me."

"Thanking Him?" asked a stupefied Emily.

Lenore smiled. "Yes, for wonderful friends such as you and Gwen. And for a home and my children and for life, stuff like that."

"You amaze me."

"Why do you say that, Emily?"

"You can actually find something to be thankful for after a night like last night? After the week you've had?"

"No matter how bad things are, Emily, there's always something to be thankful for."

"That's true," joined in Gwen, who had risen to a sitting position. "I could not have gone through my husband's departure without prayer and without looking for things to be thankful for."

"But that's crazy! How are you able to do that?"

"God," said Gwen and Lenore in unison.

"And this God you believe in, that you pray to, actually answers when you talk to Him?"

Both women nodded, and Gwen said, "Sometimes I hear a voice quite clearly in my head telling me what to do."

"How do you know you're not just imagining it? Lots of people hear voices in their heads. Many of them are in mental institutions!"

Gwen laughed. "No one can convince anyone else of the reality of God. There's a text in the Bible that says, 'O taste and see that the Lord is good.'† All I can tell you is how I have experienced Him for myself. I cannot imagine my life without God. He has always been a part of me, but adversity brought Him even closer. I think it is through trials that we learn how weak we are and realize our need of a Savior."

Emily's eyes narrowed. "Maybe your God is just for weak people then, those who can't stand on their own two feet."

"Do you consider Gwen and me to be weak people, Emily?" asked Lenore.

Emily looked chagrined. "No. I don't mean that. But from what you're saying, it seems that God is good for only the bad times, for when you can't cope. Everyone needs someone when things are bad."

"But that's the whole point, Emily," said Lenore. "When things are good, we tend to assume that all our successes and triumphs are because we have made it possible. It's *our* brains, *our* skills, *our* aptitudes. If we're so capable, we should be able to deal with every bad or ugly thing life throws at us—after all, we are mini-gods. But when death, illness, pain, and troubles come knocking, our money, brains, or built-in tenacity cannot get us through.

Personally, I think these problems can act as reminders to us that God is the capable one and only. He can help us weather the good and the bad."

"Unfortunately, many of us cannot be trusted with too many blessings. We tend to get arrogant," added Gwen.

"Plus," continued Lenore, "we need to remember that we are living in a world plagued by sin, and that the forces of evil create opportunities to pull the rug out from under us."

"Just as he did with Job," supplied Gwen.

"Who is Job?" asked Emily.

"He is a man who lost everything and still chose to depend on God. I could tell you his story, but I think you'd get more out of it if you read it for yourself. Job is the name of a book in the Bible that candidly tackles the question of why bad things happen to good people."

"The Bible talks about stuff like that? I did not know that. Show me where it is."

Lenore stood and completed the postponed stairway climb up to her bedroom. This time she was more ready, and her mission kept her mind from going to the place of too much pain. This time she went in search of a version of the Bible that would explain the complexity of the book of Job in clear English.

There, in the room she had shared with Robert, she paused to stare at her favorite photograph of him, which was resting on her dresser. "This is all your doing, you know," she told the photograph, "but I'll do my best to water the seed you sowed."

She imagined the smile that would have lit up his face at the very thought.

---

* Isa. 26:3, KJV.
† Ps. 34:8, KJV.

Chapter Twenty-five

Sunday's Coming!

Sammy and Todd cleared the table and loaded the dirty dishes into the dishwasher. Then, with a sense of purpose, they headed to the living room. Sammy, true to his word, tailed a safe distance behind Todd.

Brian sat leaning forward in Mr. Williams' recliner, head resting in the palm of his hands.

"Brian," called Todd as he walked into the room and stood in front of his friend.

"H'mm," answered Brian, fingers splayed over his face and thumbs kneading his temples.

"Head any better?" Todd asked.

"Kinda," came the muffled reply.

"Sammy and I had a little talk while we were in the kitchen, and we've come to an agreement."

"Yeah? 'Bout what?"

"You."

"Me? What did you need to agree on about me?" asked Brian, still talking through his fingers.

"We agreed that we love you like a brother. And because all three of us go way back, we agreed we've not been doing right by you over the past couple of years."

Brian's hands dropped away from his face as he slowly raised it to focus on Todd.

"Come again? What do you mean you're not doing right by me? And Sammy, why are you standing over there?"

Sammy straightened his spine and walked over to Brian. Pulling up the nearby footrest, he sat down and got straight to the point.

"Brian, Todd and I have agreed that you're messing up. We haven't said anything about it before, but you're really tripping up, guy. You're sleeping with this and that girl, and now you've started to drink. What's going down with you, anyway? So what we agreed on in the kitchen is that effective today, as in right now, we're going to hold you accountable. We're not going to cover for you anymore or ignore your, your—" Sammy struggled for the right word.

"Indiscretions," supplied Todd.

"Yes, your indiscretions and such. Last night was our wake-up call. We're going to stick with you and help you get yourself together. Enough is enough!"

Brian's eyes reflected his disbelief. "Are you guys for real? Tell me, what exactly was in the scrambled eggs you just ate?"

Sammy intervened. "C'mon, Brian. We're serious."

Brian's eyes narrowed. "And you think I'm not? You make me sound like some kind of junkie who's been blowing his brains out with drugs." Raising his hand in a placating gesture, he said, "Listen, let's just pretend this conversation never happened, OK? I agree that last night was not one of my better decisions, but I just needed something to get me through. That's all it was."

Undeterred, Sammy pushed back. "So what about tonight? What's going to get you through? How about next week when things get a little bit rough again—what kind of 'something' will you need? Brian, we've been hanging together since we were kids. We went to the same schools, got baptized about the same time, and went up front at church many times to recommit our lives to God. But lately, man, you've been sliding away. The sex, the two-faced life you've been living, and now alcohol?"

"Sammy, get outta my face right now before I kick you over. Y'all must be trippin'. Yeah, let's hatch up a little plot in the kitchen to fix up Brian. But first, why not rub his bloody nose in some salt?" Brian's eyes were spitting fire. "I would never do this to you!"

Todd closed ranks behind Sammy. "I hope you would, Brian. I hope to God you would care enough about me or Sammy to do this for us. What's going on with you anyway, man? What made you just jump into this kind of lifestyle?"

Brian jumped out of the chair and laced into his friends. Sammy bolted off his seat too, and stood beside Todd. Eyeballs bored into eyeballs. "I didn't jump into nothing! If you weren't so busy being watchdog and keeping records of my so-called sins, you'd have noticed that my dad just up and died last Friday. My dad! I loved that old man. He meant everything to me, and now he's dead!"

"We know all that, Brian, but—"

"But nothing!" Brian shouted. "What do you know about waking up for the last eight mornings and not having your father around? What do you know about the knife that twists in my gut every time I pass by his den and forget that he's not in there? Maybe you can tell me what you'd do when you see your mom walking around the house like a dry-eyed freak and your little sister bawling every time she looks at you."

"We don't know what it's like," Sammy said softly.

"Then don't you dare talk to me about nothing! You haven't walked even an inch in my shoes!"

"That's where you're wrong, guy," said Todd firmly. "We dare, and will continue to dare. We love you too much to let you go without a fight. Your dad would roll over in his coffin if he thought we wouldn't fight for you. We're gonna be here for you through all the pain. We're going to prop you up whether or not you want us to. The alcohol doesn't have as broad a shoulder as we do.

"You just don't get it," said Brian through gritted teeth. "I don't need help. I'll manage this by myself."

"So if you're managing so well, why the liquor? Tell me that," questioned Sammy. "Sorry, man. We're not buying that line. And what's with the macho attitude? Who says you have to play tough guy, Brave? What's wrong with admitting you're scared out of your skull? Is it going to kill you to admit that?"

Brian felt cornered. "I'm getting outta here." His eyes darted from his friends to the door, back to his friends.

"I don't think so," said Todd. Sammy nodded his agreement.

Brian looked at them as if they'd lost their minds. Advancing on them with a look of pure menace, he barked, "And what are you planning to do? Keep me here forever?"

"Nothing so drastic," replied Todd, his heart beating hard but his feet not budging. "We want your cooperation."

"To do what?" Brian's voice was too calm for comfort.

"To help you." Sammy grimaced internally at the slight quake in his voice, but stood fast beside Todd. He hated confrontations. He preferred words written on paper doing their work, not screamed at you from angry mouths.

Brian looked at his two best friends and felt something tickling his throat, but he bit it back. The poor brutes looked so ridiculous! Before he could stop himself, however, a hiccup of laughter escaped, followed by another and another, convulsing his body until he was completely overcome. He rolled onto the floor and whooped till tears ran down his cheeks.

Todd and Sammy looked at each other in bewilderment. Had the boy flipped out?

Brian eventually got himself under control and sank back down on the chair he'd vacated earlier.

"Well, I've got to hand it to you guys. I never thought I'd be able to laugh again, but you two jokers somehow managed it with this awful charade. You should've seen your faces, looking all determined and terrified."

His face sobered. "Am I that out of control to force my two best non-fighting friends to try to take me on?"

Todd plopped to the floor, and Sammy followed suit. "I can only speak for myself, but you've been causing me a few sleepless nights."

"I bumped you to the top of my prayer list—above my best-selling book dream," added Sammy.

Brian's throat was tickling again, but this time from a different emotion. He pinched the bridge of his nose and swallowed against the tears seeking release. "That's a serious SOS to God."

Sammy nodded.

"Thanks, guys. For everything."

The silence was beginning to become uncomfortable until Sammy returned to the unanswered question. "So do we have your agreement that you'll let us help you and be there for you no matter when or what?"

"Doesn't look like I have much of a choice in the matter, does it? All right. I'll try to cooperate."

Looking in Todd's direction, Sammy pressed Brian for more. "You need to also agree to be there for us if we ever go anywhere close to the edge."

Brian looked at his friends for a long time, then nodded. "As long as you know I'll play as tough as you two. After all, what goes around comes around."

His eyes took on a faraway look, and his jaws clenched. "This one is tough, guys. Really tough."

Sammy and Todd knew that he was talking about losing his dad, and could think of no words to help him. Then Sammy said softly, "Remember you don't have just us, Brian. There's always God. Talk to Him about whatever's on your mind."

Brian shifted in his seat. "I'm not sure about that God stuff anymore."

"What do you mean?" exclaimed Sammy. "You don't believe in God anymore?"

"I don't know what to believe. I don't understand Him and how He works. Nothing He does makes any sense to me. For instance, my dad's death. And some of the things our church says that God wants us to do. Well, He can't be serious."

"What things?" questioned Sammy.

"As I said last week—no sex until marriage, no drinking coffee . . ."

"God didn't specifically say that, the coffee thing. Course, I can't say that being buzzed on caffeine does anyone a lot of good. But God did say the other, and I'm sure He has a good reason."

"Well, how about I do what feels right for now, and when I get to heaven I'll ask Him what He meant?"

"Wow, you really have strayed from what you used to believe! How come I didn't see that happening?" mumbled Sammy almost to himself.

The doorbell chimed, and Todd left the room to answer it, his mind doing its typical detailed analysis of the discussion.

It was Scott.

Scott entered the room, waved to Sammy, and walked over to hug Brian, backslapping him bracingly. "How're you doing, Brian?"

"Other than the house arrest and the lack of food, I'm not doing too bad. Soon as they give me back my clothes, I'll be able to leave."

Scott raised his eyebrows at Todd and Sammy. Both young men shrugged.

"Our consciences are clear," Todd said, "but there are times in life that friends gotta do what friends gotta do. Speaking of food, can I get you some juice, Scott? A soft drink? And while I'm in the kitchen, I might see if I can salvage some toast for the prisoner here. He abandoned us at breakfast earlier."

Brian tossed a cushion at Todd. "They've been telling me my life is outta control, and they will not *let* me—did I use the right word, Sammy? —yes, *let* me mess it up any further without their permission."

"And you agreed?" asked Scott.

"Some." He shrugged. "I have some conditions around certain parts."

"Let me guess. The 'no sex' part?"

"Good memory, Scott. These clowns here have warned me off liquor and any other kind of assistance. But I'm going to have some trouble giving up . . . well." He gave an exaggerated wink. "How about if I just cut back a little? Fewer consequences, and no hangovers."

Scott stood up abruptly and walked away from Brian, his mind tossing pros and cons as to how to address his young friend. Making a decision, he turned back and almost bumped into Todd, who was returning with a tray of refreshments.

"Whoa," said Scott. "That was close."

Todd passed juice and toast to Brian and a soda to Scott. Brian heartily dug into the toast as if he were a starving man.

"Sammy, here's another drink, just in case you're feeling dry."

"Thanks," said Sammy, reaching for the glass and taking a long swallow. "So how have you been, Scott? Wasn't last night's program something else?" Not waiting for a reply, Sammy turned to Brian: "Your sister was great. Best performance of the whole crew!"

"Some of it wasn't acting, Sammy," replied Brian dryly.

"I know that, but it only made the message more powerful. Anyway, back to you, Scott. How's Charmaine? I saw her last night, and she looked kinda down. What've you been doing to that lovely woman?" he joked.

"I hope nothing," warned Brian. "Charmaine's one of my favorite ladies."

"I'm sure she'll be glad to hear that, Brian," Scott said softly. His gaze took in all three of them. "Listen, guys, there's something I need to talk to you about, and, well, now is as good a time as any."

"Oh, no," wailed Brian. "More preaching about my sinful ways."

"Interesting that you say that, Brian." Scott dropped to the floor, his back against the wall. "That's exactly what I want to talk to you about. Except it's not about your ways, Brian. It's about mine."

"What?" asked Brian.

"You?" asked Sammy.

"What do you mean?" asked Todd.

"There's no easy way to say this, guys, so let me give you the bald facts: This past Monday I discovered that I'm the father of a 10-year-old girl."

"You're what!" Brian jumped off his chair—then instantly grabbed his head.

Scott didn't even react to Brian's flight. "You guys may or may not know that even though I grew up in the church, I was not always a Christian. Back in the day I was just as cavalier as Brian here. Love 'em and leave 'em. Well, it seems that one of the ones I loved . . . I left pregnant. I probably would've gone to my grave not knowing, except for the fact that the girl's mother died recently, leaving instructions for the now-dying grandmother to locate me and let me know."

"You're kidding. Right?" Sammy sputtered before he could stop himself.

"Are you for real?" Brian demanded.

"As real as the nose on my face," said a somber Scott.

Brian could not believe it. *Scott?* "How's Charmaine taking this? Serious, man, isn't this gonna, like, mess up your marriage?"

"Well, to put it bluntly, Charmaine and I—she cannot deal with this, guys. I'm having my own trouble taking it in, but I don't seem to have many options here. The child is living with her grandmother, who has a very serious heart condition. She could pass away at any time."

"And then the kid will have nobody," Todd said slowly, "but you."

"You got it."

Brian gave a self-conscious laugh. "Well, this makes my little drinking binge child's play. What you gonna do, Scott? I mean, this is big-time serious!"

The look on Scott's face was painful to see. "I'm glad you, of all people, think so, Brian, because as I was trying to tell you the other night, God has a reason for what He does. When He tells us to save sex until marriage, He knows what He's talking about. And whether they happen to get pregnant or not, the girls are affected by it too. Plus, I think we shouldn't allow something so beautiful to become so tarnished. It cheapens sex. If only I'd known this back then!"

For once the three guys were speechless. Scott? It was hard to imagine.

"Obviously, if I hadn't been acting the 'player' back then, I wouldn't be in this dilemma now—and wouldn't have this threat to my marriage."

"Is it that bad?" asked a much quieter Brian.

"Let's just say it has put some large cracks in my marriage." Scott lifted a hand to his eyes, covering them for an instant, as if that would wipe away the image of Charmaine's face. "It's not just about this little girl, guys. Charmaine saved herself for marriage. I didn't. And now she has to deal with both the psychological and physical consequences of *my* actions."

"Charmaine's not gonna—" Brian began.

"I don't know if the holes can be sealed up," Scott interrupted. "I hope so. I pray to God they can, because that woman means the world to me. I don't know what I'd do without her, but she's taking this really hard."

"This is heavy stuff, man," said Sammy.

"Yeah, it is," Scott said. He pushed himself to his feet. "Listen, guys, I gotta go. I didn't come here to tell you this, by the way. I just swung by to check in on Brian. But when I heard you spouting off, Brian, about few consequences to sex, I had to tell you. I would've talked to you guys about this later anyway. Folks will find out about it soon enough, but I'd appreciate if you'd keep this under your hat. I want to be able to tell our whole group myself."

He took a deep breath. "More important, Charmaine doesn't need to have people talking about this either."

"No problem, Scott," said Todd.

"Sure, man," Brian promised.

"I can do that," replied Sammy.

Working unsuccessfully to shake his melancholy, Scott replied, "Thanks, guys. I need some time with God, so I'm going for a drive. Hopefully I'll see you later this evening at the program."

Todd rose to see Scott to the door.

"Don't bother, Todd. I'll let myself out. See you later."

The guys heard the door softly close.

"Man!" said Sammy.

But the only reaction from the other two were the shocked looks on their faces.

It was Brian who eventually spoke. "That could be me." A long pause. "Right now."

Chapter Twenty-six

"My Grace Is Sufficient" . . . Really?

"H ey there, sleepyhead," Candice greeted Samantha. "I guess a lot of us are missing from church today. Your mom and mine, Brian, Todd, Sammy, us, and no telling who else. Did you sleep well?"

"Yeah. I'm surprised I slept so well. Did you put something in that tea you made last night?"

"No, just talked you to death. That'll put anyone to sleep for a long time. Ready for some breakfast? I could make pancakes."

"Sold. I'll slice up some of these strawberries—if that's OK."

"Go ahead. I love strawberries with my pancakes. Want some eggs?"

Sam considered, then shook her head. "No eggs for me." Reaching for the strawberries, she thought out loud, "I wonder how my mom and Brian are doing. I've wanted to call since I woke, up but don't want to wake them if they had a late night."

"It's almost 11:00, Sam. Your mom, at least, will be up by now. Brian, well, that might be a different story. Call her."

"OK, I will." Sam reached for the phone and quickly dialed her home number.

"Baptiste residence."

"Morning, Sister Bolski. It's me, Sam. Is my mom up yet?"

"She's right here, Sam. We're discussing the book of Job with Emily."

"What!"

"Oh, we've been up for ages. Nobody even made it upstairs last night. We camped out on the floor, and have been engaged in a rousing discussion ever since we woke up. Mrs. Price is a mean opponent. She yields no turf, and wants to see proof for everything."

"Mrs. Price is asking about God?"

"Why is that a surprise? Questions are meant to be asked. Hold on a minute." Sam could hear mumbled voices through the earpiece. "Sam, your mom says that she's OK. You're not to worry. She'll call you back later." Gwen laughed. "I have to get back into the fray, baby girl. Emily just tossed out a doozie of a question, and I have the perfect answer. Give my love to Candy."

Samantha looked at the phone in her hand. "I think she hung up on me!"

"What was that about?" asked Candice.

"Emily Price, our neighbor, a really nice person who does not want—or at least she used to get very impatient with—any discussion about God. Well, she seems to be asking a lot of questions today. Our mothers are giving Bible studies to her as we speak."

"They didn't even ask about us?"

"Yours sent her love, and mine told yours to tell me she'd talk to me later."

"Say that again."

"Our mothers are fine. Mine seems to be surviving her ordeal of last night." Samantha clicked off the phone. "Candy?"

"Yes."

"God is kinda weird, isn't He?"

"How do you mean?"

"Well, look at all the stuff that could have gone wrong last night. I mean, I got sick, then completely lost control and bawled all over the stage, then my mom chose the same night to freak out over Dad's death, yet God took all of that and made something beautiful. Think about it. So many people were touched by the program last night, and Mrs. Price, who I am sure was an atheist, is sitting through a Bible study with our mothers!"

Candice inclined her head at an angle that told Samantha she was thinking. "I see what you're saying, but I'm not calling it weird. I'm calling it awesome."

"That's the kind of weird I mean. It's weird in an awesome kind of way!"

"Considering what your family has gone through this past week, you especially are a walking miracle, Samantha Baptiste."

"That is the weirdest part of all. How can I be functioning, let alone performing, when Daddy is dead?"

"God is holding you up. Isn't that what you said again last night before you went on stage?"

"You're right. I wonder what's going to happen tonight."

"We'd better hurry with breakfast." Noting the time on the clock, Samantha amended, "Make that lunch. And then I need to go home and get some fresh clothes."

When Scott let himself into the apartment, he was tired but more at peace within himself than he'd been all week. Like Jacob, he'd wrestled with God for the past two hours, and God had rewarded him with a blessing of peace.

My grace is sufficient for you. My strength is made perfect in your weakness. [*]

The promise had broken into Scott's consciousness and smoothed some of the lines that had recently furrowed his brow.

His first thought was to find Charmaine. He wanted to remind her of his love and share the promises he'd recently received from God. Maybe they would help her as much as they were helping him.

Seeing the closed bathroom door, he knocked softly and, hearing no response, pushed it open. The drawn bath curtain meant that she'd fallen asleep in the bath again. He called her name softly so as not to startle her, but when there was no answer, he pushed back the curtain.

The tub was empty.

Scott could still smell remnants of her after-bath talc. He inhaled the scent and went across to their bedroom, where he was sure she must be. She was not there, either. The bed was nicely made, and empty. Then, as he turned away to check the spare bedroom, something caught his attention.

On the pillow was a white envelope with his name on it—Charmaine's handwriting. Beneath the white envelope lay a large manila envelope that looked somewhat familiar. Scott felt his heart rate increase. He rushed over to the bed and tore open the white envelope.

"Please, God, please," he whispered.

My grace is sufficient for you.

Scott tore open the envelope and quickly scanned the letter. His heart rate kicked up its pace. The adrenaline rush sent him running to the next room, searching, searching, but to no avail.

She was gone.

Scott stood motionless in the middle of the room, his mind freaking, spitting out plausible explanations.

None could deny the fact that she had left.

In a fit of rage he crushed the letter into a tight ball and flung it against the wall. It bounced back and landed right beside his toe. He stared at it as if it could speak to him, then slowly bent down and picked up the balled-up page, reverently smoothing it open. He sat down on the floor, almost in the exact spot that his wife had occupied earlier, and reread her letter.

Dear Scott,

Like you, I need to get away for a while. There are many things I need to think through and make some crucial decisions about. Our relationship is at the top of the list. I can't continue this way. All day long I've tried to talk to God, but it's as if He's turned His back on me.

I love you, and want very much to be the wife you need me to be, but every time I try, it seems my failure is worse than the previous try. I'll call you once I have made a decision. Please pray for me, since God might listen to your prayers on my behalf better than He does to mine.

Charmaine

Scott's mind tried to make sense of the letter. Then he recalled the other envelope on the pillow. That had to be it. She'd found the papers Celeste's grandmother had given to him, and jumped to the wrong conclusion. But he hadn't even opened the envelope. He'd stashed it in the closet until they'd had time to work through—*O God, what could she have found in it?*

Scott rushed back to the bedroom and dumped the contents of the larger envelope on the bed. Two letters fell out. He saw the one addressed to him and the other labeled "Celeste's papers." Scott groaned. She must have thought he'd already made plans to take the child without consulting her. He dropped his head between his knees and half-prayed, half-spoke within the empty apartment.

"God, this is all my doing! She's gone because of me. Please pursue her, Lord. Go before her, and let Your Spirit sustain her. I want her back. I need her here!"

My grace is sufficient.

"OK, God. OK. You gave her to me; now I give her back to You. Please keep her safe, wherever she is. Hold me together, Father God, because I will fall apart if You don't."

Again Scott heard the same voice: *My strength is made perfect in your weakness.*

---

* See 2 Cor. 12:9.

Easter Sunday

Chapter Twenty-seven

"I Will Dwell in the
House of the Lord Forever"

E aster Sunday dawned to an overcast sky. Lenore, looking out from her bedroom window, contemplated the April gloom. Last night, after returning from church, her body had decided on its own accord that it needed sleep with or without her permission.

Another beautifully performed program had taken place at the church last evening, told this time through the eyes of Simon Peter. His guilt over his denial of his Lord, his anger at himself, the need to run away and hide. He'd been so sure he'd stay by Jesus' side no matter what! Yet he had denied Him, not once or even twice. Three times!

The program had then taken a modern twist when it showed Christians in various contexts denying Christ even now: A husband and wife in a restaurant too ashamed to publicly give thanks for a meal until their little boy asks why; a teenager riding the bus to church and disguising her Bible; a classroom student choosing not to speak of his faith in the face of vocal evolutionist ideology; a so-called Christian husband abusive to his wife and children.

The candlelight mourners in black had done the processional again. This time, after they had blown out their candles, Pontius Pilate made an appearance.

"I killed Him," he'd said, before blowing out his candle.

Mary did the same. "I killed Him," she'd said before blowing out her candle.

John came next. "I thought I loved Him, but I killed Him."

The modern-day families depicted came forward as well, and in a chorus said, "We killed Him."

Finally Simon Peter, as had Mary the night before, was left standing alone on the stage. His final words, "He's dead," followed by the outing of the candle, had ended the program on a very solemn note. It was a quiet crowd that left the church that night.

And Emily. Who would have believed that Emily Price had spent almost all of Saturday in Lenore's living room discussing the plan of salvation and the mystery of God? She had not even waited to be invited back to the evening program. Following a late lunch that she had insisted on preparing in Lenore's kitchen, she'd left for home saying she'd be back to accompany them to church.

And afterward, in the car on the way home, her only question had been "What did all those people mean by saying they killed Jesus?"

Lenore had told her that a lack of acknowledgment of Jesus was the same as killing Him. It was as if He had never existed at all.

Emily's only response had been "I see."

Now it was Easter Sunday. One week and two days without her Robert. The pain still bordered on crippling, but Lenore felt the sustaining presence of the Spirit. She would one day emerge on the other side of this tragedy, changed, but seasoned with grace.

She thanked God again for her children. Prayed for her daughter that her adventures with God would continue; prayed for her son, who seemed to have lost his way; her friends, who daily provided support and encouragement; her church family; and for herself. She prayed for strength to be an outstanding representative for God, just like Job, come what may. She prayed for God to be able to proudly say of her, "Have you seen My servant Lenore?"

She smiled in anticipation of this afternoon's program. It would be told by Jesus' mother, Mary.

Thank God for the resurrection!

■ ■ ■ ■ ■

Todd lay in bed and thought over the previous day. He closed his eyes and thanked God for giving him and Sammy the strength to face Brian. He prayed for wisdom to discern when and how to help his friend, as well as the other guys. He prayed for fortitude to be a man of God when many young men were leaving the church, choosing to enjoy the pleasures of sin for a season. Finally, he prayed that when the time was right, God would send him a fine woman to love and experience all the joys of marriage with—and that until then, he would keep himself pure.

When he'd finished his silent prayer, he got up to look out at the overcast day, then washed his face and headed toward the kitchen to surprise his parents with breakfast.

Gwen and Candice walked briskly down the sidewalk, enjoying the crisp morning temperature. Neither woman spoke, each busy with her thoughts. After they had crested the hill overlooking the park, Candice slowed, then stopped.

"Boy, am I out of shape," she panted.

"Shame on you! Less time on the computer and more exercise, missy!"

"Mom, you know I hate to exercise. But thanks for dragging me out of bed. My brain feels refreshed."

"Mine too. It's been a tough and strange and exciting week all rolled into one."

"You can say that again."

"It's been a tough and strange and—"

"Mom!"

"What? You asked me to say it again."

"Did I ever tell you that you're crazy? Certifiable. That's what you are." Candice turned and bellowed to the trees. "Hey, trees, my mother is crazy!"

A squirrel, frightened by the noise, scurried up a nearby tree.

"Look what you've done! Traumatized the poor animal." Gwen sat down on the grass, pulling at its stalks. Candice joined her.

"Looks like rain today," Gwen said, looking at the sky.

"April showers. God knows just what the plants need right after winter."

"God knows. Period." said Gwen. "Candice, before life gets too busy and I forget, I want you to know how very proud I am of all you have done with this Easter program. I know you have an excellent team to work with, but you manage to keep things organized and flowing. That must be your spiritual gift. Congratulations on a job well done."

"Thanks, Mom. I must say, however, that for a few minutes there Friday night I was completely stumped. Thank God for Sister Simms coming to the rescue and snapping me back to the task at hand. I did not have a plan B for Sam being sick. What a disaster that could have been."

"That's what I mean. God knows. He knew and provided just what was needed."

"And made us look good in the process! He's totally awesome."

"And this afternoon? Are you ready?"

Candice grinned. "Well, it's the resurrection. If anything goes wrong, I'll just tell the whole cast to run up and down the aisle shouting 'Glory, hallelujah!'"

Gwen laughed at the image. "That would work. I would have no hesitation joining the happy throng."

Sammy picked up the phone and called the Baptistes' home. He wanted to check in with Brian, even though he hoped Samantha would answer the phone.

He was not that lucky.

"Hello," answered a male voice.

"Brave, Sammy here. Just checking in to see how you're doing."

"I'm cold and sober. Will that do?"

"Grab an extra blanket to ward off the cold. It's April, not July," responded Sammy.

"Hey, Sammy."

"Yeah?"

"Thanks again for what you and Todd did yesterday. It took guts, but I'm glad you did. If I said anything to hurt your feelings, well—sorry. I was kinda upset at the time."

"We love you, man."

"Well, thanks. It means a lot."

"No problem. Soooo, what do you have planned for the day?"

"Nothing much. I was thinking of spending some time with my mom this morning. Making sure she's OK."

"Your mom's pretty strong."

"I know, but I want to check in on her and Sam. As two of my friends reminded me yesterday, even strong people need support from time to time."

"You got that right. Say hello to her and your sister for me."

"Now, why do I get the feeling, Sammy Watson, that you have a thing for my little sister?"

"Because I do. But don't worry. I am way too young for anything super-serious. Women are item 5 on my list of priorities after you, my best-selling book, a good education, and some traveling. And just in case you're wondering how come I didn't mention God, He's the title for the list."

Brian chuckled. "I wasn't wondering, but now I know. One of these days you may want to tell me how and when you got so smart."

"You got a deal. Sure your head can handle it?" Sammy teased.

"I'll let my head handle it if you'll allow me to teach you how to be relaxed around the ladies. Come to think of it, that might not be a good idea. I want you trying no moves learned from me on my sister. Then again, I'd just be embarking on mission impossible. With your head always in a book or bent over a computer screen writing who knows what, when would I be able to teach you anything?"

"A genius is without honor among his own friends. Listen, I'll catch you later."

"Cool."

Brian eased himself out from under the sheets. Before he got off the bed, however, he spoke to the ceiling.

"I'm still mad at You, but if You don't mind the yelling from time to time when I get sore at things You do, I'm willing to reconnect. You seem to be holding up the rest of the family, so I guess I could do with a bit of help too. Oh, and sorry for all the sin stuff. I'm kinda stupid sometimes."

Before crawling into bed in the early hours of Sunday morning, Scott had placed the telephone beside him on Charmaine's pillow. A shoulder-slumping weariness had settled over him since he'd left church last night, and not even to Andrew had he been able to admit that Charmaine was gone.

Eyes bloodshot and dry from too much looking inward, he stared at the telephone and willed it to ring. He checked again to make sure it was working. The dial tone told him it was.

"God . . ."

He started what he was sure was his 127th prayer. But his mind would not supply him with anything he hadn't already covered. Needing to hear a voice in the empty apartment, he began to repeat the shepherd's psalm.*

" 'The Lord is my shepherd; I shall not want . . .' "

His mind started to argue.

But I do want, Father. I want You to bring her back here. I want my wife here with me. I want the past to not . . .

What was he saying? Did he want the child, his daughter, Celeste, not to exist? Would he wish her dead? That beautiful child!

Frightened at the direction of his thoughts, Scott sat up in bed and continued on his quest to fill up the silence.

"'He maketh me to lie down in green pastures: he leadeth me beside the still waters. He restoreth my soul.'"

"Please, God! Restore her to me as You are restoring my soul.

"'He leadeth me in the paths of righteousness for his name's sake. Yea, though I walk through the valley of the shadow of death, I will fear no evil: for thou art with me; thy rod and thy staff they comfort me.'

"I deserve the punishment, God. Not her. Not her!"

Everyone needs to work out their own salvation with fear and trembling, Scott.

There it was again. The voice.

"God, what are You trying to tell me?"

Charmaine was Mine before she was yours. She needs to find her own path to Me. I love her, but you both need to trust Me.

The ringing of the telephone catapulted Scott out of the bed toward the night table to answer it.

It was not there.

Remembering in time that he'd placed it on the pillow, Scott reached for it, but in his haste knocked it clear onto the floor on the other side of the bed. With the desperation of a last-ditch rescue effort, he dived across the bed.

"Hello! Hello!"

The caller had hung up. Was it her? Quickly his fingers dialed ★69, but the number was not listed.

"'Surely goodness and mercy shall follow me all the days of my life.

"'Surely goodness and mercy shall follow me all the days . . .'"

"Surely mercy and goodness shall follow me all the life of my days."

He felt hot tears on his cheeks.

He must not cry.

He was a grown man. He must not cry.

The phone rang again.

"Thank You, Jesus!" Scott pressed the talk button. "Charmaine?"

"Scott, it's Andrew. Did you just ask for Charmaine?"

Scott could not respond. He'd been so sure . . .

"Scott?"

He heaved his body into a sitting position.

"Yeah. I'm here."

"What's going on?" asked a worried-sounding Andrew.

"She's gone, Andrew. Charmaine is gone."

"Gone where?"

"I don't know. She left yesterday."

"But why didn't you say something last night?"

"Andrew, don't take this the wrong way, but I am not in much of a talking mood right now, OK?"

Scott did not wait for a response. He pressed the off button and disconnected.

Scott let the telephone slip from his fingers and fall to the floor. Immediately it began ringing again. He ignored it and waited for the voice message system to do its work. Andrew would just have to understand.

He was lowering himself onto the bed when the voice on the answering machine started to speak.

"Hello, Scott, this is your mother-in-law. I'm just calling to see—"

Scott swooped down to the floor, and in one fluid motion grabbed the phone.

"Hello, Mrs. O'Dell. This is Scott."

"How are you doing, and more to the point, how is my daughter?"

"I was hoping you were calling to say she was with you. She's gone, Mrs. O'Dell. I don't know if she talked to you about the situation we're going through, but she left yesterday, and I don't know where she is."

"Well, she's not with me, but I wouldn't worry too much. When my daughter gets overwhelmed, she looks for a hole to hide in. She'll come out after she's sorted things through."

"But she's never done anything like this before. I'm going crazy here. She could be hurt, or dead!"

"I'm sure she's neither. I know my child. This is how she copes with her troubles. I am not saying I approve. I am just letting you know that this behavior is not atypical. I told her when she called me last Wednesday or Thursday that while your situation is a bit of an inconvenience, it was not the end of the world."

226

"She thinks I don't love her anymore."

"That's not quite it, Scott. Remember that Charmaine is an only child. She's not used to sharing. So added to the fact that a daughter out of the blue is a bit of a shock to the system, she has to wrap her brain around sharing your love. She's a bit possessive that way."

"But I do love her, Mrs. O'Dell. She's my heart."

"You don't need to convince me, young man. Even a blind and deaf person can sense that you love my daughter. Now get up, if you're still lying in bed. Go wash your face and occupy your day as best as you can. She'll be back."

"But will she want to stay married to me?"

"I'm her mother, Scott, not a prophet. Trust in your God. Doesn't your Bible say something about 'nothing good will He hold back from those that trust Him,'† something to that effect?"

Scott took a deep breath and felt the oxygen fill his lungs. Then he exhaled. "Thank you for the reminder. I let my panic overcome my peace."

"Now, son, get up," Lucinda O'Dell said kindly. "Take a shower and go occupy yourself with someone else's problem until your wife comes home. She's got to do what she's got to do, and, well, you have to be patient. Tell her to call me when she gets back."

Scott got out of bed and walked to the window. The overcast sky was enough to return him to his gloom, but he bowed his head and finished the psalm.

"'And I will dwell in the house of the Lord for ever.'"

And just like that, God allowed a section of the clouds to part and set a rainbow in the sky.

The Son had risen.

---

* See Ps. 23, KJV.
† See Ps. 84:11.

Another Sunday

Morning

Sunday Morning's Miracle

The day of the annual church picnic was one of the brightest yet of the summer. The park selected this year was a full hour's drive out of Toronto, but was worth it. There were lots of open areas in which to play and shaded trees that invited a blanket on the ground and a snooze in the open air. Six minutes of walking on the northern side of the grounds would take you to the graveled beach area, which was part of Lake Ontario. Already the air was alive with the giddy laughter of children, some learning to jump rope for the first time and others playing tag or throwing Frisbees.

Judith Simms, sitting under one of the inviting trees, leaned against the trunk and kept a watchful eye on her 2-year-old. Where had the time gone? Jess, once she'd discovered the freedom of feet set in motion, kept Judith constantly running. And that 2-year-old independence was teaching her mom and dad that they still had a whole lot of character development to work on.

"Jess, your laces are undone. Come and let Mommy help you with them, honey."

"No! Can do it by myself" was the perky response.

"Jess!" Judith's tone had changed.

Jess recognized it, and came to sit on the blanket with her back turned to her mother. She then proceeded to rectify the lace problem without assistance. She made first one rabbit ear, but could not get her fingers to cooperate in holding it in place while she looped the other. She tried and tried again, to no avail. Frustrated, but still refusing to ask for help, she walked over to her mother, plopped herself on Mom's lap, and stuck her thumb in her mouth.

"Somebody is sleepy already?"

Judith turned to the sound of the voice, her face breaking into a grin. "Charmaine! When did you get here?"

"About a half hour ago. I'm doing the walk-about. You know how long that takes. Everyone is offering me food, and of course, I had to sample Sis

Agnes's potato pudding, Brother Marcus's corn on the cob, Sister Percival's sweet bread, and of course, Emily Price's blueberry coffee cake. That one did me in. It just melted in my mouth, and, I guarantee you, automatically added five pounds to my hips."

"I've had that one," replied Judith. "It is beyond good. Makes your eyes roll back in your head. It's all the butter, you know. Anyway, enough about food! Talking about it might contain more calories than I need. Come sit down and have a chat with me, girl. We haven't had a heart-to-heart in ages."

Charmaine considered the blanket, but shook her head. "Tempting offer, but my plan is to make it down to the beach and then hike to the top of that boulder over there. Once I've done that, I'll have justified the eating of all those sweets and completed my exercise for the day. So save me a place, OK?"

"All right. Leave me here alone with Miss Independence."

"I suggest you take a nap. The fresh air seems to have done her in. Look, she's fast asleep."

"Me nap? In the outdoors? You gotta be kidding. What if an ant crawls up my nose, or worse yet, a spider?"

"You mean like the one that's crawling up your leg right now?"

Judith gave her leg a sharp jerk, startling Jess. There was no spider. She turned to give Charmaine a piece of her mind, but she was already making fast tracks toward the lake.

"I know where you live, Charmaine. I know where you live!" She shouted at the disappearing figure that turned in her sprint and blew her a kiss.

"Arrrgh!" growled Judith.

"Arrrgh," echoed Jess over her thumb.

⬛ ⬛ ⬛ ⬛ ⬛

Charmaine slowed her run into a light trot, gathered up her hair into a pony-tail, and secured it with an elastic band. She'd allowed it to grow over the past year, and now it hung at the top of her shoulders, again hiding the dimples.

She picked up her pace again, sprinting the rest of the way to the beach. After pausing to catch her breath, she walked to the water's edge and gazed off into the uninterrupted horizon.

Thank You, Father!

You're welcome, My daughter.

Charmaine smiled. It was so good to hear the voice of the Spirit speaking to her.

It's been a long road, hasn't it? Thanks for making the journey with me. And now this blessing You have given me . . .

The new direction of her thoughts agitated her feet, making her want to move again. Refocusing on the boulder overlooking the beach, which was her final destination, she turned toward it and started to climb. Finding footholds was easy, and soon she was at the top, winded but exultant.

The view from the top was breathtaking. Careful to stay far back from the edge of the drop-off, Charmaine took in her surroundings. Directly in front of her lay the full expanse of the lake, dotted in the distance with the frothy lace of crashing waves. Seagulls, perched on the downed trunk of a tree, cackled loudly to their mates soaring above. A firm wind flattened her clothes against her body and coaxed tendrils of hair from its ponytail.

Charmaine inhaled her lungs full and slowly measured out inches of exhaled air. She felt the need to sing, to shout, to do something completely outrageous to express this giddy joy. Instead, still facing the water, she lowered herself onto a smooth patch of rock.

Her mind finally decided to choose for her a mode of expression. It prompted her lips to continue with the prayer of thanksgiving.

God, You have been so good to me. You have forgiven my sins, blotted out my transgressions, and healed my wounded heart. Even when I thought You'd turned Your back on me, You were right there, looking out for me. Look how far You've led me, and now this? I don't deserve it, but I thank You from the bottom of my heart. And right here in this place today, I offer up all I have to You. My fears, my loves, my joys, and my doubts, and I accept Your amazing grace again. Thank You for my new—

The sound of falling gravel swiveled Charmaine's head.

"Celeste!" Her voice was sharp with fright.

"I'm sorry. I didn't mean to scare you," the girl answered solemnly.

Quick to reassure her, Charmaine said, "I'm sorry too. I didn't mean to sound so sharp."

"Are you sad, Charmaine? Is that why you're up here by yourself? I don't like when you're sad. It makes me sad too."

Charmaine shifted and patted a spot beside her on the rock. "Come sit with me."

Celeste did. Charmaine put an arm around her and continued to stare out at the water. "No, Celeste. I'm not sad at all. I was just thanking God for the many things He's done for me. The many blessings He has given to me. And one of those blessings is you."

The almost-12-year-old looked at Charmaine with eyes still capable of wonder. "I am a blessing?"

Charmaine pulled her close. "You are a gift straight from God."

Celeste pulled at a tuft of grass trying to grow on the rock. She was silent for a moment, then said, "I'm glad you came to see me that day, Charmaine."

The smile Charmaine directed at the child was a tender one. "I'm glad too. But you see, I had to. After I read that letter from your mom, my sad heart forgot all about my troubles and thought only of you. I couldn't stand the thought of you being left alone."

"And now both of them are gone. I miss them so much, Charmaine." Her eyes filled up with tears, not of inconsolable pain, but of remembered joy.

Charmaine felt her own eyes misting. "But God gave us a small miracle, didn't He? Well, two miracles, really. First He changed my heart, and then He kept Grandmother with us for eight whole months. That gave us a chance to get to know each other and put her mind at peace that she was leaving you in good hands."

"Yeah. I'm glad I have you and my dad. It's nice to belong to someone."

"Well, my blessing, how would you like to belong to someone else?" Charmaine asked.

Celeste's brows crinkled in puzzlement. "What? How do you mean?"

"What if I told you that close to the end of January you're going to have a brother or sister?"

Celeste's eyes popped. "Really? You're going to have a baby?"

"That's right. And I'm going to need all the help that I can get to be a good mother. Since you know what a good mom is like, will you help me, Celeste?"

"Snap!" responded Celeste in an atypical use of slang. "This is great! I get to be a sister. Super-cool!" She shot up off the ground, her excitement contagious. "Does my dad know?"

Charmaine felt her contained joy on the edge of bursting out. "Not yet. I wanted to tell you first."

"You told me before you told Dad?"

Charmaine nodded.

"But why?" asked Celeste, sitting down again beside her.

"Because sometimes when a person is used to getting all the attention and then finds out that they have to share it with someone else, it makes them think that they aren't as important. That there isn't enough love to share. I don't want you to feel that way, Celeste. Since that April evening 20 months ago when I walked into your grandmother's house and met you, I've been smitten with you. I've grown to love you as if I'd given birth to you myself. And while I can never take the place of your mom, you are a daughter to me in every way. As I said before, a special blessing straight from God Himself."

"Wow! You love me that much!"

Charmaine's arm reached out again to pull the child close to her. "Not only do I love you, missy—I quite like you. You're fun to be around."

"I like you, too," said Celeste softly. "And I've grown to love you, too."

Charmaine projected her choked-up emotion into humor. "You're kidding me! For real?"

"For real," replied Celeste with her serious face.

She looked as if she wanted to say something else, but thought better of it. Her brows furrowed, then eventually cleared. "There's something I've wanted to ask you, Charmaine."

"What's that, honey?"

Celeste looked almost shy. "Do you . . . do you . . . mind if I start calling you Mom, Charmaine?"

Charmaine was shocked. Never had she expected this.

"But honey, you don't have to. I am quite happy . . ."

"I really want to, Charmaine," Celeste interrupted.

God, not this, too. It's too much!

Clearing her throat of its abundance of emotion, Charmaine said, "In that case, yes, Celeste. I would be honored to be called Mom Charmaine."

Celeste lost her bashfulness just as quickly. Her eyes were shining. "Great! Do you mind if I start now? That way, by the time the baby is born, I'll be well practiced."

"Yes, honey. You can start now. And to mark this moment that's so rich with so many good things, I think it is only fitting that we say thanks to God for these blessings, too."

"Do you mind if I pray, Charmaine? I mean Mom Charmaine?"

O God, where did You get this child! Charmaine's heart cried while she nodded her assent.

With the wind blowing softly across the waters taking the sting out of the midmorning sun, Celeste's soft voice carried across the waves and up into the heavens.

"Dear Father God, Thank You for answering my mom's prayer and for providing a ram in the bushes for me in my dad, and for Mom Charmaine, and this new baby that's coming. Even though I miss Mom and Grandmother so much, You helped me to find love in my new home. Help me to be a good sister and to do what Mom Charmaine has asked, which is to help her learn to be a good mom. But I think she is already a good mom, because she came to find me in Montreal and took me into her home and loved me when she didn't have to. Thank You for listening to us sitting here on this rock. In Jesus' name. Amen."

"Amen," whispered Charmaine, rapidly blinking back tears.

"Amen," said a male voice.

"Dad!"

"Scott!"

"Abandoned by my two best ladies! My heart is going to break," Scott intoned.

"Oh, Dad, don't be silly," said Celeste, all proper. "We were just having some girl talk. Women need to bond with each other from time to time, you know. That doesn't mean we've abandoned you. Isn't that right, Mom Charmaine?"

"Couldn't have said it better myself."

"Good," replied Celeste. "Now that we've established that, come sit with us and complete our family circle. Mom Charmaine has news."

"News?" asked Scott, silently mouthing a question to Charmaine at Celeste's calling her Mom. She shook her head and mouthed "Later."

Quickly he hurried over, and the women shifted on the rock to create a space for him between them both.

"What news?"

"How much of Celeste's prayer did you hear?"

"Just the amen. Why?" asked Scott.

Charmaine looked past Scott to Celeste. "Then you go ahead and tell your dad the news."

Celeste's propriety deserted her. "Me! You want *me* to tell him?"

"Tell me what?"

Charmaine smiled at Celeste. "Yes, I want you to tell him."

"What do you want her to tell me? Will somebody tell me something, anything!" cried Scott, head ping-ponging from one to the other.

Celeste, overcome with the task, stuttered. "But, but . . . it's your news."

Charmaine was firm. "No. It's our news, and I designate you to be the one to tell your father."

"ARRRGH," Scott bellowed, the sound echoing off the waves below.

"Scott!" scolded Charmaine.

"Dad, is that any way for a soon-to-be father of two to behave?" scolded Celeste.

"You women are going to drive me to—a what?"

"You're going to be a daddy again, Dad." Celeste's eyes were shining. "And I get to be a big sister."

Charmaine leaned into her husband and kissed his cheek. "Please tell me that you're happy about this."

Scott bowed his head for a long minute. When he looked up, his face split into fissures of pure rapture while his eyes did a crazy dance with tears of joy.

Celeste, not taking her eyes from her father's face, said to Charmaine, "That's what happiness looks like."

⚑ ⚑ ⚑ ⚑ ⚑

Pastor Al and his team had been edged out of the Winner's Cup at the annual touch football game last year. Brian, Larry, Damon, Les, Todd, and even Sammy had played them hard, and in the final minutes of the game the score was close. Because of an early lead in the game, however, Pastor Al's team was pretty much assured a win.

However, a bad throw in the final two minutes had resulted in an interception by Todd. That had secured the young men's team the victory, and they'd been insufferable then and ever since. It was time to teach those young pups a lesson. This year Pastor Al and his "over the hill" gang, dubbed thus by the younger men, were prepared to yield no quarter or entertain no excuses of creakier knees or slower reflexes.

After checking to see that Judith and Jess were doing fine, Pastor Al decided to take a jog along the beach to limber up for the afternoon game. It was not one of his better ideas. The beach was too pebbly for running, and he would not give the young men any reason to say that he purposefully twisted an ankle so that he would not have to play. Deciding to settle for a brisk walk instead, he turned to his left and stopped dead in his tracks.

Before him was a scene reminiscent of the biblical description of the disciples' faces as they descended the Mount of Transfiguration. This time, however, the shining faces belonged to Scott, Charmaine, and Celeste, who were walking arm in arm toward him. Scott in particular looked as if he'd been visited by the angel Gabriel himself, so joyously shell-shocked he seemed.

Pastor Al took in the picture and felt his heart utter a prayer of thanksgiving. *Just look at them, Lord! Another one of Your miracles.*

The trio stopped in front of him, and Pastor Al exclaimed, "You guys look radiant. What's up?"

Scott, at last capable of speech, looked squarely into the eyes of his through-thick-and-thin friend and pastor. Then drawing his family even closer, proclaimed, "God is, my friend. God is!"

Discussion Questions

On sex and sexuality . . .

1. In your opinion, do you think that Brian's statement in the first chapter (that most of the young people in the church are sexually active) is true? What arguments do you have to support your position?

2. Brian argues: "Why did God give me these strong urges [for sex]? If we shouldn't have sex before we get married, then we shouldn't crave sex before we're married!" How would you respond to this?

3. One of the young men indicated that the "come hither" outfits that some young women wear make it difficult for men to keep their minds from "straying." Discuss with your group your opinion of dress and its effect on sexual temptation.

4. What is your definition of sexual promiscuity? Support your position.

5. What would you need to do in your dating relationship to keep from falling into sexual temptation? What steps might you take?

6. Do you believe there will be sex in heaven?

7. If a couple is engaged and will be getting married shortly, is it OK in that situation to have sex with this person, who is soon to be your spouse? Why or why not?

8. How difficult is it to say no to sex? Who has the greater struggle with this temptation, males or females?

On pain and suffering . . .

1. From all reports, Robert Baptiste was a good man, yet God allowed him to die fairly young. Brian, his son, is angry with God over this very issue. If Brian was *your* friend, what would you do to help him? Is it OK to feel anger toward God? Why or why not?

2. After Lenore Baptiste's passionate defense of God, Emily Price asks Lenore, "And what if this God takes Samantha, and Brian, too, and

then gives you a lingering and painful disease? Will you still believe?" How could you know for sure that your faith would hold up under these circumstances?

3. Samantha talks of having the feeling of God "holding" her up. Have you ever experienced anything like that? If so, what were the circumstances?

4. Why are the problem of pain and the belief in a God of love such difficult concepts to reconcile?

On how God communicates . . .

1. Charmaine prays, but feels that God is silent. She leaves a note for Scott to say that maybe God will answer his prayer instead.

   - Have you ever prayed and felt that God was silent? How did you deal with it? Did it have an impact on your faith?

   - Do you believe that some people have better "pull" with God than you do, and that He will respond to them more quickly than to you? Can you find any biblical evidence to support your position?

2. Different characters in the book (Lenore, Scott, etc.) experience instances in which they hear God speaking to them with words of comfort or directives. Have you ever personally experienced God in this way? If yes, how do you know, as Emily Price argues, that what you're hearing is not a figment of your imagination?

On forgiveness . . .

1. What does it mean to forgive? Do you think that some things should not be forgiven? If yes, what things?

2. If you were in Charmaine's situation, how would you handle Scott's "bombshell"? Do you think she behaved appropriately for a Christian? What if you cannot forgive the mistakes of your spouse or a significant person in your life?

3. Are women more forgiving than men? Defend your position.

4. How do you know for sure that you've forgiven someone? If you've truly forgiven someone, does that mean you should be able to fully trust the person again—even with the situation that you had to forgive them of?